Christians in the City of Nairobi

CHRISTIANS IN THE CITY: STUDIES IN CONTEMPORARY GLOBAL CHRISTIANITY

Series Editor: Dyron B. Daughrity

Christians in the City looks carefully at Christianity in many of the world's great cities. It draws on interdisciplinary methods including anthropology, ethnography, sociology, phenomenology, and history. The series marks a significant contribution to the growing body of scholarship on world Christianity, lived religion, material religion, urban studies, and globalization as it engages people on the ground, in their local setting. The cities covered are drawn from around the world: North America, Latin America, Africa, Asia, Europe, the Middle East, and Oceania.

Books highlight how Christianity is changing particular metro areas, as well as how those areas are impacting the Christian religion. Most major forms of Christianity are discussed: Pentecostalism, Roman Catholic, mainline Protestant, non-denominational megachurches, Eastern Orthodox, immigrant forms, and house churches. The net is cast wide in order to understand what is happening with Christianity as it engages the great urban centers of the world.

Books in this series

Christians in the City of Hong Kong, Tobias Brandner
Christians in the City of Shanghai, Susangeline Y. Patrick

Christians in the City of Nairobi

An African City and the Future of World Christianity

**KYAMA MUGAMBI AND
MARK SHAW**

BLOOMSBURY ACADEMIC
LONDON • NEW YORK • OXFORD • NEW DELHI • SYDNEY

BLOOMSBURY ACADEMIC
Bloomsbury Publishing Plc, 50 Bedford Square, London, WC1B 3DP, UK
Bloomsbury Publishing Inc, 1385 Broadway, New York, NY 10018, USA
Bloomsbury Publishing Ireland, 29 Earlsfort Terrace, Dublin 2, D02 AY28, Ireland

BLOOMSBURY, BLOOMSBURY ACADEMIC and the Diana logo are trademarks of
Bloomsbury Publishing Plc

First published in Great Britain 2025

Copyright © Kyama Mugambi and Mark Shaw, 2025

Kyama Mugambi and Mark Shaw have asserted their right under the Copyright,
Designs and Patents Act, 1988, to be identified as the Authors of this work.

Series cover design by Rebecca Heselton

Cover images © amani nation/joecalih/mustafa omar Zkao/ Unsplash

All rights reserved. No part of this publication may be: i) reproduced or transmitted in any form, electronic or mechanical, including photocopying, recording or by means of any information storage or retrieval system without prior permission in writing from the publishers; or ii) used or reproduced in any way for the training, development or operation of artificial intelligence (AI) technologies, including generative AI technologies. The rights holders expressly reserve this publication from the text and data mining exception as per Article 4(3) of the Digital Single Market Directive (EU) 2019/790.

Bloomsbury Publishing Plc does not have any control over, or responsibility for, any third-party websites referred to or in this book. All internet addresses given in this book were correct at the time of going to press. The author and publisher regret any inconvenience caused if addresses have changed or sites have ceased to exist, but can accept no responsibility for any such changes.

A catalogue record for this book is available from the British Library.

A catalogue record for this book is available from the Library of Congress.

ISBN: HB: 978-1-3502-9653-4
PB: 978-1-3502-9652-7
ePDF: 978-1-3502-9654-1
eBook: 978-1-3502-9655-8

Series: Christians in the City

Typeset by Deanta Global Publishing Services, Chennai, India
Printed and bound in Great Britain

For product safety related questions contact productsafety@bloomsbury.com.

To find out more about our authors and books visit www.bloomsbury.com
and sign up for our newsletters

In loving memory of Elizabeth Nyathira Mugambi (1948–2024).

Contents

List of Figures viii
List of Maps ix
Series Introduction x

Introduction 1

1   The Cathedral and the Kiosk: Historic Protestant Churches in Nairobi 7

2   The Mass and Its Masses: Catholic Presence in Nairobi 23

3   A Place to Feel at Home: Independent Churches 37

4   "Fire": Pentecostalism and Evangelicalism 53

5   Ancient Altars: Orthodoxy 69

6   "Youth Arise": Nairobi Christianity as a Youth Movement 85

7   "Your Daughters Shall Prophesy": Women's Role in Shaping Christianity in Nairobi 97

8   Rival Cities: Nairobi Christianity and Public Life 109

9   The Kiosk, the Cathedral, and the Mosque: Christians and Muslims 125

Conclusion 141

Notes 147
Bibliography 168
Index 179

Figures

1.1   All Saints' Cathedral. Photo: Mark Shaw 8
2.1   Holy Family Cathedral. Photo: Kyama Mugambi 24
3.1   All Africa Independent Pentecostal Church Cathedral Bahati. Photo: Mark Shaw 38
4.1   CITAM Valley Road. Photo: Clara Koimett 65
4.2   Jesus Is the Answer Ministries. Photo: Clara Koimett 66
5:1   Coptic Orthodox Church. Photo: Clara Koimett 76
5.2   Ethiopian Orthodox Church. Photo: Clara Koimett 78
8.1   Nairobi Parliament by dreamstime, commercial and editorial licence obtained 110
8.2   Jomo Kenyatta statue by dreamstime, commercial, and editorial licence obtained 112
0.1   Aga Khan walkway. Photo: Kyama Mugambi 142

Maps

1 East Africa 4
2 Nairobi area 5
3 Nairobi central business district 6

Series Introduction

Dyron B. Daughrity, Series Editor

Christians in the City is a fascinating and cutting-edge series that looks carefully at Christians in many of the world's greatest urban centers. It draws on interdisciplinary methods including anthropology, ethnography, sociology, phenomenology, and history. The series marks a significant contribution to the growing body of scholarship on world Christianity, lived religion, material religion, urban studies, and globalization as it engages people on the ground, in their local setting. The cities are drawn from around the
world: North America, Asia, Africa, Europe, Latin America, and Oceania.

The Series' books highlight how Christianity is changing particular metro areas, as well as how those areas are impacting the Christian religion. Many different although often overlapping forms of Christianity are discussed in the volumes: Pentecostal, Roman Catholic, mainline Protestant, non-denominational, Eastern Orthodox, immigrant churches, megachurches, charismatic, evangelical, independent, and house churches. The net is cast wide in order to understand better what is happening with Christianity as it engages the great urban centers of the world. Christian organizations in the city—universities, private schools, and faith-based charities—will be explored as well.

The series features established as well as rising scholars. We have taken great care to choose authors who live in the cities under consideration, or at least have lived in those cities in the past. There is an intimacy that comes through in these volumes, and readers from those cities will recognize the streets, the sounds, the vibe, and the cultural accents that make cities unique. The volumes are written with crossover appeal—for audiences both inside and outside the academy.

Each volume contains interviews with leading figures from the city under consideration—as well as a broad array of laypeople—in order to gain a well-rounded perspective on these cities. There will be no shortage of material, as Christianity is not only the largest world religion in terms of adherents, but is also extremely widespread geographically, making it a diverse and complex religion that takes root in the soil of the cities it has been planted in.

The series will consist of monographs on 25 of the world's great cities, with carefully chosen, exceptional authors who have an intimate understanding of the city they write about. As the list of books in the series expands, a global balance will be maintained. The current list of cities/volumes that have either been contracted or are under consideration are:

- *In North America*: New York, Los Angeles,* Boston, Houston,* Montreal*
- *In Asia*: Shanghai,* Hong Kong,* Seoul, Delhi, Manila
- *In Africa*: Cairo,* Addis Ababa, Kinshasa,* Lagos,* Johannesburg,* Nairobi*
- *In Europe*: Moscow, London, Athens
- *In Latin America*: Sao Paulo,* Rio de Janeiro,* Havana, Santiago, Mexico City
- *In Oceania*: Sydney*

   Books already contracted.

This series has been several years in the making, and we are excited to see it now coming to light. Over half of the books are contracted, but the search continues for authors for the remaining volumes. We are open to proposals of other cities from potential authors.

Over half of the world's population lives in cities, and the expectation is that in coming years the number of people leaving the countryside for the city will only increase. Since its earliest days, Christianity was a religion of the city: Jerusalem, Alexandria, Antioch, Damascus, Corinth, Thessaloniki, and Rome. Established by the apostles themselves, that pattern continued. As Christianity expanded further, it gravitated towards cities: Aleppo, Edessa, Seleucia-Ctesiphon, Aksum, Etchmiadzin, and Constantinople.

The pattern continued, as the energy of the city attracted Christian missionaries, scholars, and laypeople in search of opportunity. As cities developed, Christians established bishoprics, cathedrals, and centers of learning in cities. Today, the great centers of Christian thought and influence are located chiefly in cities: Seoul, Addis Ababa, Rio de Janeiro, Dallas, Athens, Rome, and Moscow.

A series on Christians in the cities is timely, and promises to break new ground. There is an undeniable power in cities—a power to attract. And Christians continue to make their way, bringing with them manifold Christian practices, routines, rituals, and beliefs. In all of their diversity, they are united in one thing—they consider themselves Christians. And they live in the city.

For more information about this series, contact the Series Editor:
Dyron B. Daughrity
Professor of Religion
Pepperdine University
dyron.daughrity@pepperdine.edu

Introduction

Nairobi, like many great cities around the world, is a mirage. Its steel and concrete skyline speaks of a place that will stand the test of time. Though Nairobi projects an image of permanence, the city is always changing. Hidden beneath the shadows of its concrete skyscrapers, Nairobi is also a city of mud, brick, sticks, and metal sheets housing most of the city's residents and the shops in which they do business.

Nairobi appears to have fixed boundaries that have lasted for decades. On the ground, however, the "lived" boundaries of the city are porous and expanding. New people constantly move into the city, spilling across old boundaries and expanding communities into an ever-widening arc. The word "metropolitan" means that ultimately, people on the ground decide the "real" boundaries, much to the consternation of city planners.

Nairobi is, at first glance, a place of power elites and enormous wealth. University campuses, expensive office towers, and sprawling government buildings run through the city like a central nervous system. Yet "people" power really controls the city. The negative side of "people" power is crime and violence. The positive side is the vast sea of ordinary people, making all the systems of power and wealth work daily. As Adam Smith (the guru of capitalism) said, the wealth of the nations is not just wonderful stuff. It's working people.

Perhaps Nairobi's greatest mirage is its modernity. Cities are the epitome of the modern, the symbols of the secular. Yet they're fundamentally religious in nature. Artists paint what they worship and cities build what they worship. There is a deep and pervasive religiosity in cities. The existence of thriving, vibrant faith in the secular city may seem like a contradiction. In fact, it just reveals that the city, like humans, has more than a body. It has a soul. Nairobi's millions have found another way to be modern. The West became modern by marginalizing God. The non-West is becoming modern by bringing him back into the center. Every day, millions of Nairobi's citizens crunch their spreadsheets, navigate their internet, teach their classes, and raise their families by tapping the power inherent in a higher world. Cities like Nairobi look just like any other city of man from the top down. From the bottom up, however, the real Nairobi pulses with a longing to become the city of God and shape the city (from below) with this spiritual power. This book is the story of a city struggling, and often failing, in that sacred quest.

The numbers related to Nairobi and its faith are important. Consider but a few:

1. The city itself is home to 4.3 million people.[1]
2. The most densely populated sections of the city are Embakasi (near the Jomo Kenyatta International Airport), Kasarani (north of the central business district), and Njiru (in the Eastlands area).
3. The city is home to 1 million Catholics, 2.3 million Protestants and Evangelicals, 300,000 African independent churches, and 23,000 Orthodox.[2]
4. Other faiths represented in Nairobi are Traditionalists (7029), Muslims (323,809), Hindus (38,141), and atheists/agnostics (54,841).[3]

Christianity in Nairobi does not happen in its own silo but interacts with the religious diversity that marks this modern African city.

While numbers matter, this book takes a "bottom-up" perspective on the city of Nairobi. The story and characters on the ground tells us more about Christians in the city than statistics alone. Founded in 1899 as little more than a train depot for the Uganda Railway, Nairobi has come a long way. Metropolitan Nairobi now boasts a population of 10 million and is the continental headquarters for both the United Nations and the World Bank. Nairobi is also one of the most religiously pluralistic cities in the world. Mosques, megachurches, and temples compete with gleaming skyscrapers to define Nairobi's skyline. Christian pluralism runs deep with the 85 percent of Nairobians who claim allegiance to one of the different thousand Christian churches. This makes the city a laboratory of a new global pluralism, a concept promoted by Peter Berger in his *Many Altars of Modernity: Toward a Paradigm of Religion in a Pluralist Age*. Nairobi is the vital center of a new global Christian pluralism. It is a kind of pluralism that is reshaping religion in the majority world. Our book examines the diverse expressions of Christianity found in Nairobi and how they relate to each other. The threads and themes that emerge from this study provide a perspective on how Christians in the city come to terms with modern urban realities, including religious pluralism, through their faith. As such, Nairobi's faith story may shed light on how this process of pluralism and re-sacralization of secular space could unfold in other parts of the world.

The two authors of this book are both colleagues and friends. We have both made Nairobi our home for several decades. Kyama writes as an insider who has lived much of his life in the mix of the traditions we describe in this book. He was raised Anglican, married a former Roman Catholic, has an extended family who belongs to the independent churches, went to school with Coptic Christians, and pastored Pentecostal/charismatic churches. Mark came to Nairobi as a missionary outsider whose discovery of the rich diversity of urban Christianity has not only given him a front-row seat to the story of

World Christianity but also enriched his personal faith journey. Our method uses historical narrative, telling fact-based stories gleaned mainly from primary sources, interviews, and archives, to illuminate the life of Christians in Nairobi. We tell the story of the city from below by looking at one of the many faith traditions that flow through the heart of the city.

Chapter 1 begins with Nairobi's dominant form of Christianity, historic Protestant churches. Missionary Christianity dominated the new city of Nairobi from its founding in 1899 until independence in 1963. The growth of indigenous leadership within the historical churches is a main part of the story in the post-independence period. Chapter 2 tells the story of Nairobi's particular form of Catholicism. Catholicism in Nairobi is not static but ever-changing, from its early years as the product of European missionary orders to the role of Catholic charismatic Christianity in modern Nairobi. Chapter 3 examines Nairobi's African Initiated Churches (AICs). Beginning with churches like the rural-oriented *Roho* churches of Western Kenya, this chapter tracks the AICS shift to the city and the role of churches like the African Independent Pentecostal Church of Africa (AIPCA) in helping marginalized urbanites to "find a place to feel at home."

Chapter 4 details the variety of forms of urban Pentecostal churches found in the city. We examine a variety of types, from progressive Pentecostals to churches of deliverance. Chapter 5 surveys the three major expressions of Orthodoxy in Nairobi. This ancient form of Christianity has found new life in the city in its Coptic, Ethiopian, and more indigenous forms. The key role played by young people in urban Christianity is the subject of Chapter 6. In contrast to Christianity in the West, young Nairobi Christians are translating their faith into their culture at the speed of the internet. Chapter 7 focuses on the role of women in Nairobi's vibrant Christian scene. The involvement of women has influenced and altered every aspect of Christianity in Nairobi at the local and national levels. Chapter 8 looks at the volatile story of church and politics in Nairobi. The varied responses of the church to political life under the nation's five presidents are surveyed and new directions in the church-state relationship are explored. The final chapter examines the relationship between Christians and Muslims in Nairobi. Muslims struggle with deep feelings of alienation and marginalization. Christians struggle with fear and hostility toward many sections of the Muslim community. The chapter highlights efforts to bridge these differences. Throughout the story, we chart the rise of at least two recurring themes: an ever-evolving religious pluralism and the re-sacralization of the secular.

If no man is an island, then that is surely true of authors. Kyama is grateful for his wife, Wambui, and the many sacrifices she has made to make both this book and his teaching career possible. Mark can't imagine life or work without Lois, who is a constant inspiration. Both of us are grateful to our families, our institutions (Yale Divinity School and Africa International University), and the expert editorial services of Irene Mugambi. We also thank our hardworking research assistant, John Musumbi. This book would not have happened without the vision and creativity of Dyron Daughrity of Pepperdine University, the general editor of this series. Emily Wootten and the team at Bloomsbury have guided us every step of the way. Much appreciation to them all.

Nairobi, like other great cities, may be a mirage, but it is not just a mirage. Beneath the clouds of glass and steel exists a solid world of vibrant faith that daily nurtures the city's millions. Nairobi's story is intensely local but also achingly universal. How can one use the diverse spiritual resources of the Christian faith to live fully human lives in an urbanizing world full of dehumanizing forces? The story of Christianity in Nairobi is but one partial answer to that persistent question.

This book is dedicated to Kyama's mother, Elizabeth Nyathira Mugambi, of blessed memory, who, together with his father, Jesse Ndwiga Mugambi, were first-generation Christian residents of Nairobi, where Kyama was born.

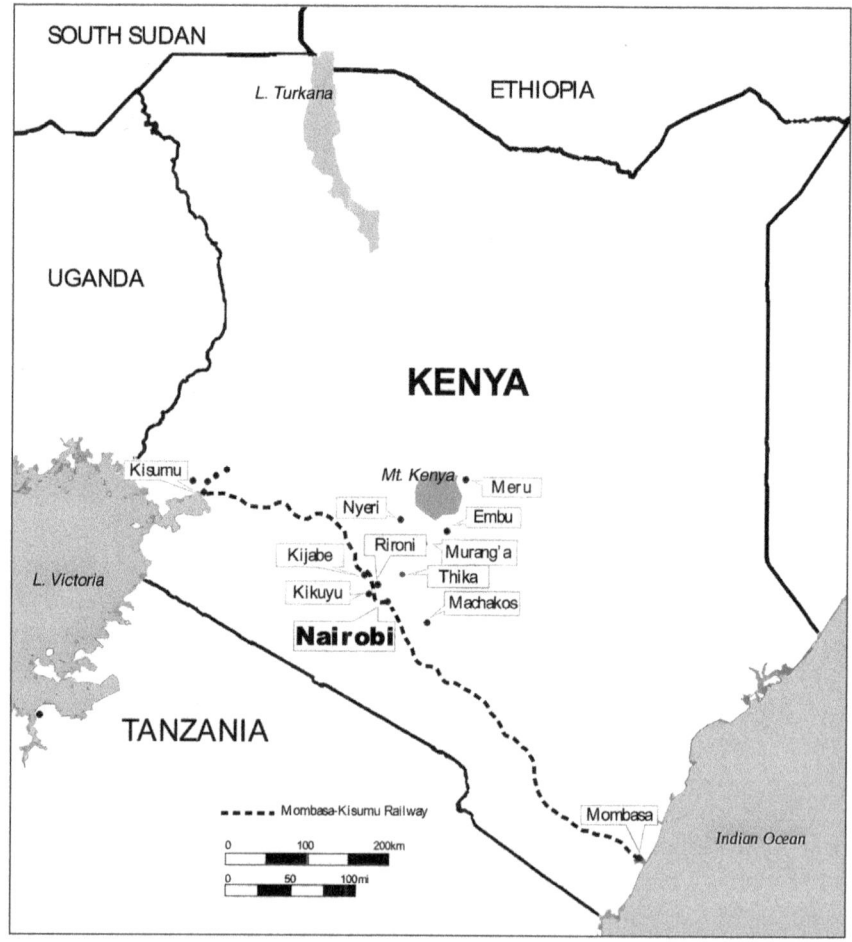

MAP 1 *East Africa. Credits: by Kyama Mugambi.*

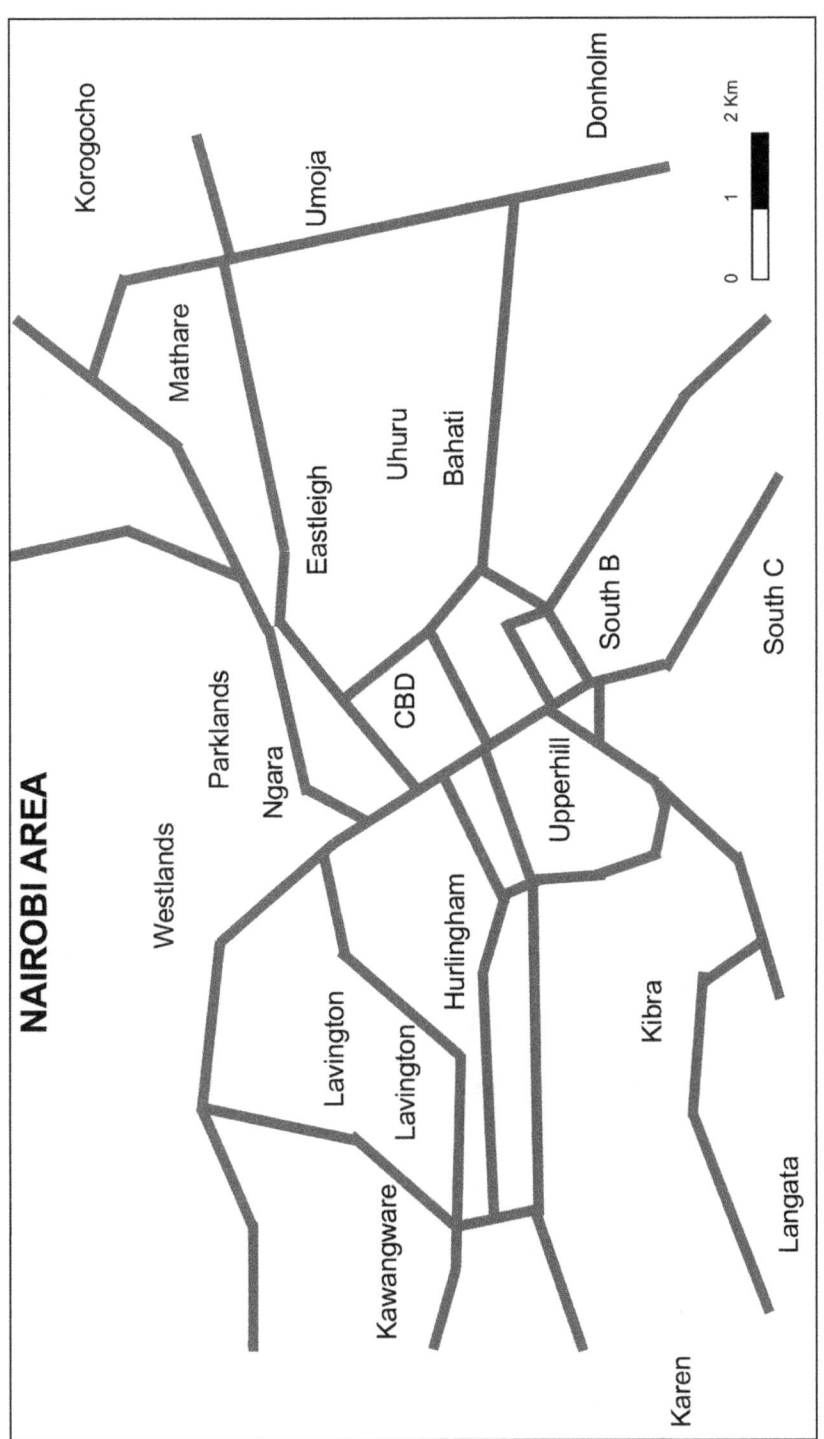

MAP 2 *Nairobi area. Credits: by Kyama Mugambi.*

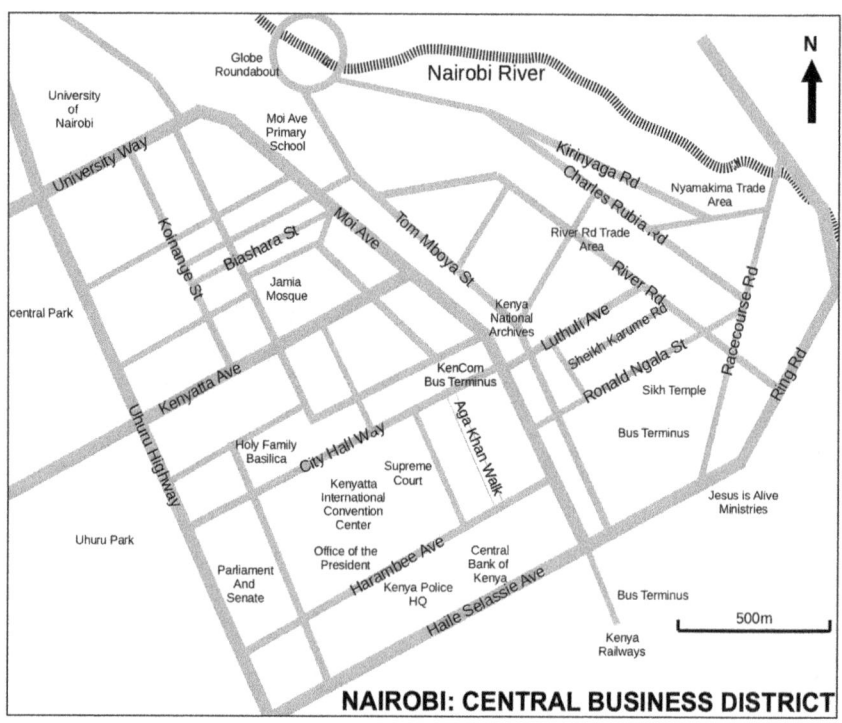

MAP 3 *Nairobi central business district. Credits: by Kyama Mugambi.*

1

The Cathedral and the Kiosk
Historic Protestant Churches in Nairobi

Christianity in Nairobi is the story of two structures. One structure stands uniquely on a hill and was built at a significant cost. The other is found everywhere throughout the city and is cheap to construct. The first structure is a cathedral, and the second, a kiosk.

The foundation of All Saints' Cathedral was consecrated in February 1917 on a quiet hillside overlooking central Nairobi. Designed by British architect Temple Moore just before he died in 1920, it captured the Gothic revival style that Moore had perfected in the forty churches that made up his professional portfolio.[1] It took several decades before All Saints' was completed and consecrated in 1952 (Figure 1.1). To worship today in its somber interior or contemplate its medieval style is to gaze upon a form of Christianity deeply rooted in a European past. Its soaring liturgy, visual beauty, and timeless appeal speak of one kind of Christianity that has helped shape Nairobi—missionary Christianity. Kyama Mugambi describes the Cathedral as a "monument to the success of the missionary enterprise and the colonial backbone on which it stood." Ironically, it was also a testimony to "a missionary Christianity that was not yet enculturated."[2]

Surrounding the Cathedral and spread throughout Nairobi is a second symbolic structure. Hundreds, if not thousands, of food kiosks (*Kibanda* in Swahili) pepper the city like the savory seasonings that flavor their dishes. Kiosks offer affordable servings of fish and meat stew, *sukuma wiki* (collard greens), *madondo* (beans), *ndengu* (green grams), and *chapati* (a popular flatbread). This

FIGURE 1.1 *All Saints' Cathedral. Photo: Mark Shaw.*

popular cuisine is washed down by large quantities of local tea. Food kiosks are popular hangouts and play a key role in feeding Nairobi's working class.

Most of Nairobi's Christianity today is more like the Kiosk than the Cathedral. Its residents bring with them local questions, seeking a "word from God" in ways they can understand and apply to their life situations. Still, Nairobi's urban faith is a fascinating mix of both cathedral and kiosk. While one might say some of the main ingredients, "the meat and potatoes," of Kenya's Christianity are from the missionary Christianity represented by the Cathedral, much of the flavor and spice come from "Kiosk Christianity." This local Christianity is found primarily in the newer churches, descendants of indigenous movements such as Revivals, African-initiated churches, and newer Pentecostal churches, both homegrown as well as international. Christianity in Nairobi can only be understood as a rich and ever-changing mixture of both the Cathedral and the Kiosk.

The story of kiosk Christianity comes later in the book. Cathedral Christianity commands our attention in the opening chapters. Protestant missionary Christianity is the focus of this opening chapter. Catholic Christianity makes up the story of Chapter 2.

In this chapter, we first look at the broad background of the rise of Nairobi and coming of missionary Christianity, before giving profiles of a few specific denominations. We will end the chapter by analyzing how these forms of Christianity, deeply rooted in European and American cultures, became localized and helped move the Cathedral ever more closely toward the Kiosk.

The Story of Nairobi Protestantism

Before there was a Nairobi, there were churches. And, many of them. While Catholics (the subject of our next chapter) planted their flag on the Kenyan coast in the 1500s, it was not until 1844 that Protestantism gained a foothold in what would become Kenya. Ludwig Krapf and Johann Rebmann were the two Europeans sent by the Church Missionary Society (CMS) and planted the first Protestant church in Kenya just outside of Mombasa in that year. Their conversions were few but their travels were many. They extensively explored eastern Kenya doing translation as they went. The first Swahili bible and dictionary were the product of Krapf's pen. It would be hard to imagine two more effective table setters for the future of Christianity in Kenya.

Methodists, Presbyterians, and independent missions like the Africa Inland Mission (AIM) soon followed the Anglicans and helped the gospel penetrate deeper into the heart of the country. The development that changed everything was the so-called "Lunatic Express," the name given to the East African railway built from Mombasa to Kisumu on Lake Victoria between 1896 and 1902 with the help of some 32,000 Indian workers. The "lunatic" part of the nickname came from the real reason for the railroad: to ensure that the British Empire could control the source of the Nile and consequently the passage to India, the crown jewel in her imperial crown. In 1899, the railway opened to the public when it reached mile 326, making a death-defying safari of many weeks an overnight affair. Mile 326 was named Nairobi, and a city was born.[3]

By the turn of the century, mission churches were gathering around the new railway depot like many moons around a planet. New arrivals were the Church of Scotland Mission (CSM 1898), the Holy Ghost Mission (HGM 1899), the Church Missionary Society (1901), and the African Inland Mission (AIM 1901). Land and infrastructure seemed easier to come by than converts. AIM struggled for converts outside Ukambani, their rural center well south of Nairobi. The Presbyterians baptized their first convert, Philip Karanja, in 1907.

As more converts slowly trickled in, missionaries kept tripping over each other. This awkwardness inspired a true milestone in the history of Nairobi's historic churches in 1909—The United Missionary Conference, which was held in the emerging city. Issues such as zones of influence and degrees of cooperation were thrashed out, inaugurating a period of cooperation between the agencies and related churches that seemed to be far in advance of what was happening elsewhere on the continent.[4]

In June 1913, the United Missionary Conference met again in Thogoto, just outside the city limits. The bold proposal debated over five days that June was the possibility of the mission agencies forming a single church. By the end of the conference, five of the missions had agreed to accept this proposal including CMS, AIM, and CSM.

The First World War, however, interrupted the merger plans of the leading mission churches. Nairobi went off to war, fighting in German East Africa (GEA) in a game of hide-and-seek with the numerically inferior German army led by the wily General Lettow-Vorbeck. Nairobi grew due to the war, as white settlers and British allies swelled the ranks of the European settlers. Despite the Allies' vast superiority in numbers and resource, the German general eluded both defeat and capture, surrendering his forces only after the general armistice had been announced in 1918. Kenyans tended to be the biggest losers in the war, as white settlers took advantage of the conflict to take over the economy, moving from 15 percent ownership of land in Kenya to some 70 percent by the war's end. The seeds of future internal conflict were sown by this dramatic economic shift.[5] The white settler influence on the colonial regime was pervasive. Winston Churchill's observation in 1907 when he visited Nairobi proved true during the years of the war: "Every white man in Nairobi was a politician, and most of them leaders of parties."[6]

The immediate aftermath of the war seemed apocalyptic to many. A deadly flu epidemic claimed tens of thousands of lives locally. The bubonic plague claimed even more lives in Kenya and over a million across the continent. A famine swept through the young colony, claiming the lives of thousands more. The missionaries were kept busy mourning the tragic loss of countless many. Yet their dreams of a united church were kept alive even amidst the tragedy of war, disease, and famine. In 1918, the Alliance of Protestant Missions (APM) was formed, pledging to build a united church across the nation. The experiment persisted until 1935. One of the abiding achievements of 1918 was the plan to form Alliance High, soon to become one of the elite educational institutions in greater Nairobi.[7]

In 1919, the Alliance of Missions (AIM) became an advocate of Kenyan rights. The great white settler land grab of the war years led to the great labor grab of the postwar years. To help the new settlers farm their fields, the colonial regime passed a "hut" tax on every Kenyan family unit required to be paid in cash. For many Kenyans, cash was a hard commodity to come by. The new policy amounted to forced labor. The alliance took up the measure before the colonial council. CMS missionaries such as Harry Leakey became sincere and effective advocates for "native rights."[8]

In 1920, Kenya became an official colony of the British Empire with Nairobi as its capital. What had once been little more than a railway depot had become a growing city replete with all the urban challenges that came with that status. The Salvation Army, founded in London in 1865, testified to the growing social and spiritual crisis of Kenya's capital by seeking out "Thieves, prostitutes, gamblers, and drunkards" in Nairobi in 1922.[9]

Nairobi Churches in the 1920s

For the Protestant churches of Nairobi, much of the "roaring twenties" was taken up with matters of education and ecumenism. The Phelps-Stokes Commission studying education in the British colonies of Africa visited Kenya in 1924. Their conclusion regarding the mission-founded schools was sharply negative. They put considerable pressure on the mission agencies to increase the number and quality of schools in the colony. The Alliance of Missions responded quickly with the establishment of Alliance High School in Kikuyu in 1926. G. A. Grieve was the first principal overseeing a total student body of twenty-six. It would be under the leadership of the second principal, Cary Francis, like Grieve, a CMS missionary, that the Alliance would reach its celebrated heights.

The 1920s also saw new developments in the quest for ecumenical unity. The Alliance's triumph in establishing a joint high school was somewhat compromised by the theological divisions growing within the alliance. The forces of theological modernism and conservative revivalism were contending for the soul of the Western world. Nairobi was not exempt from this culture war. Earlier divisions in the Alliance (such as those posed by Bishop Weston of Zanzibar) were more denominational in character. AIM, as the foremost representative of conservative revivalism (or what was soon becoming known as fundamentalism), found the theological conflict within the Alliance so disturbing that it resigned from the group for several months before rejoining.[10] By 1932, theological tensions declined sufficiently that the four main missions in the Alliance (CMS, CSM, Methodist Mission Society (MMS), and AIM) drafted a proposal for a united church. The dream never materialized. Part of the reason was the growing number of indigenous converts that were less inclined to give up the distinctives of the new churches which they had left culture and kin to join. But perhaps a deeper explanation was the most pressing issue of the 1930s—race. Race and racism set not only Kenya but the entire world on fire by the end of that decade.

War Within and Without: Historic Churches since the Second World War

Looking back on the 1930s in Kenya, it is easier now to see how race conflicts that strained the social fabric of the city and its nation were not simply local, but continental and international. Similar racial tensions that inflamed Nazi

Germany, South African Apartheid, and Segregated America were at work in Nairobi in the years leading to the Second World War. It was in the 1940s that African Christian converts responded to the perceptions of discrimination by colonial and missionary leaders.

One response to racial tension was separation. New breakaway churches popped up around Kenya and in the city. The African Israel Church Nineveh (AICN) broke away from the Pentecostal Assemblies of God (PAG) of Canada in Western Kenya in 1942. The Presbyterian Church of East Africa (PCEA) became self-ruling in 1943. In 1945, AIM's Africa Inland Church (AIC) ruptured, and the African Brotherhood Church was formed among the Kamba. In 1946, one of the oldest African independent churches, the African Orthodox Church, was recognized by the Greek Orthodox Patriarchate of Alexandria. Thereafter, in 1950, a host of Kikuyu independent churches were born. These movements of separation were indicators that the power center of Kenyan Christianity was shifting from missionary to local convert. In recognition of this shift, the Kenya Missionary Council (KMC) became the Christian Council of Kenya (CCK) to accommodate these new churches. The CCK eventually adopted in 1984 its current name, the National Council of Churches of Kenya (NCCK).[11]

A second response to racial tensions in the church was revival. In 1947, the first mass meeting of the Uganda-based East Africa Revival was held just 40 miles north of Nairobi in Kahuhia. The revival swept across Central Kenya in the postwar period, changing the face of the church. The city was encircled by revival fervor in the 1940s and 1950s. In 1949, 8000 gathered to hear revival preaching and testimonies in Kabete, about 9 miles north of Nairobi. In 1950, 15,000 gathered in Kikuyu, 12 miles west of the city.[12]

In 1952, the revival was interrupted by a declaration of a state of emergency in what became known as the Mau Mau rebellion, seeking independence from British colonial rule. The lives of many Kikuyu were turned upside down through the forced detention of thousands in mass compounds during the emergency. Revival Christians were targeted by the rebellion for their refusal to take the tribal oath of allegiance to the cause. Church after church was divided over Mau Mau. The movement was eventually defeated, and the state of emergency was lifted in 1960. The revival fervor continued throughout the emergency. The strength of the revival brotherhood was demonstrated in 1956 when some 12,000 gathered at the Maseno Convention in Western Kenya. By 1964, the revival was in full swing as 20,000 gathered in Mombasa.[13]

The postwar period was years of decolonization and growing African agency. In retrospect, the revival was an important agent of decolonization in the churches. The career of Bishop Festo Olang' (1914–2004) serving as the first African bishop of Nairobi and archbishop of Kenya, illustrates the power shift from missionary to indigenous leader. Born in Western Kenya, Olang' spent years as a teacher before becoming a priest. A year of training at St. Paul's Divinity School in 1944, followed by a year of training in Oxford, England, opened him up to the wider church. Olang' was exposed to the East Africa Revival and its message of confession and repentance. It became central to his preaching and leadership. On August 3, 1970, Olang' was enthroned in All Saints' Cathedral as the bishop of Nairobi and the first archbishop of Kenya. Olang' became a networker. He traveled extensively to visit churches in various countries. He was also instrumental in Billy Graham's Nairobi Crusade in 1960, which drew huge crowds. He organized conferences, networked internationally, and helped make the Anglican church a place where Kenyans could feel at home. The revival heritage was visible in Olang's life and work up to his death in 2004.

Rising Kenyan nationalism between 1940 and 1960 was yet a third response; a sign of growing African agency and rejection of the second-class status imposed by colonialism. The Kikuyu reserve, created during the early years of colonization, became restless over issues of land and economy. Nairobi became, in Ese and Ese's phrase, a "magnet of hope for many."[14] Missionary education raised indigenous expectations about better jobs and more say in their lives. Those jobs and that greater autonomy all pointed toward Nairobi. The number of African residents doubled during these years from 41,000 in 1939 to an estimated 95,000 by 1952.[15] After the state of emergency was lifted, the nation moved quickly toward independence and achieved its autonomy in 1964 with Jomo Kenyatta as the nation's first president.

Church and State Tensions in the 1990s

The decades since independence were marked by growing political action by the Protestant churches and more attention to issues of social justice. The death of Kenyatta in 1978 and the regime of Daniel arap Moi, which lasted until 2002, were the catalysts for this change. Nairobi Protestantism underwent a noticeable shift from revivalism to social justice that was sweeping the church internationally. A milestone in this shift was the 1975 World Council of Churches General Assembly in Nairobi. Six hundred and sixty-four delegates and many observers attended.[16] The Nairobi assembly and the rise of a secularized Christianity only concerned with social, economic, and political matters. This theme came through strongly in the play *Muntu* ("man" in several African languages). Here, an idyllic African past is interrupted by the white missionary who comes with a Bible in one hand and a gun in the other as the vanguard of colonialism. The need for social action to adjust these historic wrongs was the clear, albeit exaggerated, message of the play.[17]

How did churches respond to this shift from revivalism to social justice? The story of three churches may illustrate the range of views. The Anglican church was (and remains) the largest Protestant denomination in Kenya.[18] Since independence, the church has moved from a focus on indigenization to a focus on contextualization—understood as a concern for justice in the social, political, and economic context. A key agent of indigenization was a series of activist bishops who altered the church's traditional supportive role with the government to a more prophetic stance. The shocking death of Bishop Alexander Muge in a suspicious road accident in 1990 was the most dramatic sign of growing tensions between the church and the state. Throughout the 1980s, Moi's Kenya African National Union (KANU) party had become more repressive, at one point declaring Kenya a one-party state. Anglican leaders met this development with outspoken condemnation; 1989 was a year of political arrests for those who championed political pluralism. Bishop Muge, along with Archbishop David Gitari, was vocal in his opposition to the loss of freedoms and violations of human rights under Moi's regime. Muge's death was widely believed to have been orchestrated by the government and deepened the distrust of the Moi regime by an ever-wider Christian community.

A second church influenced by social justice was the Nairobi Baptist Church. In the 1950s, twenty individuals from a variety of local and international origins attempted to form a truly urban church—one not defined by ethnicity but plurality. Its series of international pastors brought a higher level of preaching to the pulpit than many attendees had experienced back in their rural churches. The first Kenyan pastor was Mutava Musyimi, who led the church from 1979 to 1993. He preached openly against the abuses of the Moi regime. Themes of justice emerged from his carefully crafted expositional sermons. His political concerns led to him leaving Nairobi Baptist in 1993 to become the Secretary General of NCCK. He publicly campaigned for the constitutional revision and led an interfaith "Ufungamano" initiative (named after the meeting place) that played a key role in the eventual revised constitution of 2010 (see Chapter 7).

A third response is that of the AIC. The second-largest Protestant denomination in Kenya, the AIC was strongest among the Kamba people. The parent mission, AIM, spent much of its first fifty years of existence building churches and schools but delayed the ordination of Kenyans until the 1940s. Likewise, the full autonomy of the AIC from AIM took place in 1970, when a formal handover of the property to Bishop Wellington Mulwa (1918–79), head of the new church, finalized the transition. One of his first actions was to move the church headquarters to Nairobi. The church flourished under his watch. Between 1970 and 1979, the AIC in Kenya went from an estimated 300,000 to 1.5 million, making it, for a time, the largest Protestant denomination in Kenya by some estimations. Mulwa was in a running conflict with the Mission leadership over their attempts at control. He was a fundamentalist in theology but not in ecclesiology, participating fully in the NCCK despite AIM's concerns about the connection with the World Council of Churches. He insisted on changing the name of the denominational head from president to bishop, arguing that it was both more biblical and readily understood by people in the villages. When Presbyterian church moderator John Gatu (also general secretary of the Presbyterian Church of East Africa) called for a moratorium on new missionaries to Kenya in 1971, Mulwa, despite his contentious relationship with AIM, disagreed, and under his watch, the AIM missionary presence grew from 250 to 300.[19] AIC's work in leadership training, however, had been strong in the rural areas of Kenya but weak in Nairobi. In 1983, they joined with the Association of Evangelicals in Africa in the formation of Nairobi Graduate School of Theology. AIC churches were supporters of President Moi until his retirement. The AIC eventually pulled out of the NCCK and joined the Evangelical Alliance of Kenya (EAK), originally formed in 1975.

Relations between church and state continued to be rocky at the turn of the century. The violence that attended the 2007 elections united the churches behind an agenda of healing, unity, and nonviolence, as later seen in this book. The 2010 constitutional debate also revealed where Nairobi Christianity was going, particularly in its relation to Muslims and power sharing in the modern Kenyan state.

An additional issue facing the churches of Nairobi in the early 2000s was the growth of the Islamic terrorist organization, Al-Shabab. They confirmed their mission in Nairobi in 2013 with the Westgate Mall attack that resulted in over seventy deaths. Living with terrorism became a daily part of the Nairobi experience.

Despite the distraction of church and state tensions and the earlier war on terror, Nairobi Protestantism continued to grow in the Moi years. The 1990s saw Protestant church numbers skyrocket in Nairobi as immigration swelled the number of residents from the thousands to the millions. As Ian Shaw writes,

> Just after independence in 1963, the population of Nairobi was 400,000. By 1990 it was officially 1.3 million people, but most considered it above two million. In the late twentieth century, Nairobi's rate of population growth was around 7 percent per year.[20] The number of Christians has doubled each decade since the 1990s. Philip Jenkins has argued that with Kenya's increasing birth rate, the prospect for continued growth of the nation, the city, and the faith should continue well into the 21st century:

> That growth has plainly transformed Kenyan society, notably in the form of urban expansion. Nairobi began the 20th century with barely 5,000 people—it was a poor relation of the thriving port of Mombasa. Nairobi

grew to 100,000 by the early 1950s, and today its larger metropolitan region includes more than 5 million people. By 2050, the city alone could have 14 million.[21]

Nairobi's Historic Protestant Churches Today

Nairobi's historic Protestant churches today are more than just a monument to their past. The explosive growth of Christianity in the city is not only because of the rise of the additional streams of Christian faith and practice—which we explore in subsequent chapters—but is also the result of continuing revitalization within the historic churches. Let us look at the features of historic Protestant churches in modern Nairobi.

The first feature of the ongoing strength of historic Protestant churches is not only the number of churches but also the high concentration of parachurch ministries or NGOs. Julie Hearn has documented the growth of evangelical agencies operating in Nairobi. World Vision, World Relief, All Africa Conference of Churches (AACC), AIM, and CMS are but a small sample. In the early twenty-first century, the number of such institutions continued to grow.[22] Historic churches have been behind the rise of private universities throughout the country with Daystar University, Africa International University, St. Paul's University, International Christian University, Kenya Methodist University, and Africa Nazarene University a few of many examples available. Each has grown from a few hundred in the 1990s to several thousand today.

Faith-based NGOs have been criticized for competing with government programs, shifting the focus of Christian mission off of evangelism and church planting, and taking too large a slice of the world's charitable giving. Reverend Fred Nyabera, a former Protestant pastor at Nairobi Baptist Church and Karen Community Church who is now director of End Child Poverty, a Nairobi-based initiative of Arigatou International, responded to these criticisms. Reverend Nyabera readily admitted that many of these challenges have been true of some NGOs but they are not the whole story. "What if we remove faith-based NGOs from places like Lodwar and Kibera?" he asks. The answer would be large numbers of people descending deeper into the abyss of poverty and poor health. "NGOs have had a greater positive impact than a negative one. We work with the government not in competition with it and have seen a far more meaningful difference in the lives of children and the poor," he adds. What about the future of the historic mission churches and the NGOs they create in a city like Nairobi? "The city isolates people," he says. "It creates social and spiritual challenges. Historic churches and Faith based NGO's will continue to be a positive force for hope and change." He adds that the great challenge of historic churches is not external but internal.

We must focus on the discipleship and spiritual formation of urban believers. We must learn to love God with all of our heart, as agents of comfort and love, all of our mind as we speak truth into the difficult intellectual challenges the city generates and to love God with all of our strength by becoming a strong and healing community like the early church in the book of Acts.[23]

A second feature of historic Protestant churches is their engagement in global Christian debates. Discussions of women's ordination and the global debate regarding human sexuality have agitated the churches of Nairobi as they have in the West. The response of historic Protestant churches in the city has covered the spectrum but with a decidedly more conservative leaning than in Europe or North America. GAFCON 2013 (Global Anglicans Future Conference) was held in Nairobi, recommitting itself to upholding the Lambeth standards of 1998 on human sexuality and opposition to same-sex unions.

A third feature of Nairobi Protestant Christianity shared with other churches' expressions is the poverty divide. One feature is growth on both sides of the economic divide, but with historic churches more heavily concentrated in middle- and upper-class urban estates. In a comparative study between church growth between contemporary Nairobi and nineteenth-century Glasgow, Ian Shaw notes that in much of Nairobi, church attendance and middle-class identity often go together:

> The wealthy Karen and Langata areas, which had one church for every 500 people and an urban density of 4 persons per hectare, saw church attendance of 50.6 percent; appearing to confirm the thesis that high levels of church attendance are connected to proximity to churches and high levels of disposable income. So too with middle-class Kilimani. In Ngara and Eastleigh, areas of low-income, high-density housing, with up to 200 or 300 residents per acre and 5,000 and 9,300 persons per church, low levels of church attendance, at just 1.4 percent and 2.5 percent respectively, were recorded, again suggesting a clear correlation. However, the pattern was reversed in the case of Kibera, Nairobi's largest informal settlement, with a population density of 826 per hectare, but with one church for every 1,100 people and church attendance as high as 18.2 percent.[24]

Even though church attendance is often higher in more affluent churches, volunteerism is not. Shaw points to higher levels of church involvement among those in the informal settlements:

> Another factor observed of churches in Nairobi is the very high level of active engagement in church activities found amongst the poor, compared

to those in more affluent congregations. For more than 60 percent of those who attended churches in Nairobi, their only involvement was attending one Sunday morning service. Overall, only 4 per cent of affluent church members reported high levels of engagement, but this was 25 percent in low-income areas. In the poorest areas, church members are more likely to be involved in activities such as teaching, catechizing, visiting homes, running church projects of development and relief, organizing worship and Sunday schools, and running meetings in their homes compared to affluent members. There were especially high levels of engagement by women.[25]

Next in fourth place is that the gap between Christian profession and church attendance is significant. It reflects a similar gap in Western Christianity, the gap between believing and belonging. Studies conducted at the end of the century showed that while a third of the city declared themselves members of a church, only less than half showed up on Sunday morning with any regularity. This may show the unfinished task of discipleship or may just reflect the employment demands of Nairobi's working class. Perhaps some of both are involved.[26]

Moreover, Nairobi church life reflects a trend throughout majority world Christianity, the gender gap. Shaw notes that "With around 70 percent of migrants being male, the city's population in the late 1980s included 100 men for every 72 women. However, only 10 percent of men in Nairobi attended church, compared to 14 percent of women. The result is a gender imbalance in congregations unrepresentative of the wider population."[27] The reasons for this gender gap are unclear. One possibility is poverty itself. Women, with their responsibilities to care for the home and families, may feel the force of poverty more sharply than men. They are therefore more likely to seek the hope and comfort provided by the Christian message. If this observation proves to be true, it would counter the argument of some sociologists that poverty and low church attendance are corollaries.[28]

Finally, Nairobi's historic Protestant churches experience the phenomenon of double affiliation. Protestant Christianity accounts for 55 percent of Kenya's Christian population—if one does not include what the World Christian Encyclopedia (WCE) calls independents. It becomes two-thirds if independents are included. Charismatic expressions within the historic mission churches give rise to a great deal of double affiliation. The WCE estimates as many as four million Christians belong to multiple churches. It is not uncommon for an Anglican or Africa Inland Church member to also attend a charismatic deliverance church for healing or help not offered in their home church.[29]

Nairobi's Christian past and present, at least through the lens of the historic Protestant churches, has been powerful, rich, and varied. But what does this all mean and what does it have to say to the rest of the world about the future of world Christianity?

The Impact of Nairobi Protestantism

In what ways has Nairobi's particular brand of Protestantism shaped the urban Christian landscape of the city? While the newer Pentecostal churches often grab the attention of observers, Protestant missions and churches have defined Nairobi Christianity in many ways. We mention three.

First, the historical Protestant churches of Nairobi act as bridges to the past and to the global church. Missionaries, to the degree that they are effective, are bridge people. Their role is to network. They connect new converts to the scriptures, to the global church, and to the story of the Christian past. We will look at examples of "diffuse" Christianity in subsequent chapters, some of it new and vital. The remarkable thing about even the new churches of Nairobi is their basic commitment to historic Christian orthodoxy. This has not been by government decree or Episcopal edict. The Christian framework established by the historic churches has provided room for innovation while at the same time providing enduring foundations.

Not that the historic churches are all on the same page theologically. They differ, as churches in other parts of the world differ, on theological matters, on the authority of the scriptures, on aspects of salvation and church government, and the sacraments. The polarities between Liberal and Conservative Protestants, however, do not seem as sharp as in Europe or the United States and Canada. A strong if fluid evangelical core provides common ground for most, if not all, historic Protestants in the city.

Secondly, and connected to the first point, is that historic Protestantism has been a force for unity. This may seem to be a contradiction. How can a movement so splintered and so committed to the multiplying of distinct organizations be a force for unity? The answer is something called pluriformity. The early twentieth-century Dutch philosopher-theologian, Abraham Kuyper, argued for pluriformity as the proper form of church unity. Kuyper opposed uniformity on the one hand and sectarianism on the other. He saw a third way—unity in diversity. As one theologian explained:

> Appealing to the diversity of creation, the variety of circumstances within God's providence, and the limitations of human knowledge and understanding, Kuyper articulated a doctrine of church pluriformity that approved the diversity of churches and denominations. Rather than being regarded as a sinful deflection from the biblical standard of unity among the

churches, Kuyper regarded the diversity and pluriformity of the churches to be a kind of necessary, even inevitable expression of such factors as the diversity of creation and the variety of God's providence. That the churches are pluriform in confession, in church order, in practice, and in so many other ways, is not something to be viewed with dismay or regret, but with benign approval.[30]

From the early missionary councils and comity agreements to the modern ecumenical organizations of the NCCK and the EAK, the historic churches have steered a middle path between oppressive uniformity and exclusive sectarianism. This commitment to a functional pluriformity has given a fundamental dignity to the new churches that a more centralized church culture would withhold.

This pluriformity must be more than just an academic idea. Bishop Rose Okeno, the second female bishop in the Anglican Church of Kenya (ACK), consecrated in 2021, was asked how historic Protestant churches like the ACK can best face the future. Her answer anticipated many of the themes of this book.

> There are many large challenges facing the church. Muslims continue to grow in number and influence. Young people continue to drift from the church. What we must not do is push people away. We must not disconnect with people where they are and how they are. We must not let the clergy class separate from the people below. We must learn to eat sweet potatoes with the people.[31]

Unity is not just about organization. It is fundamentally about love, humility, and building relationships.

Thirdly, historic Protestantism in Nairobi helps contemporary Christianity in Kenya to navigate global secularization and religious violence by embracing an emerging pluralist paradigm.[32] Protestants believed that the truth of the gospel was bigger than any institutional structure and could not be contained within it. Only multiple institutional expressions of the church, acting cooperatively, could adequately bear witness to the gospel. Sociologist Peter Berger speculates that it is this very fractious Protestant practice of allowing institutional diversity and theological argument that may well shape the twenty-first-century global religious landscape. Berger's current position represents a major shift from his years subscribing to the secularization thesis and its belief that modernization erodes faith and promotes science and secularization as a substitute for religion. In 1999, Berger confessed his intellectual error in a book entitled *The De-secularization of the World*. "The world today . . . is as furiously religious as it ever was, and in some places, more so than ever."[33]

Berger argues that though modernization has affected Africa and other places in the majority world, it has not produced the decline of religion and a scientific revolution such as Europe experienced in the eighteenth and nineteenth centuries. It has instead produced pluralism, an increase in faith as a whole and in a diversity of faiths. The reason for this, for Berger, is clear: "Modernity . . . undermines all the old certainties; uncertainty is a condition that many people find very hard to bear; therefore, any movement (not only a religious one) that promises to provide or to renew certainty has a ready market."[34]

Berger speaks of a double pluralism involving, on the one hand, "the pluralism of diverse religious traditions and institutions" and, on the other, "the pluralism of secular and religious discourses." This second form of pluralism is key to understanding its positive social, economic, and political impact.

Berger's view of both modernity and pluralism makes clear that these dynamics produce more than diversity. They also produce peaceful coexistence. This double pluralism creates, to use Berger's phrase, "the co-existence of different religions and the co-existence of religious and secular discourses." Pluralism as a formula for peace and progress not only creates civility between religions and a deepening of Christianity within religious tradition, but it also creates a non-coercive secular space, free of sectarian control, in which all traditions can have more or less equal access to public goods such as governance and education. Pluralism is therefore a key to progress.

Ian Shaw notes that "In their 1997 study of Nairobi, Shorter and Onyancha claimed that secularism is rapidly becoming a more generalized phenomenon on the African continent, spreading from a small circle of privileged individuals to a whole society which is undergoing a spectacular evolution."[35] If Berger is correct, then Nairobi's prospects for weathering both religious competition and secularization are excellent.

Karen Community Church is located on the outskirts of Nairobi, daughter of the megachurch Nairobi Baptist. It is a church of about 300. Young people attend special services in a large tent on the campus. Children flock to the Sunday school program housed in an attractive educational building. The family service is packed with families of all ages and is led by an enthusiastic worship team of mixed generations and genders, alternating English and Swahili choruses. Prayers and Bible reading punctuate the order of worship. The Senior Pastor, Reverend John Paul Mugendi, preaches an animated and probing sermon from the scriptures. He speaks of the need to engage unreached people groups with the gospel of Christ and reminds his people of the great commission to go into all the world and make disciples. People are challenged to accept Christ as lord and savior or to renew their commitment to his worship and service. In many ways, this service not only represents historic Protestant churches in Nairobi today but reflects the DNA of Protestantism in Kenya's past. At the end of the day, historic Protestant Christianity in Nairobi is a word-based faith, emphasizing preaching, teaching, and singing the message of the Scriptures and bringing that saving word to the lost. Importantly, Karen Community Church realizes it cannot fulfill the great commission alone. God works in other churches besides their own. They practice an evangelical pluralism of word and mission. This is not the pluralism of the ivory towers but a pluralism of the street and the city, of a church balanced between the cathedral and the kiosk.

2

The Mass and Its Masses
Catholic Presence in Nairobi

At 10:00 a.m. on a Sunday morning, the Catholic faithful exit the church after Fr. Kamau's benediction. They gather in a wide concrete courtyard at the front of the church. The large cross atop a round pavilion at the center of the courtyard is a vivid reminder of the sacredness of the church grounds. This is significant for a church located in the middle of the most important secular business and political establishments of the nation. Those leaving the Sunday mass mingle with those coming in. The roads are empty and there is little activity in this part of the city, save for a large curio market some 200 meters east of the church compound, next to the Supreme Court building.

The Holy Family Minor Basilica (Figure 2.1) stands in the central business district (CBD), half a kilometer east of Uhuru Park. It is an imposing building of cast cement, 70 meters long and 40 meters wide. Its walls are eight stories high, while the free-standing bell tower is three times the height of the walls. This chapter explores how Catholicism touches the life of the city through ritual spirituality, education, and in the homes of Nairobi residents. The chapter explores how Catholicism remains relevant despite its commitment to ancient ritual rooted in Western European ritual heritage.

A stone's throw away from the basilica sits the Parliament, the Supreme Court, and the County office in the President's office. The basilica complex houses the Main Church building that holds eight chapels. Its concrete form is reminiscent of 1960s architecture. The building is the creative work of Dorothy Hughes, a devout Catholic, and one of very few female architects in Kenya's colonial era.[1]

In 1899 at the time settlers founded Nairobi as a colonial town, French bishop, Emile Augustine Allgeyer, a Holy Ghost Father, spearheaded a Catholic mission beyond the coastal region.[2] Holy Ghost Fathers were the

FIGURE 2.1 *Holy Family Cathedral. Photo: Kyama Mugambi.*

first to establish successful missions in the nation's interior. This mission was a triumph after several earlier missions that were unsuccessful in penetrating the Savannah, a vast grassland south of Nairobi. Nairobi was the natural place to build the Holy Family Cathedral. It was a business center and the colonial government's administrative seat. It housed the largest rail station after Mombasa. The Holy Ghost Fathers set out to build a church and the priests' residence in Nairobi. The growing congregation was active by 1907 when Nairobi was declared the capital of the colony.[3] The work brought together Catholic Indians from Goa, Europeans from the colony, and a small but growing number of Africans.[4] These were the beginnings of the Nairobi Diocese, which extended in a triangle with Thika in the east, Rironi in the west, and Nairobi in the south. In 1918, the Holy Ghost mission established another church in Nairobi for Africans, the mission of St. Peter Claver. The mission set it up east of Nairobi's railway station. In the meantime, the Holy Family congregation grew steadily with Europeans, Indians, and Africans. Following this prolific growth, in 1963, the church demolished the old building to make way for a new larger building. Acknowledging the prominent place of Catholicism in the emerging nation, the Vatican elevated the status of the new building to be one of only 1,800 minor basilicas in the world.

By 2020, Catholics accounted for 12.1 million Kenyans. One million of those live in Nairobi and make up almost a third of the Christians in the city.[5] Roman Catholicism is the single largest Christian denomination in Kenya. So significant is the presence of Catholics that it has merited papal visits in 1980, 1985, 1995, and 2015. Pope John Paul's visits to Nairobi in the mid-1980s inaugurated a decade's long era of large open-air Christian gatherings in the city.

Pope John Paul II's mass in 1985 provided an opportunity for the use of Uhuru Park, a secular space, for religious gatherings. Not only was this the largest Catholic mass ever celebrated in the city at the time, it was also the largest religious gathering of any kind ever witnessed in Nairobi. Pope Francis's visit in 2015 continued with this trend. A different secular ground was selected. The university grounds also along Uhuru Highway. With these visits, the Catholic church in Kenya demonstrated the use of secular spaces for religious purposes on a national scale. In this way, the Catholic church offered leadership in the sacralization of secular spaces in the city.

The Catholic church is institutional in its approach to engaging with society. Its different expressions model the Cathedral and not the "kiosk." Whatever the local situation politically, economically, or culturally, the Catholic church remains integrated in every way with the global denomination. Their expression of Christianity in Nairobi is not marginal to mainstream city life. Catholics are at the center. Their schools, mission hospitals abide by the strict rules of the final authority in the Vatican. Through the transformations of Kenyan history, Catholics modeled in concrete ways the institutional authority of one of Christianity's oldest and most powerful bureaucracies. As we shall see later, from early post-independence Kenya, Catholicism rose to occupy a significant place in the country. The colonial separation of religion from other structures of society sought to create a secular Kenya in the mold of modern Europe. Even then, secularizing forces in the city of Nairobi in those early years did little to reduce religious commitment among indigenous people. The growth of the church continued unabated. The basilica's rising significance represented the steady upsurge of Catholicism's profile in urban areas.

The minor basilica's lofty plain gray walls and narrow stained-glass windows house a community for worship that is far from dull. Each Sunday, a multigenerational congregation gathers for two Swahili and two English masses. The worship services are multigenerational. Majority, however, are young people aged below thirty-five. They resonate with the vibrant Christianity evident in the rest of the country. The traditional mass incorporates local elements such as occasional dances for processions of special masses. The music of the services employs the use of drums to accompany choir music.

The liturgy includes Swahili songs composed for various parts of the mass. The choir leads these songs, joined by the congregation which sings them extemporaneously.

Music at the minor basilica is typical of Catholic mass in Kenya. A distinctive tone in Catholic congregational music is the sound of the electronic organ played in a characteristic percussive style. The percussion section adds to the drums, the sound of the *kayamba*. This is a flat shaker made of elephant grass, with dry ground gram seeds in it. This is a traditional instrument originating from Kenyan coastal communities. A combination of drums, organ, and *kayamba*, along with a Swahili vocal chorus, makes the distinct sound of Kenyan Catholic worship. The congregation is familiar with the sound because recordings of this type of music sell by the thousands in music shops in the older part of Nairobi CBD, less than a kilometer east of the church.

The church is active every day, bustling with attendees coming for mass early in the morning, at lunchtime, and in the evening. A small portion of the pavement is a driveway which serves as entrance and exit from an expansive parking lot below the courtyard. The parking, which accommodates hundreds of cars, is one of the most technologically advanced in the city. The parking is fitted with one of the first automatic sensor, electronic metering, and payment systems.

These pieces of technology are a testament to the Catholic church's futuristic pragmatism. This is among the first fully automated parking lots of its kind in the country. It serves the congested central business area of the city. The site is also home to two other important examples of Catholic pragmatism: a school and an office block.

The minor basilica is a physical symbol of Catholicism's growth to develop its now highly visible, pragmatic presence.[6] Catholic impact comes across in schools, hospitals, and social work. Catholicism here, as in its native Europe, stands for the well-established presence of Christianity in society. Its commitment to liturgical worship and church tradition does not stand apart from but complements its robust development agenda for a dynamic context. Contrary to what critics might argue, the development agenda still is subservient to the evangelization goals of the Catholic church.[7] Education is a factor in the rise of secularizing forces in urban Africa. Western education introduced the concepts essential to sustain the secular state. Roman Catholic Christian ritual is one of the religious elements running counter to secularizing forces introduced through education. Nairobi is the site where this Christian expression lives out the tension between the sacralizing and secularizing influences of education.

The eight-floor business block next to the church houses a bookshop and Bishops' offices. Pacis Insurance Company, owned by the Catholic church, also has offices in the building. The Catholic church founded Pacis Insurance

Company in 2004 "with the aim of providing sustainable funding for projects in the Catholic Church in Kenya."[8] The company has the support of affiliated institutions of the church which includes the Association of Catholic Nuns, the Catholic Missionary Priests, the Dioceses, and Archdioceses. The concept behind Pacis points to the church's openness to business enterprise with and for its membership. Profits from Pacis Insurance go back to the sponsor for investment into community projects.[9] This block illustrates how the Catholic church connects with society beyond the religious to the social and economic life of the nation.

Catholic Parochial school hosted within the basilica counts as one of three primary schools found in the central business district of Nairobi. The school is smaller than most public schools with only a few hundred children. The school, however, maintains a vibrant presence in the city, active with students throughout the school year. The yard doubles up as a playing field for the pupils.

Catholics, Political Power, and the City

The minor basilica's proximity to the numerous sites of government power is striking. This is especially so given the history. Drawing from its European origins, Catholicism did not make an overt attempt in Kenya to engage with the state during the pre-independence days. Kenya's British colonial heritage established Protestantism and especially Anglicanism by default, as the official Christian expression.[10] Anglicanism firmly entrenched itself in the life of the country through this colonial contact point. Scottish Presbyterian missions also enjoyed some privilege and protection from the colonial government. The Kikuyu alliance of missions produced a Kikuyu Bible in the 1910s. The collaboration of Anglicans and Presbyterians also left a lasting legacy through the Alliance school, so named because of this collaboration. Catholic mission into the country's interior came an entire half century after the Anglicans had established themselves.

Catholicism charted a different path. It tried to establish a Christianity that was institutional but separate from the structures of colonial power. French and Italian missionaries stayed out of the government's way in their missions, focusing on their work. Their voice tended to be muted in government matters.[11]

Catholic missions busied themselves, seemingly staying away from the workings of the largely British colonial enterprise in Kenya. Though the relations were cordial, there was little if any formal connection with English speaking Protestant missions. Engagement with the government was limited to bureaucratic functions. This allowed Catholic missions to operate as somewhat independent institutions in the colonial government era from 1900 to 1960.

Catholic work in the Nairobi Diocese bore fruit through many baptisms and confirmations in the Kikuyu dominated areas of Thika, Gatundu, Limuru, and Nairobi. Many Kikuyu luminaries in the independence struggle came from predominantly Catholic mission areas. Kenyatta and Kibaki are two prominent examples. Unlike the Anglican counterparts in the Kabete-Kikuyu area, Catholic missionary voices were largely quiet during the independence struggle. Kenya's first president Jomo Kenyatta and his son Uhuru, the fourth president, hailed from Gatundu, one of the early Catholic strongholds. Mwai Kibaki, a pioneer politician and the third president, from Nyeri was also a Catholic. His education at Mang'u, the foremost Catholic mission school of his day, reflects his heritage. He and Uhuru were especially public about their Catholic religious roots in the years between 2002 and 2022.

The rapidly growing city of Nairobi provided a live context within which members of society conceptualized their multiple identities in this rapidly changing reality. Within this context, Catholicism did not confront modernity. Instead Catholicism enhanced the impact of modernity on the society—primarily through education.

Catholics in Kenyan Public Life

Catholics in post-colonial Kenya sought to harness their numeric and institutional influence to address governance issues in the country. The conspicuousness of Catholic religious and social infrastructure became more prominent in the public sphere. This made Catholicism politically visible, leveraging its institutional presence in the city of Nairobi and, by extension, the nation of Kenya. The church, through its bishops, challenged government dysfunction through strategic engagement and calls for dialogue. In the context of upheaval, Catholic leaders actively commented on sociopolitical issues at various points from the 1990s.[12]

The Catholic mission operated unobtrusively, moving in the shadows of political power during the colonial and post-independence season of Kenyan political history. Unlike its colonial season, Catholic voices were eventually heard speaking truth to power during the Moi era in the 1990s through the Kenya Conference of Catholic Bishops (KCCB). Often speaking from Nairobi, the body of prelates would meet twice a year and issue regular statements addressing the State of the Nation in a wide range of topics.[13] The aim of the issuance of these statements is to harness the collective power of Catholic polity in providing religious input on national issues. The Apostolic Nunciature of the Holy See in Nairobi acts as the embassy of the Vatican. The office offers an additional means through which the Holy See gives oversight to Catholics in a nation.

As religious offices operating in a secular state, neither the KCCB nor the Nunciature sought to directly influence the political and social affairs of the country. That said, through the family of the first president and, especially, in the tenure of the third president, Catholicism enjoyed twenty years of a subtle but visible presence close to the vestiges of power. These years saw the most regular public display of Catholic worship in the mass media.

Whenever there were eruptions of violence, electoral unrest, or national disasters, Nairobi often served as the location for intense deliberations on public issues. Bishops' gatherings produced thoughtful, firm calls for peace and harmony motivated by the gospel message. Ndingi Mwana a'Nzeki, a Catholic archbishop, famously stood against the Moi regime in the early 1990s.[14] He urged an end to corruption and, together with others, championed a new constitutional dispensation. The economic downturn of the mid-1990s was another occasion for the Catholic prelates to raise their voices on behalf of the poor and marginalized. The post-election violence saw the Catholic bishops join with other religious voices in condemning the violence, calling for dialogue and humanitarian aid.

Over time, the Catholic church has also faced criticism, coming under fire for its stand on certain current issues. The Catholic stance on contraception is one such issue. The other is the resistance by some bishops to vaccine initiatives before and during COVID-19 pandemic, which cast aspersions on their conscientious attempts to protect the citizenry.[15]

Catholicism as a highly visible institutional Christian expression has not been without opposition. Though it is better tolerated in Kenya relative to other African countries, Catholicism does experience religious violence. In the few instances experienced, opposition by other faiths, especially Islam, is more overt than the denominational conflict between Protestants and Catholics.

Instances of destruction of property and loss of life in the context of religious conflict involving Catholics is rare. One instance stands out. Our Lady Queen of Peace located in Nairobi's South B area is one such incident.[16] For the first time since its establishment in 1968 by the Holy Ghost Fathers, Our Lady Queen of Peace experienced serious interreligious violence in November 2000.[17] This was a time of transition as the nation came to terms with the end of Moi's regime. Muslim and Christian youth engaged in running battles resulting in the burning of the church. Christian intervention by Kenyan church leaders, among them the Anglican archbishop, did not yield fruit immediately but spurred more violence. After the conflict subsided, the church was rebuilt and opened in 2003. The community engaged in interreligious dialogue in this area populated by both Christians and Muslims.[18] This eruption of violence in the church was unusual in Nairobi. This flashpoint exposed the fragility of religious tensions in Kenya at a time of transition. These tensions can quickly escalate in a time of social, political, and economic transition such as there was in Kenya in 2007.[19]

Through the times of stability and of change, the Catholic institutional infrastructure—through worship, education, and medicine—remained an important participant in the public life of the country.

Catholicism and Education

Catholic education initiatives in Kenya have never been far from church missions. Our Lady of Mercy Primary school is a stone's throw from Our Lady Queen of Peace church.[20] Catholic education institutions in Nairobi began from mission origins such as the Italian Loreto sisters early in the twentieth century. The Loreto sisters launched their ministry in the 1920s to establish vibrant schools for girls in a segregated Kenya.[21] This legacy of education lives on in such schools as Catholic Parochial at the minor basilica. The school models the Catholic commitment to education from early childhood to advanced degree institutions.

More examples of this commitment can be seen closer to the CBD. A kilometer west of Catholic Parochial Primary School lies Loreto Convent, Valley Road. This convent is also home to a leading girls' school situated on the main transport artery going westward. The complex includes a primary and secondary school. This relationship between the church and schools can be seen all over the country, and it extends beyond secondary schools into tertiary institutions.

One of the private universities closest to the business district is Strathmore University. It is located near Upper Hill's gentrified area turned business hub, 3 kilometers southwest of the CBD. Established in 1961 as an accounting school, this university gained a reputation for its premier law and business schools.[22] While the university is not an official ministry of the Catholic church in Kenya, it encapsulates the Opus Dei vision, under the Pope, to catalyze a community of Catholics devoted to excellence. Strathmore considers itself a "corporate undertaking of Opus Dei, inspired by St. Josemaria Escrivá." Opus Dei religious community of lay people attracts educated young adults to a life of devoted service to society. It seeks to "spread the message that work, study, sport, family life, and other ordinary activities are occasions for spiritual union with Jesus Christ."[23] The community also maintains libraries and reading rooms situated in several parts of the city.

The largest Catholic university in the country is found in the Nairobi metropolitan area, 12 kilometers southwest of the CBD. Catholic University of East Africa is the largest Catholic university system for them in the region. Launched in 1984 by the Association of Member Episcopal Conferences of Eastern Africa (AMECEA), it comprises of multiple constituent colleges.[24] Its colleges include such institutions as Hekima University college. This is a Jesuit training institution situated on the west side of Nairobi off Ngong Road, one of the main roads leading to Karen and other areas.

Catholic institutions serve as incubators of thought from which important African scholarship has emerged. Catholic scholars in the region are known for their work on the relationship between Christianity and traditional culture. Catholicism in the church, as in the academy, has sought not to antagonize traditional religion. Its scholars did not present its opposition in openly contentious terms as Protestant Christianity. At the same time, Catholicism also did not romanticize traditional religion. Its engagement with traditional religion was one of study, respect, and mutual coexistence.[25]

Their scholars argued for a greater understanding of the resources traditional culture had to offer Christianity. Catholicism found ways to engage culture and religion. Catholic theologians, many of them writing and teaching in Nairobi, put forward the thesis that it was possible to be African and Christian at the same time. Important East African theologians such as Magesa and Nyamiti carried forward the contextualization agenda.[26] These theological initiatives involved decades of discourse around the topic in ecumenical collaboration with Protestant counterparts.[27]

Ministry to the Sick and the Poor

Healing is an important theme in the Catholic mission and so hospitals form an important part of Catholic outreach to society. The Mater Misericordiae Hospital in the South B area of Nairobi is just a few meters from Our Lady Queen of Peace Hospital. It is well-known for the care of middle-income residents of that part of the city and beyond. The hospital also hosts one of the oldest maternity wings serving the area of Nairobi. Founded by the Irish Sisters of Mercy, the Mater Hospital has expanded from a health center, in the 1970s and 1980s, into a fully fledged hospital providing all the essential services. It was during this time that the government chartered it as a school of midwifery. In the early 2000s, Mater began to undertake heart procedures. As a charity devoted to the well-being of the poor, the hospital raised money for these procedures for children and the underprivileged who could not afford the operations. The hospital instituted the Mater Heart Run in 2002. This is a charity event which brings together thousands of schoolchildren, their parents, and corporate sponsors from all over Nairobi.[28] The walk remains a major city event held annually in June. It is one of the most visible events in the city marked by road closures and the characteristic green T-shirts of the participants.

There are numerous smaller Catholic hospitals and clinics distributed all over the city. Jamaa Mission Hospital, run by Catholic sisters (Order of nuns), is in Uhuru estate, in the east side of Nairobi. This area became one of the most populous after being designated in the 1960s as a housing area for the emerging middle-income populations.[29] St. Mary's Mission Hospital in Langata is on the west side of Nairobi. Langata is a more recent development. It is adjacent to the Karen area, reserved for white populations in colonial Nairobi. The Langata estates were built in the 1980s to cater to the upper-middle-income government and private sector workers. St. Mary's serves the Kibera population, providing a full range of medical services. St. Francis Mission Hospital serves the Kasarani area, northeast of Jamaa hospital. This area began growing in the 1990s and is one of the most densely populated areas for middle-income residents. The mission hospital serves this population as well as the low-income communities of Mathare and Korogocho informal settlements.

These provide medical care to complement and sometimes stand in place of government medical services. In many rural areas, Catholic hospitals and clinics are the only medical centers available, providing affordable health care for a population in need of it. Catholics' commitment to the urban poor is evident in hospitals, schools, and churches located within or near informal settlements. Catholic missionaries devote their time to the poor in Nairobi's informal settlements such as Kibera, Korogocho, and Mukuru. The Jesuits run the St. Joseph's Church in Kangemi informal settlement.

This deep devotion to the poor is evident in such places as Our Lady of Guadalupe Parish, which serves the Kibera informal settlement and St. Bakhita, next to the Mukuru informal settlement. Here, the church's duty to justice and intellectual rigor meets the commitment to mission amongst the least of these. Though keen on education and health, the Catholic church retains its priority of evangelism.

Charismatic Catholicism

Catholicism's strength is really in its people, not just in the institutions. Thousands congregate in churches in the city, saying mass in English or Swahili. The long-held Catholic mass liturgical traditions find a new lease of life—with more engagement in prayer—through the Vincentians. The Vincentian Prayer House near the Kawangware informal settlement highlights the charism of prayer albeit with a charismatic bent. The Vincentian Prayer House began in 2001 with Eastern Catholic priests from Kerala in southwest India. The movement is a part of the Syro-Malabar Church that is in full communion with the Vatican.[30] The movement is a Koventha "based on the Common Rules of St. Vincent de Paul and on the model of the Congregation of the Mission, founded by him in 1625."[31] Varkey Kattarath founded the Koventha (religious group) along with three diocesan priests in 1904. The Vincentians came to Nairobi in 2001.[32] In their worship and practice, they aim to "give expression to the spirit of Christ, resplendent in the five virtues of simplicity, humility, meekness, mortification and zeal for the salvation of souls."[33] Their vibrant worship and attention to the context draws many to their prayer programs. At the heart of their approach is relevance to the needs of the people through prayer and evangelism.

This expression's achievements in Kenya illustrate the possibilities that lie in Catholic mission from outside Western cultural roots. The South Indian origin of its missionaries and the relevant themes contextualized for their worship service is unique. The success of these global south missionaries against a historical background of mostly European missionaries speaks of the global nature of charismaticism in historic mission churches. The missionaries from India have struck a chord with the local communities who relish this highly relevant Catholic ministry.

The Vincentian center in Kawangware is vibrant with activities throughout the week. The day begins with silent meditation from 6:30 a.m. to 3:00 p.m. daily. The priests celebrate mass every weekday at 5:30 p.m. The Saturday service lasts the whole day from 8:00 a.m. to 4:30 p.m. The emphasis on prayer in different forms, silent and oral, in the format of the Catholic mass, provides opportunities for Nairobi residents to express their Catholicism in ways that make room for extended worship. The sermons often emphasize God's immanence in concrete ways in the lives of the audience. This is one expression of missionary Christianity in Nairobi which responds directly to the challenge of indigenous charismatic Christianity.

The uncharacteristic setup in a tent is a departure from the usual permanence of Catholic buildings. However, the mass here is even more energetic than in other Catholic churches. Catholics and other Christian faithful wishing to experience divine healing find one another in this gathering. The services here provide liturgies for prayer together with healing to cater to the needs of the faithful. Those who gather here seek the gifts of healing without stepping outside their expression of faith. The success of the Prayer House in Nairobi as a site for Catholic renewal serves as an illustration of the enduring strength of Catholic Christianity in urban Africa.

The Vincentians provide for the Nairobi Christian, a prayer dimension of Catholic diversity. Prayers for healing find an expression along with ancient liturgy and familiar music. Vincentians host gatherings with prayer liturgies that resonate with the prevailing contexts of African Christian spirituality. Through these gatherings, Catholicism in Kenya has tapped into the vibrant possibilities of pneumatic expressions. This charismatic vitality is also evident within small group communities. Here, a strong spiritual vitality quietly invigorates the traditional ritual of historic mission Christianity.

Big Churches, Close Communities

Catholic congregations tend to be fewer and larger than Protestant ones. They tend to have bigger buildings in strategic places. The institutional resources enable the denomination to purchase lots in places otherwise unaffordable for smaller Protestant congregations. Many Catholic churches have several hundreds who gather for worship. This illustrates the visible component of the Catholic "cathedral" component. While these larger churches illustrate the numeric and economic might of the Catholic institution in the population, it is their small groups that point to Catholicism's rootedness in the local community.

Small Christian communities, or *Jumuia* as they are referred to in Swahili, supply relational contexts for people who share the Catholic denominational affiliation.[34] Within these groups, individuals live their lives together in small, urban kinship units. Here, families and individuals meet, eat, and share in life's milestones together. They care for each other by providing social support in times of bereavement and illness. They also celebrate childbirth, weddings, and other social events. It is in these groups that Catholics in the city exercise entrepreneurial, "kiosk," faith.

The groups are often led by women, and their attendance outstrips that of the men by far. The groups jointly raise funds for business ventures and personal family needs. Within these groups, the members complement and, in some instances, substitute the role of family in an increasingly urban life. The groups display a kind of functional ecumenicity. They invite people of all denominations, allowing non-Catholics to share and participate in their activities. Occasionally, the parish priest will attend the small groups in his parish and offer prayers or even communion.

The vitality of these small groups buttresses the place of Catholic Christianity in the Kenyan religious landscape. These groups open up their worship space, inviting their members to freely express themselves. It is common to see, mingled within Catholic rituals of personal worship, groups break into charismatic prayers. Group members are at ease carrying their rosaries, saying their "hail mary's" and raising their voices in prayer for healing or provision. These activities infuse vitality into the members spirituality.

Conclusion

Catholicism, within its liturgical and institutional frameworks, demonstrates how secularizing forces in modern Africa can be countered by the institution. The Catholic church as the religious cathedral shows that through education, health care, and worship, the negative aspects of secularizing forces in society can be moderated if not counteracted. Despite its historical exclusion from colonial power structures, Catholicism in Kenya demonstrates how the Cathedral can maintain religious power and relevance without necessarily invoking the instruments of political power. The Catholic church models constancy and resilience in its growth, despite the ebb and flow of political changes.

The Catholic church is institutional in its ethos and function. It is the cathedral and not the kiosk. Even within its smallest establishments—the kiosks—Catholicism stands for and defers to the cathedral. Its schools and mission hospitals submit to the ultimate authority in the Vatican. At its furthest distance from political power, the Catholic church remains united with the worldwide institution, theologically, ecclesiastically, and even diplomatically. In Kenyan history, Catholic presence remains committed to and representative of the institutional power of the religious establishment.

The Catholic church in Kenya is more than a religious institution. Its infrastructure presents it as a force of religious engagement and change in society. Not only does it provide a vibrant vitality of faith through its diverse religious, social, educational, and medical offerings, but it models the steady presence of Christianity in history. It infuses the constancy of liturgy with tradition for the three of ten Nairobi Christians who profess Catholic faith. It blends a vibrant spiritual engagement with the social, economic, and political life of the nation centered in the city of Nairobi. Catholicism's internal diversity nuances our understanding of its unity. It defies the institutional tendency toward uniformity. Catholicism in Nairobi, as representative of the Cathedral, negotiates space for its members without sacrificing its commitment to its institutional whole.

Far from being a religious remnant whose impact is only apparent in development initiatives, Catholicism in Nairobi is a highly visible and active presence.[35] Its impact is felt within nongovernmental initiatives in the spheres of medicine, education, and social work. It affirms the value of liturgical worship and church tradition, while advancing a development agenda in a rapidly changing environment. Catholic influence in urban Africa is on the rise despite the secularizing forces that exert themselves in the urban environment. The adherence to the rhythm of liturgy and the enduring celebration of ritual establishes Roman Catholicism as a "cathedral" religion in the Kenyan spiritual landscape.

3

A Place to Feel at Home
Independent Churches

Buried deep in the heart of Nairobi's Eastlands is Bahati estate, the city's most densely populated community. Founded in 1951—as an unofficial detention camp for Kikuyus suspected of being Mau Mau sympathizers—the estate has retained its largely Kikuyu population, 70 percent of its estimated 130,000 residents.[1]

Originally built by the government as one-room hostels for single men, the houses of Bahati teem with families, sometimes two-family units in one room. Only 17 percent of the residents are in paid employment, which is mostly in the nearby industrial area. Another 41 percent are self-employed, seeking to make ends meet by their work in the "*jua kali*" sector (literally in Swahili, "under the hot sun," meaning informal outside labor), often by the side of the road. The final 42 percent have no paid employment at all. The explanation for these critically low employment numbers is complex. One key factor is education. Among heads of households, 54 percent only have primary school education or less. Some 44 percent have finished high school. Only 2 percent have completed college.[2]

Living in Bahati means not only struggling with poverty and housing shortages but also dealing with the challenges of the environment daily. Bahati is hemmed in from the north by the Nairobi River, heavily polluted by the daily dumping of industrial and residential waste. It is boundaried on the west by the industrial area with its toxic fumes and belching factories. In Swahili, the word "*bahati*" can either mean "luck" or "accident." One could be forgiven for wondering if most residents understand the name of their estate more as the latter than the former. Yet at the very heart of Bahati is a cathedral of hope, the AIPCA's (Africa Independent Pentecostal Church of Africa) Bahati Cathedral and Academy, consecrated in 2019 (Figure 3.1). On a Sunday in August 2023, the church was packed with 1,200 enthusiastic

FIGURE 3.1 *All Africa Independent Pentecostal Church Cathedral Bahati.* Photo: Mark Shaw.

worshipers. Parts of the service were conducted in Swahili while other parts were in Kikuyu. Dozens of TV monitors spread throughout the cathedral were full of close-ups of the front, and texts from well-wishers online. The songs to which the congregation danced and ululated, spoke mostly of victory over evil. When the archbishop and his entourage of bishops arrived, they were led by around 100 young people, marching sharply in their carefully pressed uniforms and caps. During the service, there was preaching. There was the celebration of the Eucharist. There was even an enthronement of a new bishop. But one of the most dramatic moments came when the bishops moved up and down the aisles, first sprinkling the congregation with holy water and second, filling the air with holy incense. We were being not only purified in preparation of the Eucharist but also being protected from the evil one. For some, this protection from evil may have been the highlight of the service.

The AIPCA has always been a political church, standing behind Kikuyu politicians running for elected office. For over a decade, they have been in the press over the "Archbishop wars," in which three separate archbishops claimed supreme power over the church, each eventually forming rival denominations when others refused to submit. It was not uncommon for Nairobi's newspapers to run stories on the AIPCA's court battles or clergy fistfights, almost on a weekly basis. The public reputation of the church took a nosedive from these disgraceful headlines. Former president, Uhuru Kenyatta eventually settled the dispute by suggesting that each of the three rivals serve as the sole archbishop for one year each. This unusual solution seemed to work. Peace was restored. The third and final bishop served his one year of supremacy. A recent broadcast in November of 2023 reported that Samson Muthuri will remain as the presiding bishop of the church.

But the AIPCA and its Cathedral are more than their politics. We have earlier described Christianity in Nairobi as both a Cathedral and a Kiosk. The city is a place for the educated and upwardly mobile but also for those Nairobi residents living in poverty. The Bahati AIPCA Church represents the Cathedral as Kiosk. The Africa Inland Church (AIC) churches like Bahati Cathedral with their highly ethnic appeal, have long been described as "places to feel at home." While this is still true, the Cathedral, which is also a Kiosk, is "a place to get ahead" and "a place to get delivered." As a full-service church (the kiosk) with an academy and programs for all ages, it seeks to meet the spiritual, social, and economic needs of those who come. As a Cathedral, it is also a place of power (Cathedral literally refers to a throne of spiritual authority occupied by an anointed leader—usually a bishop) where one can be protected and delivered from evil. Bahati Cathedral is not just a monument to a church tradition but a movement of change and growth that touches every aspect of one's life and community. It taps into one of the deepest and most powerful convictions of the African soul—that "real world" power flows from spiritual world realities.[3] The AICPA represented by Bahati Cathedral is not just a "separatist" church that broke away from missionary Christianity in the 1930s. It is a power broker that can transfer spiritual power into real-world problems.

This chapter explores some of Nairobi's key spiritual power brokers, past and present. AICs and the renewal movements they belong to are places not only of feeling at home and getting ahead but also as places of protection and deliverance from evil. Every Sunday in Nairobi, thousands of members of independent churches march, sing, preach, give, witness, and worship in every corner of the city. This chapter cannot tell the story of the living witness of every Kenyan AIC but it can tell the story of a handful of some of the pioneers who have sought to revitalize the city and its soul through the unleashing of spiritual power. Joseph Ng'ang'a and the Akurinu, David Kivuli and the African Israel Church Nineveh, Matthew Ajuoga and the Churches of Christ in Africa (CCA), John Gatu and the Revival Brethren, and John Gichimu and the Organization of African Independent Churches. We begin our exploration in the highlands of Central Kenya.

Joseph Ng'ang'a and the Rise of the Akurinu

Jocelyn Murray classified AICs in Central Province into four categories. First were the "Nationalist" churches. These churches followed the "Ethiopian" church pattern where religion and politics were intertwined. The African Orthodox Church of Kenya (AOCK) would be an example of this type of church, but it belongs more to the orthodox family of churches in Kenya even as it bleeds across the classification boundaries into the realm of the AICs. The second type were "Secessionist churches" that split from a historic church but remain patterned after their mother church in worship, government, and theology. In our cluster of case studies, the Churches of Christ of Africa (CCA) most closely represents this type. The third are the "Revival-Pentecostal" type. These may break away from parent churches, not primarily over issues of power or culture but more over spiritual fervor and a quest for a deeper connection with God. The Revival Brethren never broke away from their parent churches, but they became little churches within larger churches in order to satisfy a deeper hunger for spiritual reality. The fourth and final classification were the "Spirit (in Swahili, Roho) churches." The Roho churches of Western Kenya would come under this classification. For Murray, the Arathi prophets and the Akurinu churches they became were the clear example of this type.[4]

The origin of both Joseph Ng'ang'a and the Akurinu movement took place in Kiambu district, now part of Metropolitan Nairobi. Born in the early 1900s, Ng'ang'a had a life-changing encounter in 1926 after a drinking binge that was followed by sickness. During his time of illness, he dreamed of someone calling him and giving him a new name, Joseph. He interpreted this dream as the call of God. He was to leave his old life and begin a new life of spirituality. Ng'ang'a also believed his dream and call constituted his baptism in the Spirit, making irrelevant the rite of water baptism. In addition to his personal call, God revealed the true condition of his people. Like the ancient children of Israel, the Kikuyu were "suffering under alien rules and crying for liberation."[5]

Ng'ang'a had gone to the primary school at the nearby Gospel Mission Station but questions bigger than grammar or mathematics dominated his thinking. How was he to help liberate his people? Ng'ang'a spent the next three years searching for that answer. He withdrew from his former life and confined himself to his hut. He took a Nazirite vow, refusing to cut his hair for those three years.[6] His days were spent in Bible study, prayer, and fasting. Gradually the message came, and he began preaching in nearby villages. The message was the declaration of a new exodus "freeing. . . . The Agikuyu from their colonial rulers." Ng'ang'a boldly proclaimed that God was "sweeping the Europeans aside and ushering in a Kikuyu golden age."[7]

Ng'ang'a called for a purified Christianity, freed from the corruption of both Western missionary Christianity and traditional Kikuyu religion. Witchcraft, sorcery, and sacrificing to the ancestors must stop. Western medicine, food, and dress must be rejected. Replacing these heathen ways would be a new life of Bible study, prayer, holiness, and experiencing the Holy Spirit.[8] The response to Ng'ang'a's preaching was not immediate, but by 1930, a group of disciples joined his movement. They were visible by their white robes and constant talk of the coming millennium in which the Kikuyu would rise again. Other prophets with similar messages, such as Musa Thuo, rose in other parts of Central Province, adding credibility to Ng'ang'a's new message. Emboldened by the growth of his movement and the voices of support in other parts of the province, Ng'ang'a declared that the new Golden Age would dawn in 1935. Nairobi would experience an earthquake that would swallow all the Europeans. The Kikuyu would be left to be masters of the city and of their ancestral lands.

Colonial officials reacted sharply to this new movement and its millennial message. By 1931, Ng'ang'a's followers numbered about 400 with many living in large communities of both young men and women. The government assumed the worst about the lifestyles of Ng'ang'a's followers. By March 1931, the District Commissioner expelled a number of *Arathi* leaders from Kiambu district. When the Provincial Commissioner overruled the expulsions, the DC ordered the arrest of Ng'ang'a and his leading disciples. During their trial, they refused to answer any questions put to them but chanted prayers throughout the proceedings. Their prayers made it clear that they were not attempting to topple the government but only to preach the gospel. They were convicted of participating in illegal meetings and sentenced to six months of imprisonment with hard labor.[9]

Waves of government harassment and arrests altered the *Arathi* strategy. Many followers began to carry weapons to church. On January 25, 1934, Ng'ang'a, again a free man, had an angry confrontation with the police while preaching in a market. Both sides dispersed without incident. In mid-February, Ng'ang'a and two associates were preaching outside his house when the police arrived once again. This time there was bloodshed. Shots were fired and Ng'ang'a and his colleagues were killed. In the subsequent trial, the police were acquitted of any wrongdoing. By April 1934, the *Arathi* movement was proscribed under the Native Authority Acts. The *Arathi* group meetings were prohibited. They were not permitted to carry arms. The Act further gave the government the right to detain *Arathi* followers without trial.[10]

The movement migrated beyond Central Kenya to escape government persecution. During the 1940s, it spread to Meru, into the Rift Valley, as far as Nakuru. Leaders of various factions came and went. The movement's unity was hindered by this migration and also by leaders seeking to reintroduce polygyny, a practice Ng'ang'a had declared forbidden.

A controversial leader emerged in the late 1940s and 1950s attempted to unite the *Arathi* under a new code of conduct. Joshua Kimani had studied under Musa Thuo. He settled in Kiambu and sought to bring all *Arathi* together under a strict code of laws that included a ban on political activity, shunning non-*Arathi*, no handshaking, and allowance of polygyny. The movement's reaction to these laws was mixed. Some were attracted to Kimani's revelations and others were repelled. The overall movement inched their way forward. Musa Thuo's group registered with the Kenyan government in 1960 as "Kenya Foundation of the Prophet's Church." By 1973, they numbered over 41,000 followers in 17 different congregations. In 1968, Musa's church split again, and the splinter group formed the "African Holy Ghost Christ Church." Githieya writes that "between 1960 and 1978, there were as many as 14 different *Arathi* groups registered by the Kenya government."[11] By early 2000s, a movement was underway to unite the Akurinu into one church. An undated document, "all Akurinu Churches Assembly Constitution and Rules" was circulated by Akurinu leaders. It declared that "there is no difference between Akurinu and Arathi. They are one and the same group but there are three groups alike." The document goes on to identify the Atumwo Church disciples as a sister group. It also names a Roho or Spirit church from Western Kenya, the "Dini ya Roho." A third church is mentioned as belonging under the Akurinu umbrella, the "African Israel Church." We turn now to this church and to its founder David Kivuli.[12]

David Kivuli and the African Israel Church Nineveh

The Luo of Western Kenya are the second-largest ethnic group in Kenya following the Kikuyu. Christianity came early in the twentieth century to the decentralized villages that made up the Luo community. In 1902, Catholic missionaries came, in 1906, Anglicans and Seventh Day Adventists, and Africa Inland Mission soon thereafter. Barrett writes that "by 1920 all four had large followings."[13]

In 1907, Pentecostal missionaries arrived from the Apostolic Faith Mission in Iowa in the United States. By 1924, their work had merged with the Pentecostal Assemblies of Canada (PAOC).[14] New believers soon took the initiative in starting their own movements. In 1914, Johana Owalo left the Church Missionary Society to form the Nomiya Luo Mission.[15] In 1916, Alfayo Odongo founded the Roho (Holy Ghost) movement. Odongo, an Anglican, kept his movement within the Anglican church until 1934. In that year, riots broke out, and Odongo was murdered. His followers left the churches and formed the Dini ya Roho (Religion of the Holy Spirit).[16] The new movement spread. Philomena Mwaura writes that "by 1927, there had been a public outpouring of the Holy Spirit in the Quaker Mission that led to the formation of several spiritual or Roho African Instituted Churches."[17]

David Kivuli grew up in Western Kenya in the midst of this spiritual ferment. Born in 1896 as a Luo in Nyanza, Kivuli's clan viewed itself as more a part of the Luhya community than the Luo. Kivuli grew up speaking Luo, Nandi, Luhya, and Kiswahili. He married in 1921 and continued his schooling at the Nyang'ori mission. Baptized in 1925 at the Pentecostal Nyang'ori mission, Kivuli showed promise as a student. In 1927, he was sent to Nairobi for further training to become a school supervisor. By 1931, the 35-year-old Kivuli was fully settled with a young family and a reliable teaching career ahead of him.

In late 1931, everything changed. Kivuli became sick and was incapacitated for six months. During this time, he sensed a deep conviction of sin and realized that he needed a savior. According to his own account, he received the Holy Spirit on February 12, 1932. He described the moment: "As I was singing in my house, something lifted me up and threw me on the ground. . . . Everything became dark and I was temporarily blinded." Kivuli spent seventeen days without sight and could not eat. He heard a thunderous voice from above that healed him. God commanded him to take the name Paul and not to shave his beard. He resumed his responsibilities with the PAOC mission, but more and more of his attention was focused on prayer, preaching, and healing the sick.[18]

Kivuli's movement grew even as he tried to balance the demands of his followers with his commitment to the PAOC mission at Nyang'ori. In 1940, Kivuli was elected as a pastor in the PAOC, but strong opposition on the part of other indigenous believers led to his leaving the mission altogether in February 1942. Kivuli moved to his own farm and began holding meetings in his home. Two of his brothers who were early followers eventually became priests in the new church. A group of ex-Anglicans led by Philomena Orwa joined his movement. The first name that he gave to his movement was the Huru Salvation Church (Huru in Swahili meaning "free"). The name was eventually changed to the African Israel Church Nineveh to emphasize its African roots and missionary calling.[19]

Kivuli remained involved with the PAOC work in Nyang'ori. Even after the founding of the AICN, he was asked to serve as chair of the African Church Committee of the Pentecostal mission and from 1939 was an authorized evangelist for the mission. John Padwick wrote of Kivuli's rare ability "to combine a Roho Spirituality with a particular concern for grassroots development and considerable political wisdom."[20]

Despite the distraction of the war years, the emergency in the 1950s, and the struggle for final national independence in the 1960s, the AICN under Kivuli's leadership continued to grow and expand. By 1967, it was flourishing in Nairobi with a total estimated membership of almost 27,000. One feature of the movement that was not always true of AICs was its multi-ethnic composition. Kivuli was an effective administrator, pastor, and evangelist. He was also a gifted networker. Kivuli embraced relations with the Akurinu churches out of Central Province and recognized in them the same quest for a deeper spirituality and more serious engagement with African culture and identity than many of the mission churches demonstrated. He worked closely with organizations like World Vision. In 1970, the AICN became a member of the National Council of Churches of Kenya. By 1975, it was an associate member of the World Council of Churches and became a founding member of the Organization of African Instituted Churches (OAIC) in 1978.

Kivuli died on November 10, 1974. Prior to his death, he had made plans to pass along his position as high priest of AICN to his son Moses, newly graduated from St. Paul's Theological College, Limuru. Moses's untimely death dashed those plans. Kivuli appointed a council of seven elders, charging them with the task of appointing a leader for the church after his death.

The period of council rule following Kivuli's passing was marked by power struggles and disunity. The solution for reuniting the AICN was the appointment of Kivuli's widow, Mama Rebecca. She led the church until 1982. Her grandson, John Mweresa Kivuli II, became her successor. In 1991, his title became archbishop. Under Archbishop Kivuli's watch, the church grew to 178,000 by 2005, in three countries, 125 regions, and 447 centers (with 8 local churches in each center). Though included as an Akurinu church, the AICN has tried to keep alive the charismatic passion of its founder but with his cooperative spirit, emphasis on training and ecumenical networking.[21]

Matthew Ajuoga and the Churches of Christ in Africa

In 1927, the fires of the East Africa Revival were ignited in Rwanda and Uganda. By the 1930s and 1940s, it became a full-scale wildfire, sweeping over a region encompassing five nations. The movement, known as the *Balokole or* the "saved ones," emphasized the necessity of the new birth for eternal salvation. A generation of Ugandan Anglicans particularly (reflecting on the fervor of the forty-five Christian martyrs murdered by Kabaka Mwanga II between 1885 and 1888), repented of their lukewarm faith and sought to revive the passion of that earlier generation who had paid the ultimate price for the gospel. But guilt alone did not drive the recommitment and public confession that characterized the revival. The movement was inspired by a joy that despite their spiritual crisis, the blood of Christ continued to cleanse them of any and all sin. And so they repeatedly sang their revival anthem, *Tukutendereza Yesu* (We thank you Jesus) and its critical line "Glory Glory to the Lamb, All the Blood, has cleansed me, Glory to the Lamb of God." Washing away the guilt of their spiritual deadness and dryness was the Blood of Christ. This blood was not only a washing for sin but a transfusion and infusion of new life and power to live like Christ in the rough and tumble of the new convert's life.

This new vision of the Christian life spread to Kenya in 1937, when the first evangelists of the revival came to the outskirts of Nairobi in what is now Kabete. A second revival team came to Nairobi proper in 1938. George Mambo describes their impact: "a small group of Christians including a prominent Anglican clergyman experienced a deep sense of salvation. Within the same year another group of Christians had been similarly converted in Nyanza [Western Kenya] through direct contact with members of the Revival from Uganda."[22] After the Second World War, the revival spread rapidly across Kenya, greatly affecting the Anglican, Presbyterian, and Methodist denominations. Among the Luo, the revival movement took the name of *Johera* (people of love). Tensions with the Anglican church leadership gave the movement another name, *Wahamaji* (those who leave). For the *Johera*, the established churches, particularly the Anglican, were spiritually dead and oppressive. Unlike the Anglicans of Uganda who were rapidly moving toward self-government, the Anglican church of Kenya was tightly held in missionary hands with little prospect of change. Conservative Anglicans resented the critique. Opposition arose. Luo critics of the revival called the revivalists *lalruok*, meaning band of thieves, stealing sheep from their flocks. By the 1950s, tensions reached a new level. For the young Matthew Ajuoga, future founder of the CCA (a Secessionist church), navigating these tensions became the central calling of his life.

Abednego Matthew Ajuoga was born in December of 1925 in Central Nyanza, the only child to a sub-chief, Oguna Ajuoga, active in local politics. The young Ajuoga was educated at the CMS Maseno School and attended Anglican services. After finishing his schooling, he left for Nairobi to attend the Railway Training School to become an Assistant Station Master. But his Nairobi years were haunted by a decision he made in 1948. He became "saved" and felt a strong inward call to preach the gospel. This tension between calling and career grew through the two years of training. By 1950, his decision was clear. He left the Railway and joined St. Paul's United Theological College. During his training, he was ordained deacon in All Saints' Cathedral. During his theological studies, the figure of Martin Luther influenced his thinking and the importance of reformation in the church. After graduation, he was posted to Eldoret but became caught up in the conflict in Maseno between the revival and the church. The young cleric weighed in on the dispute by writing to the Vicar General of the Anglican church, offering his take on unity, the central cry of the conservative anti-revival group. "People like nowadays to speak about unity, but unity without the gospel truth is a worthless one."[23]

Ajuoga became a leader of the *Johera* movement in the mid-1950s. Tensions within the church grew. Ajuoga resented the control that white settlers had on the Anglican church in Kenya. He felt this was the major obstacle to true self-government of the church. When five pro-revival bishops were ordained, Ajuoga and his *Johera* fellowship were pleasantly surprised. Perhaps the Kenyan Anglican church had turned a corner.

His hopes were dashed in 1957. Almost without warning, the Anglican leadership initiated a police action to suppress the *Johera*. All clergy sympathetic to the *Johera* were suspended and barred from their churches. Violence broke out. Twenty-five churches were destroyed. A stunned Ajuoga left with 7 other clergy, 130 churches, and 16,000 members.[24]

Ajuoga registered his movement in 1958 as the Church of Christ of Africa (CCA). He sought recognition from the World Council of Churches but was rejected twice. The new bishop eventually connected to the International Council of Christian Churches (ICCC), an American-based fundamentalist organization.

Ajuoga became archbishop of his church and served until his death in 2020. Under his leadership, the movement spread to several African countries, founded hundreds of schools, and numbered over 200,000 members.[25]

John Gatu and the Revival Brethen

John Gatu was an unlikely champion for the East Africa Revival. Born in Kiambu in 1925, he grew up in an outwardly Christian home but identified little with the faith so vividly embraced by his mother. What did inflame his passions during his youth was Kikuyu nationalism. He saw his home area turned increasingly into the "White Highlands" and his own people excluded from their native lands. He writes in his autobiography, "I became increasingly aware of these political and social injustices in my early teenage years."[26] He spent the Second World War in Ethiopia as a sergeant in the King's African

Rifles. After the war, he returned to Kiambu and took a job, "purely for the money" as he later stated, at a Gospel Missionary Society (GMS) station near his home.

During the day, he served the church. At night, he served the Mau Mau. Many of the returning Kikuyu soldiers who fought for the freedom of Ethiopia against the colonial invasion of Mussolini and the Italians had little trouble continuing the liberation battle for their own homeland. Not only did Gatu gladly take the Mau Mau oath but also became one of the oath administrators.

Other winds besides nationalism were blowing through Kikuyu land. Gatu describes his encounter with the East Africa Revival:

> In the midst of all this, in the early 1950s, the spirit of Christian revival, which had started in Uganda and Rwanda, was spreading to Central Kenya. I learnt about a big convention in Kabete and how during the event, people confessed their sins and some even returned items they had stolen from their employers. This revival movement was commonly known as "Dini ya Rwanda" (Religion from Rwanda). People in Kambii strongly identified with the movement. Mbiri Mare, my former teacher who had abandoned the church for many years, and Walter Maitai Mathenge, a renowned agricultural scientist, had taken up leading roles in the movement. Being born again through the blood of Jesus Christ was at the core of the popular movement. The opposing forces, the traditionalists, derided the movement, stating that Jesus was the name of a ship that brought white people to colonise Africans.[27]

Matters came to a head one Sunday morning in 1950, when he read James 1:21 and was struck by its appeal to "lay aside filthiness and wickedness." During the subsequent church service, the words of James drowned out the words of the preacher that morning. By the end of the service, Gatu had joined the ranks of the "born again." He described the various reactions from family and friends:

> Some just watched as I was hugged by members of the Revival Movement and others wondered whether it was a genuine turning of the heart or pretense meant to help me keep my job with the mission. When the service was over, many said they would give me time to see whether I would abide by my words. Looking back, I am glad that I proved all those doubting Thomases wrong. I joined the Revival Movement and have stayed in it all my life.[28]

Gatu spent the rest of his life as a member of the Revival Brethren, meeting regularly in their small groups, participating in their citywide conventions in Nairobi and elsewhere. Even as his commitment to the Revival and its values deepened, his roles and responsibilities in the Presbyterian Church of East Africa (PCEA) multiplied.

After his theological training at St. Paul's Theological College in Limuru (1951–5), and New College, University of Edinburgh (1958), he served as a local church pastor. In 1964, he was elected the first African general secretary of the PCEA, a position he held for the next fifteen years. He became moderator of the PCEA in 1979 until his retirement in 1985.

One feature of revitalization movements according to its leading theoretician Anthony Wallace is that they are driven not by irrational fears but by a "desire for a more satisfying culture." The Mau Mau movement and the East African Revival share that feature in common. Where they are different is about means to that end. For Gatu, the path to a Kenya liberated from colonial power and control, and a church liberated from overdependence on missionary personnel and resources was the path of revival.

When Gatu called for a moratorium on foreign missions to Kenya in 1971, he was applying a principle practiced by the Revival Brethren. Gatu summarized what he really meant, not in the word "moratorium" but in the Swahili term *jitegemea* or self-reliance. Gatu explains: "Self-reliance as I saw it then, and still do today, is consistent with the ethos of the East Africa Revival Fellowship, which knows the freedom that comes from raising and using one's own resources. Jitegemea believes that God will supply the money to do the things He wanted done."[29] Gatu was not calling for an end to mission, but for the renegotiating of relationships. Again, the Revival was his model. "The East African Revival Movement encouraged a relationship of mutual respect between brethren. They addressed each other as "Ndugu na dada katika Yesu" (brother and sister in Christ), even among wives and husbands. This was a revolutionary thing among my people—to hear a husband call his wife dada, or even apologize to her."[30]

Gatu's views on church and state were likewise influenced by his Revival values. Revival Brethren saw the key to healthy relationships as "walking in the light" with one another. This meant not only confessing one's sins and seeking forgiveness but also keeping one another informed about one's actions, plans, and ambitions, particularly when it might affect others in the fellowship. His clashes with the government in the 1980s were motivated by the application of transparency and open communication that he had learned among the Balokole.

Gatu also saw his ecumenical work as another expression of his Revival heritage, although not all Revival Brethren agreed.

Being an ordained Presbyterian minister and a member of the East African Revival Movement, my involvement in the Ecumenical Movement would, to some brethren, seem to be a contradiction of terms. However, to the best of my ability, and by the guidance of the Holy Spirit, I have aspired to live Christ's command in John 17:11: "That they may be one even as I and the Father are one." This exposure to the Ecumenical Movement has been a blessing to me as I have gained deep insights into the cultural, denominational, racial, ethnic, socio-political, and socio-economic dynamics that underlie the practice and conduct of our Christian faith.[31]

Gatu was not a Spirit-inspired prophet like Ng'ang'a and Kivuli nor a founder of an independent church like Ajuoga, but he was as much a spiritual power broker as these other pioneers in harnessing the dynamism of an indigenous Christian revival and applying its principles to church and society.

John Gichimu and the Organization of African Instituted Churches

The meeting with Reverend John Gichimu occurred at the headquarters of the OAIC, less than a block away from the Junction Mall on Ngong Road in Nairobi. John is a tall man with a big smile and an engaging personality. He made it clear from the outset of our interview that he was a man of several different worlds. He is an African Christian, rooted in the Kenyan experience. He is also an archdeacon of the AIPCA. He speaks of the power struggles that have rocked his church in the past with obvious pain but also deep affection for his church.

He is also a theologian and theological educator. His father, a committed leader of the AIPCA, encouraged his son to become a theologian after witnessing an educated friend resolve a number of issues in the church with his wisdom and training. John obeyed his father's wish. He studied theology at Kima Theological College in Kenya and at the Lutheran Theological College in Makumira, Tanzania. He has done advanced degrees at the University of Birmingham. He says with a smile that both Kima and Makumira did not know what to do with a student from a strange and suspect church. But it was through his training, he believes, that he discovered who he was, an African Christian who belonged to a church that was both unique and truly African.

Coming to work at the OAIC in 1995 helped him bring these different worlds together. As of this writing, he serves as the director of the Programme for Theology and Ministerial Formation. He built on the work of Augustino Batiya, who started the Theological Education by Extension (TEE) program for AICs in

1982. There are currently over a hundred TEE texts that can be used to train emerging AIC leaders in the field.

A big challenge in his work is the fading of vision that comes with the institutionalization of second- and third-generation AICs. New leaders are tempted to make to make their churches too much like many current churches that overemphasize the individual and his or her needs, says Gichimu. This new individualism "almost killed the spirit of the independent churches." AICs were all about community, not individualism. How do we recapture that original ethos yet apply it to the current realities on the ground?

Gichimu leans forward with his answer: workshops that recover the founder's vision. These workshops have become a signature part of theological education in OAIC. Gichimu held the first "Founder's vision" workshop in South Africa in 1996. The workshop was built around three key questions: "What were our founder's vision? What signposts came from the Bible? How can we recover and articulate the founder's vision for our current situation?" These workshops led to a threefold curriculum that encouraged churches to firstly, document historic practices, secondly, engage the Bible through textual study, and firstly, contextualize pastoral practice.

He pointed to this work with the Holy Spirit Church of East Africa, now three generations removed from their founders. Gichimu led a group of thirty HSCEA leaders through a series of studies to refresh their roots, engage the Scriptures, and update their pastoral practice. In his workshops, participants act as reporters as they do oral history with older church members who remember the origins of the movement. His goal? To produce a new generation of leaders with what he calls "critical solidarity," an appreciation of the past coupled with an openness to refresh the vision in light of both the scriptures and the current situation. One such example is on educating about the HIV/AIDS crisis. Tradition may treat it simply as a curse to be shunned. New perspectives that interact with older convictions open the door to reenvisioning the pastoral call to minister to the cursed, as Jesus did.

The OAIC was founded in Cairo in 1978 by Pope Shenouda of the Coptic Church of Egypt. Twenty AICs made up the original membership of the organization. John Gichimu and the current secretary general oversee a growing organization composed of 60 million members in hundreds of churches in every part of Africa. Kenya alone has over sixty churches that are members, with many of them having parishes in Nairobi.

Where are these churches in Nairobi? Gichimu describes their social location: "These churches are not found at the power centers of the city but at the margins." At the same time, they represent the majority of the city, not only in numbers but in economic and educational status. These AICs are churches of the people. AICs work among people who move to the city with a rural mindset, says Gichimu. For them, "work is Nairobi, money is Nairobi, and the good life is Nairobi." Sadly, few of those convictions are supported by their experience in the city. Through the educational programs of OAIC, people on the peripheries begin to see themselves in a new light. They occupy a key economic niche in the city. They are the labor force. They make up most of the population. People of the margins begin to see themselves as people of the true center of the city. John Gichimu, like the other independent church pioneers we have mentioned, is a spiritual power broker by virtue of empowering people on the margins through new approaches to theological education.

Conclusion: Deliver Us from Evil

What caused these Kenyan spiritual pioneers to create Kenyan independent churches? Francis Githieya describes two prevailing views about the origins of African Indigenous Churches (AICs). One view sees independent churches as a revolt against European spiritual and cultural domination. A second view plays down the reactionary aspect of AICs and stresses their creative quest for a more satisfying spiritual and cultural life. The more nationalist or separatist type AICs (AIPC, CCA) would seem to support the first view. The Spiritual or Prophetic type AICs (Roho, Akurinu, Revival) seem to favor the latter view.

Richard Gray proposed another lens through which to view African Christianity in general and AICs in particular. In his analysis, what missionaries said and Africans heard were not always the same thing. Missionary preaching may have proclaimed that sin and a condemning conscience were taken care of by Christ's sacrifice in our place. What Africans heard was that Jesus wrestled with the dark forces of evil and won. Evil, in many African minds, was more about the supernatural forces that destroyed health and prosperity than an interior moral calculus of sin and guilt. Faith in Christ meant defeating the cosmic forces of evil (often wearing the masks of bad leaders, foreign intruders, and rival ethnicities) which threatened to destroy one's life, family, and general well-being.[32]

We can extend Gray's insight slightly by breaking down the evils from which Kenyan AICs sought deliverance. One form of evil was *disrespect*. A lack of deference toward African leaders, initiatives and self-determination was more than a clash of personalities. It was an attack on a cosmic order of ancestral respect. Archbishop Ajuoga's separation from Anglicanism or the AIPCA's departure from the PCEA was not just about wounded egos. It was an evil that sought to destabilize the social order, one stretching back for generations.

A second form of evil was *demonic deprivation*. The loss of a job, a baby, a loved one, or health could not be explained simply by pointing to a physical or visible cause. Cosmic spiritual forces were at play that must be dealt with. For a Ng'ang'a, a Kivuli, or a typical worshiper at Bahati Cathedral, Christ defeated the powers that bring sickness, decay, poverty, and death. To cry out to him and experience his gospel meant deliverance from radical evil that shrivels and destroys life.

A third form of evil was spiritual *deadness*. To feel distant from God, alienated from his presence after previous generations had testified to their profound encounter with their creator, was to long for a return to those days of fire and light. For a Gatu or a *Balokole* who longed to be reborn, to be made alive again, to be filled with the very life and love of God, revival was to be delivered from evil.

Urban Africans in a city like Nairobi are still Africans. The witness of the AICs and the kiosk Christianity that meets one on the deepest level of identity and worldview is a Christ who defeats evil lurking behind its ever-changing masks. For AICs, the pluralism of Nairobi Christianity is the diversified search for spiritual power to overcome evil. Pluralism is not just part of an academic discussion, it's part of a cosmic war. The priests and the people at Bahati's Cathedral would certainly agree.

4

"Fire"

Pentecostalism and Evangelicalism

At 6:00 a.m. on the eastern side of Nairobi's central business district (CBD), the streets are already teeming with people walking briskly in many directions. Secondary and primary school children rush to take the next bus to school. Workers rush to their places of work. This volume of human traffic pales in comparison to the crowds that will fill the streets in three hours. Movement in the crowded streets is further complicated by vendors hawking all kinds of goods, from cutlery to handkerchiefs, umbrellas, and used clothes.

In a backstreet in the congested Eastern side of the city, a voice of a female lead singer pierces the sounds of commuting buses and minivans. The lyrics are in Kiswahili, and the voice is both pleading and celebratory. She is backed by one male singer and two other female singers in the call-and-response musical format. This is an early morning prayer meeting in session in a room on the third floor of a business building. A guitar and keyboard with preprogrammed percussion completes the sparse ensemble. The passersby on the street are not bothered by the blaring music. The sounds of worship blend into the Nairobi residents' "soundtrack" of the city's morning life.

The city is already awake and bustling with activity on this Thursday morning. It is a crowded part of the city along Munyu Road near Sheikh Karume road. The traffic consists of buses and minivans known as Matatus. These buses ferry people into the city center to work or to catch other buses transporting to other parts of the city. The area, known generally as River Road, is named after the most famous road in the east of the CBD that runs diagonally in a northwest direction.

The buildings here are closely built in blocks with narrow two-way roads in between. Each building has dozens of shops from the ground floor up to the fifth or sixth floor. Each floor has a balcony around it, covered with advertising signage. Several have restaurants on the first or second floors. Others have guesthouses which offer accommodation for travelers or revelers who find themselves in town late into the night. The ground floor shops sell electronics of different types. The smaller shops specialize in selling cell phone handsets and their accessories. Others peddle small household appliances such as hot water kettles, irons, blenders, and juicers. Other shops in the area sell flat-screen television and home entertainment sound systems. Higher up the building are a few shops that sell closed circuit television (CCTV) camera units and electrical fittings. This commercial context also carries the marks of vibrant spirituality. The shops names often include words like "Blessed," "Favor," or "Victory."

Christ Church Assemblies, Jesus Gospel Transformational Centre, and many others in this River Road area actively seek to bring two worlds together—the sacred and the secular. Their daily services are an attempt to integrate vibrant Christian spirituality into the lived realities of the marketplace. In doing so, they introduce a spiritual vibrancy into the commercial world. Nairobi's 1.1 million Pentecostals are constantly dreaming and speaking about the possibilities available for Christians amidst the challenges of the African urban city.[1] While there are large churches with tens of thousands of members, most Pentecostals attend small churches scattered all over the city. They are creating what Nimi Wariboko calls the charismatic city, which lies "between a real global city and utopia, the actual and the not-yet, the here-and-now and the future."[2]

As the day is breaking, a few of these busy people will climb the dark winding stairs to the third floor to attend early morning prayers known from the 1980s as "morning glory." This is the generic name associated with prayer meetings held in the morning for busy workers. In this gathering, the song leader sings loudly into the microphone with the sound almost overwhelming the small public address (PA) system. One part of the sound system points into the room, while another is strategically placed next to the window pointing outwards.

With only ten people in the room, the music starts with a high tempo beat and rhythmic guitar. After about fifteen minutes of fast-paced music with vigorous dance, the songs suddenly turn to mellow ballads. The song leader and her backup singers are deeply engrossed in their singing, often with their eyes closed and swaying to the rhythm of the songs. The room is now a fifth full, with about two dozen young people mostly in their twenties. Then just as suddenly as the tempo had changed, the singers and the congregation erupt into a cacophony of speaking sounds while the music plays on. Some in the group burst into glossolalia, loudly voicing unintelligible sounds that don't conform to any language spoken there. Others cry out their prayers in Kiswahili, and others in English. A young man comes up to the microphone and begins directing the prayers. The volume of prayer rises, with a few rocking while they stand. One or two men can be seen pacing back and forth, while several others are kneeling on the ground shaking violently as they pray. Those gathered wear semiformal clothes. A suit jacket for the men and dresses for the women. They come clad ready to go to work in the small business shops and offices scattered all over the city.

The prayer session pauses when the prayer leader starts reading a passage from the book of Acts. He narrates the story of how Peter and John called on the name of Jesus to heal a man lame from birth. He emphatically declares that Jesus is there to heal and provide for those present. Then summons the community to more prayer. The group immerses itself into prayer once more. This time the prayer leader calls out the prayer needs. The guitarist and keyboardist once again play the accompaniment to a familiar song. The group resumes their fervent prayer for another ten minutes. The meeting ends with a hopeful, triumphant call to trust in God's healing and provision. Most of the group leaves the room quickly to attend to the business of the day. Three or four are left in the room talking as they dismantle the microphones and keep them away for the evening's "revival" meeting.

Christ Church Assemblies, Jesus Gospel Transformational Centre, and many others in the River Road area envision the street corner not just as a commercial space but as a place where religion meets the public. This chapter focuses on such Pentecostal churches found all over the city. They use public shared spaces such as the one described above to gather and grow communities through a brand of evangelism that involves very public expressions of faith. They punctuate the working and rest rhythms of city life with these public sacralizing activities.

The rented church venue, next to a pharmacy, asserts the holistic cosmology which appreciates the contributions of modernity without sacrificing the place of divine encounters. Their integrated worldview affirms that God acts in both the secular and sacred spheres. A majority of these churches rent space for their gatherings. Their entrepreneurial street corner approach to ministry contrasts sharply with the institutional permanence of their historic mission counterparts.

Their pluralist engagement with their world invites their members to view a wide range of secular activities in their lives as compatible with their religious experience. The power encounter through healing, miraculous provision, and the ever-present glossolalia is evidence to them of God's immanence in the city. Pentecostal's unwritten liturgy animates the worship with spontaneous elements that address the immediate needs of the audience.

The churches grew in the 1970s and 1980s through their quest for a more participatory, contextual worship experience. In their view, the written liturgy of historic mission churches (HMCs) is a step away from essentials of Christianity. Their rhetoric often invokes images of the Holy Spirit at work in the moments of the service. To them, the most important element of the Christian experience is the work of the Holy Spirit.

HMCs were initially skeptical about Pentecostalism.[3] They doubted Pentecostal theology which they thought to be overly emotional. They were suspicious of oral liturgies which did not adhere to time-tested practices. One of the contentious issues was the Pentecostal insistence on baptism by immersion, even for those who had been baptized as infants.[4] Despite the strong opposition by older leaders, the younger members of HMCs embraced this charismatic strand of Christianity.

The vibrant worship in local languages allowed these young people to participate in the worship in ways that were more relevant to them. Pentecostal churches offered viable alternatives to HMC worship. Pentecostals excelled in their ability to connect at a deep level with their publics. Pentecostal worship welcomes local music and oral liturgies. This vitality makes room for those from the margins to have their needs addressed. HMCs were slow to develop the vitality seen in Pentecostal charismatic expressions.

Pentecostals also took the worship to the people. The numerous churches scattered around the city rented venues that were accessible to people as they went through the rhythms of urban life. Well-resourced HMCs owned venues in the residential areas and the upmarket parts of the city. These included Westlands, Karen, and the CBD. HMC infrastructure did not have sufficient "room" to maneuver the emerging life and work patterns in the city. Pentecostals adapted well to urban rhythms and mobilized resources for mass evangelism. The crusade culture of the 1980s and the conference culture of the 2000s navigated the urban rhythms well. Crusades were a mark of Pentecostal's eschatological urgency in mission. Though there had been large evangelistic meetings in the 1960s and 1970s, the culture took root in the 1980s.

The 1988 Evangelistic Crusade left a lasting impression on Pentecostals in the city. The event consisted of a series of gatherings held at Uhuru Park. The main venue in Uhuru Park is a large outdoor space resembling an amphitheater. It was designed on the side of a hill overlooking Nairobi's CBD in the east. The meeting place sits at the edge of a recreational park with waterways and extensive lawns. These lawns are populated by families and children over the weekends. Over weekday lunchtimes, the lawns host itinerant evangelists who preach to passersby and lunching listeners from offices nearby.

This park was the site for the 1980s and 1990s crusades. Preparations for evangelist Reinhard Bonnke's gatherings were meticulous. Bonnke's Christ for

All Nations organization brought together pastors from all denominations—with mainstream and independent represented. It was the independent Pentecostal churches that most identified with Reinhard Bonnke. His message, connecting fervent preaching with live miracles, found resonance among these pastors. This was a fortunate meeting of minds between foreign evangelists and the local Pentecostals.

The centerpiece for the week of meetings was the open-air preaching. The German televangelist spoke with a live translation into Kiswahili. The translator for each session would be a well-known or up-and-coming Pentecostal pastor with good command of both English and Swahili languages. These meetings were important national launching grounds for prominent Pentecostal bishops; J. B. Masinde, Joe Kayo, and Mark Kariuki and others.

The meetings also featured healing and deliverance sessions. The sessions were very popular with local attendees. The events featured testimonies from people who claimed healings through the preaching and prayer. The meetings harnessed new large-scale PA technology, some of which had not been seen in Nairobi before. The group also made use of mass media to publicize the meetings to the wider Kenyan community. This huge gathering ushered in what one may call the "crusade era." Crusades became a hallmark of Pentecostalism in the coming decade.

The success of large-scale meetings depended on the use of PA systems and the mass media. Pragmatic Pentecostal evangelists invested heavily in portable large-scale PA technology which enabled large gatherings in urban centers and in the rural areas. When not in use for outdoor evangelistic meetings, the equipment found use in churches. Liberalization of mass media opened the opportunity for evangelists to create a media profile, and develop a following around the country. Though initially intended for Christian evangelism, the use of technology gave Pentecostal preachers unprecedented reach around the country and beyond. Many established their base in Nairobi. Their itinerant ministries gave way to churches.

As it catalyzed Pentecostalism at the time, the 1990s Crusade era brought into the open the growth that had been going on in the background. Indigenous denominations like Pentecostal Evangelical Fellowship of Africa (PEFA), Deliverance Church (DC), Full Gospel Churches of Kenya (FGCK), which had all began in the 1970s, became widely visible in the crusades and in the mass media and gained recognition ten to twenty years after they had formed. Uhuru Park, a secular space, became the "platform" upon which what was hidden was announced in the "roof tops." It became the site where Pentecostals staged their most public example of the sacralization of secular spaces. While this might be the most prominent example, Pentecostal sacralization of public secular spaces is a common feature all over Nairobi.

Reinhard Bonnke's crusades were not so much a sacralization of the space, but the affirmation of the sacred nature of all spaces within the urban Pentecostal's mind. This is a unique contribution of Pentecostal spirituality. HMCs Protestant, Catholic, and Eastern Orthodox preferred to build their own spaces which they consecrated for sacred use. This dedicated space in theory should not be used for secular functions.[5] This new and energetic phase of Pentecostal urban life brought themes of deliverance and provision to the city and revitalized older forms of Evangelicalism and Pentecostalism in Kenya. The preaching emphasized the eschatological vision and mission urgency found within Pentecostal churches.

The energetic disposition of these new churches also carried with it serious pathologies which posed a threat to the very challenges they sought to address. Charismatic leaders sometimes focused on material outcomes in a kind of transactional faith that has come under criticism. Pastors are known to argue that faithful followers are not supposed to experience any troubles.[6] Pentecostal emphasis on charisma as the sole leadership legitimizing factor introduced many leaders without adequate theological training. As a consequence, it is not unusual for sermons to stray from orthodoxy and for leaders to venture into practices that harm their congregations.[7] Earlier iterations of Pentecostal churches did little to use their sermons or rally members to critique government failures.[8] In other instances, Pentecostals were co-opted into political machinery, becoming a part of mainstream politics.[9] Whereas HMCs were central to the inauguration of the Kenya president from independence to the early 2000s, the 2022 inauguration incorporated an overtly Pentecostal ceremony. The spontaneous, entrepreneurial Pentecostal spirituality stood in contrast to the institutionalized posture of HMCs.

History and Diversity

Nairobi's diverse neighborhoods are the home to various expressions of this movement of the Spirit. Rather than refer to them as Pentecostalisms, we refer to their shared attributes. Pentecostals are churches which affirm the doctrine of baptism of the Holy Spirit. They believe in the immanent presence of God in people's lives through the Spirit. In their view, it is not enough to claim conversion. They expect something more: a profound encounter with the Holy Spirit produces results not only in a changed life but manifestation of the miraculous. Their worship makes room for the phenomenon of "speaking in tongues." This is a spontaneous "speech" which may or may not conform to actual languages, often occurs during prayer. They welcome miraculous occurrences of healing, prophecy, and exorcism which they claim is the work of God in their lives.

The first expressions to welcome the occurrences of healing and prophecy were the early African initiatives in Christianity.[10] These movements were inspired by indigenous leaders who interpreted the Christian message in local languages and idioms. The resulting Christianity was lively and resonated with the semiliterate Africans. These Christians creatively incorporated their own music and dance into their worship.[11] They wore monocolored robes on Sunday to signify their distinctness from others of their ethnic communities.

These communities emerged in Kenya in the early twentieth century and are still found in the informal settlements of the city. The sprawling Kibera area is home to several congregations of the Africa Israel Church Nineveh (AICN) community. On Sundays, their congregations can be seen making their unique weekly pilgrimage to their places of worship in Kibera and Nairobi's Eastlands. Their march from Kibera to Eastlands is half walk, half dance, with members joining them along the way.[12] With a flag bearer at the front and one or two drummers, each congregation of about fifty make their way along the empty roads and sidewalks. Their drumming rhythms are distinctive of communities from Western Kenya. Their services are conducted in Luo, the language of a Nilotic community found on the shores of Lake Victoria, in Western Kenya.

The Nomiya church, for example, conducts its worship almost exclusively in Luo language.[13] The church started in 1912 under its prophet leader Yohanna Owalo. He claimed to have received instructions to start the church after an encounter with the angel Gabriel. Unlike AICN, the Nomiya community is more sedentary, meeting in small gatherings of twenty to fifty in their church premises in lower-income areas all over Nairobi. They don white robes. The women sit separately from the men. Unlike AICN, the women in Nomiya do not speak in church. The men and women sit in different sections of the church to signify their gender-specific roles that come together to make the church. Visitors to the community need interpreters to follow the proceedings. This is however not unique to the Luo community. Other similar African initiatives in Christianity can be found among the Kikuyu, such as the African Holy Spirit church, more commonly known as the Akurinu.

These communities might not use the term "Pentecostals" to refer to themselves. Their emphasis though on the immanence and work of the Holy Spirit through the miraculous is the reason they serve as antecedents to modern African movements of the spirit.[14] The trance-like episodes that accompany their worship, along with exorcisms, faith healings are not unlike elements of Pentecostal churches of more recent denominations. Their dress codes and observance of social codes of behaviour affirm their efforts to assert a visible spirituality in the secular environment of the city.

NPCC-Classical Pentecostal Roots

Newer Pentecostal Charismatic churches (NPCCs) are more recent. These are the churches that most identify with the crusade movement of the 1980s. Their sermons announce the present epoch to be the last days which require an urgent evangelistic response. This inspires their heavy investment in money and personnel to run mass evangelism events, both in and out of church.

Of these, one group emerged from classical Pentecostal missions from Europe and North America. The others are independent churches founded by indigenous leaders. Most of these independent churches have a clearly articulated theology of the baptism of the Spirit that aligns with the classical Pentecostals. Though classical Pentecostal missions established a strong presence in the rural areas, it is in the cities that the impact of NPCCs can be felt most.

NPCCs with classical Pentecostal roots are the most connected to their counterparts in the rural areas. Pentecostal Assemblies of God (PAG) came out of the Pentecostal Assemblies of Canada (PAOC) in early 1914. Its rural stronghold in Western Kenya is near the Nyang'ori area where PAOC established its mission headquarters. PAG churches in Nairobi are not as large or influential as they are in rural Western Kenya. Assemblies of God from the United States established its mission nearer Nairobi in Magina among the Kikuyu people in 1967. Peter Njiri, first indigenous superintendent of Kenya Assemblies of God (KAG), reshaped the denomination during his tenure (1982–2018).[15] His effusive personality brought leaders together and inspired the entrepreneurial environment characteristic of NPCCs. He was careful to maintain ties to the American Assemblies of God while building a distinctly indigenous movement. KAG mission's proximity to Nairobi provided for a stronger presence in Nairobi. KAG has a large church and college in Buruburu in Eastlands. International Christian Center is also affiliated to KAG, sharing its missionary history.[16] Pentecostal Evangelistic Fellowship of Africa (PEFA), a similar NPCC, comes out of Elim ministry which is an Apostolic Faith mission offshoot. PEFA has a large congregation in Gikomba, east of Nairobi's CBD.

These movements might differ from their classical mission roots in at least two ways. Some like KAG, transformed their church governance structures and episcopized. They now have the bishopric whereas Assemblies of God in the United States and Canada have a different structure with a flatter, more congregational polity. The other feature of these indigenous churches is the presence of women pastors. From early on, long before the discussion, KAG incorporated women pastors in their polity, especially in rural Kenya. Some NPCCs are large and sophisticated and some are small. At the core, they are indigenously led, self-sustaining, and self-governing churches. They have slowly but consistently been embracing technology. The churches in cities maintain ties with their rural counterparts through the frequent movements of their members between these places.

NPCC-Independent Pentecostals

These are indigenous independent denominations and congregations which do not trace their origin to Euro-American Pentecostalism. These include Deliverance church (DC) and Redeemed Gospel churches (RGC) of Kenya. Joseph Kayo (1936–2023) instituted DC as an independent movement in 1970. Similarly, merging from itinerant evangelistic ministry, Arthur Kitonga founded RGC in 1974. From its headquarters in the lower-middle-income area in Huruma, Kitonga built a denomination that spans across Kenya. These churches model African Christianity that is indigenously led. They have evolved robust structures to sustain themselves financially. DC and RGC have a denominational structure which encourages churches to support themselves. The churches also encourage church planting through informal mentorship and training programs. In the 1980s and 1990s, DC and RGC developed into formidable denominations with hundreds of branches around the country. DC Umoja is one of the largest and most influential churches in Umoja residential area in Nairobi's Eastlands.

They readily identify as Pentecostal and articulate a contextually adjusted Christianity well adapted to the urban setting. Many hold on to the classical Pentecostal doctrine of tongues as initial evidence of the Holy Spirit. These churches devote a lot of attention to themes of prosperity and well-being. In their quest to provide hope, some of their leaders manipulate their congregations. Some draw criticism from the public for their displays of materialism.[17] The movement of the Pentecostal church culture usually starts from cities and flows into the rural areas. Independent NPCCs have several variations within the expression.

Evangelistic Ministry Churches

They represent the fervor stirred up by an eschatological telos. They show how the city provides religious social capital to transform small movements into church institutions. They are the "quintessential kiosk turned cathedral communities" and "shop stewards turned executives." The driving force behind these communities is the entrepreneurial commitment to mission through evangelism. They take every opportunity to motivate conversion and reconversions into their vibrant expression.

Evangelistic ministry churches (EMCs) did not start as churches. They are the product of itinerant ministers who travelled through cities inspired by their vision for conversion. The evangelists' sense of call (in the earlier iterations of the churches), came out of the 1990s crusade movement. They drew inspiration from what they heard, what they read, and what they saw in the mass media. Many of them credit their call to their profound experiences at the Crusades. These leaders focused their work away from the church and on itinerant ministry. They did their own planning and raised their own resources to do this.

These movements later morphed into churches. Prominent examples of these are led by women. Margaret Wanjiru is the leader of Jesus Is Alive Ministries (JIAM). Teresia Wairimu leads Faith Evangelistic Ministries (FEM).[18] There are other ministries as well. Pius Muiru, Maximum Miracle Centre— Kuna Nuru Gizani. These founders were traveling evangelists who then planted churches coming out of the itinerant ministry in schools, churches, and open-air settings. These EMCs retain that culture of evangelism with frequent calls for conversion in the services. Their Sunday worship service takes a form similar to an evangelistic meeting. At the end of the service is an altar call inviting the attendees to consider "making a decision for Christ." The church leaders take every opportunity in their services to encourage people to convert.

This sense of urgency motivated them to learn how to harness television, radio, and, in the 2010s, social media for evangelism. In the late 1980s and 1990s, the evangelists were willing to raise and use indigenous funds for evangelism through mass media. They often paid for time on affordable radio slots in the weekends, late at night, and early in the morning. The liberalization of media came as a boon for their entrepreneurial spirit. TV and radio stations were initially willing to offer these slots for free in a bid to gain viewership.

EMCs espouse a theology of concrete religion where God acts in the here and now. They speak into Harvey Cox's idea of God active in the city's lived realities.[19] To these Pentecostals, God's voice is everywhere. God speaks in their finances, in health. God speaks in every facet of people's existence within the urban city. High points in their worship service are the miracle moments, the prophecies, and the call for conversion. These moments act as the portal between the physical and metaphysical. They gear the thrust of their sermons toward these transcendent moments. Prayer is an important aspect in the life of the churches. Prayer is the opportunity to access the divine promises they believe to be theirs by faith.

Pius Muiru, is one of the leading lights in this type of Pentecostalism. He adopted the crusade model, applying it throughout the country. Pius Muiru's

Maximum Miracle Center is in the eastern side of Nairobi along Thika Road. When mass media was liberalized in the early 1990s, he took advantage of it for the new opportunities. He became well-known through his TV broadcast in the 1990s. He adopted the crusade model including live language translation within his services. Muiru pushed further, developing an active strategy for missions in the rural areas while remaining connected to Nairobi. His crusades featured translation from English to Swahili and sometimes from Swahili to English. Other leaders include Margaret Wanjiru and Teresia Wairimu who had a similar ethos. These leaders evolved a type of Pentecostal church that mingled evangelism with a concrete theology of provision and healing.

Media and Entrepreneurial Churches

Media and entrepreneurial churches (MECs) emphasize media or entrepreneurial empowerment initiatives. These churches harnessed liberalized media and moved the mission field from the street corner into the virtual world of media technology. They "professionalized the kiosk" beyond what EMCs did. In their sophistication, MECs never lost their entrepreneurial spirit.

The founding and, especially, the growth of these churches relies on media initiatives.[20] Kathy and Allan Kiuna founded Jubilee Christian Center (JCC) in 2004.[21] These churches established themselves as highly urban in several ways. Their church services highlight an impressive professionalism of their worship service production. The churches have elaborately decorated setups occasionally held up market venues. Their ministry strategy takes advantage of media. Leaders at the front maintain a flawless appearance with meticulous grooming. Their hair is carefully put together, they apply makeup, and their brightly coloured clothing is coordinated. They aim to project an image of a God of order and beauty. There is also a very strongly aspirational theme in their message.[22] The leaders model through their appearance and public life, what their congregations would like for themselves.

They emphasize business and entrepreneurship. The churches emphasize personal success in the spiritual social and financial areas of life. Empowerment is a common theme in the church services, conferences, spiritual emphasis weeks, and workshops. Church leaders such as Allan Kiuna and Niyi Morakinyo prepare talks and write books focusing on entrepreneurial activities such as starting businesses and thriving in the market place.[23] They teach their members how to thrive in urban financial settings and generate content about an empowered Christianity lived in the marketplace. The Lucy Natasha's Empowerment Christian Church embodies this concept in its name as well as its approach. Lucy Natasha presents herself as an inspirational figure through her social media posts and sermons online.

These churches encourage entrepreneurship in business and life in general. They constantly encourage their members to pray that God will help them do something for themselves; that they will not perpetually be employees. Life for them is not just spiritual exercise but also a concrete lived reality. The churches evolved a conference culture. They put together regular conferences, inviting speakers to address inspirational themes.

The churches engage the youth with sophisticated media technology. They broadcast their services online. Their services can be found on live stream on YouTube or uploaded afterward. The churches use the latest technology for the PA systems. Their meeting venues are often rented venues. They model the sacralization of urban secular spaces. Purpose Centre church conducts many of its meetings at the ballroom of the upmarket and luxurious Villa Rosa Kempinski Nairobi.

Despite their seeming appeal to individual success, NPCCs are the most overt with regard to their public expression of kinship. They articulate their communality most visibly. The pastor and his wife are considered mother and father (mum and dad) of the community. Their members use these familial terms for their leaders. The leaders also use the terms to refer to themselves. The church (JCC) founding pastors, Kathy and Allan Kiuna, refer to their mentor, Teresia Wairimu, as their spiritual mother.[24] As is the case in JCC, the members of the congregation see themselves as spiritual grandchildren of their pastors' mentor. Despite the modern outlook, the churches retain these references to kinship in ways that are distinct from other areas in modern, secular society. They rely on their communality to construct and make meaning of their religious social reality. Their relationships express a relational perspective which broadens kinship beyond blood relations. Through their faith and under their leadership, these communities embrace a pseudo-family structure linked to their spirituality.

Progressive Pentecostal Churches

Progressive Pentecostal churches engage with questions that other types of NPCCs have been slow to answer. The Progressive Pentecostal churches represent a more recent iteration of Pentecostal churches. The term was used by to describe urban, socially aware Pentecostal churches which are charting a different path beyond the forms described above. They deliberate what can be done with structures in society that have failed the society.[25] They are the harbingers of institutional Pentecostalism. Examples include the Nairobi

Chapel, CITAM, International Christian Centre (ICC), and Parklands Baptist. These all grew in the late 1980s and the 1990s from diverse backgrounds. They question the efficacy of the secular structures upon which modern society is built. They examine alternatives for education and health institutions that are not addressing the societal needs. They explore solutions for an economy that is failing within an African context. In terms of their doctrine, the churches carry on as Pentecostals or charismatic. Some might not use the term Pentecostal on themselves though they carry the defining characteristics outlined above (Figure 4.1).[26]

Christ is the Answer Ministries have in the recent past, challenged the government on policies and governance.[27] They have been known to ask questions about transparency in governance, accountability in elections, corruption, and the economy. During the election period, they encourage people to pray for the nation, but also to go out and vote for the right kind of leaders. In this regard, they are more willing to work with secular pathways to find solutions to society's problems. They find ways to articulate their reality in spiritual terms. For example, they emphasize that voting is a citizen's responsibility but the outcome belongs to God. They exhibit a greater political awareness because their constituents understand the levers that move business and government (Figure 4.2).

The churches are also concerned about their responses to the questions they raise in society. These churches model what they ask of society. Large Progressive Pentecostals, unlike other NPCCs, post their audited accounts online or present them to their members during their congregational business meetings. They have defined their leadership succession plans.[28]

FIGURE 4.1 *CITAM Valley Road. Photo: Clara Koimett.*

FIGURE 4.2 *Jesus Is the Answer Ministries. Photo: Clara Koimett.*

These churches attract educated, middle-income urban dwellers. Their annual budgets are considerably larger in relation to some of the other Pentecostal churches. In Kenya, for example, CITAM has an annual budget of about $2 million.[29] They account for this money which is used to run their schools, an orphanage, a media station, and a university. They challenge the notion that Pentecostal spirituality is for the economically challenged.

Progressive Pentecostal churches recognize the value of accountability structures in an era of institutional opacity within the African economic, political, and church contexts. They recognize the need for structural change and value theological education for their leaders. In so doing, they moved away from "kiosk" level and ended up with established structures that, in and of themselves, resemble the established nature of the cathedral. These are the most prominent signs of the potential for Pentecostalism to institutionalize. These churches develop elaborate bureaucratic systems to regulate their use of money, leadership succession, and property management. They also deploy extensive training programs for their leaders.

The churches synthesized the sociopolitical and economic context and formulated Christian responses. They infuse their teachings with references to sociopolitical engagement.[30] They question the institutions and usually, demand accountability. They are larger institutions with substantial material resources. In their ethics, they strive for accountability and transparency.

The leaders provide solutions drawn from their interpretation of the Bible. The churches attract highly educated congregants. They are committed to financial accountability and transparency. They espouse a different kind of conference culture. The conferences are not centered around evangelism and power encounters. They focus on sociopolitical and economic reengineering of society. The conferences promise teachings to promote excellence "both in church and in the marketplace."[31] The churches invite the conference attendees for "great networking opportunities, solid and respectable speakers, financing, and investment deals."[32]

Charismatic Christianity

Pentecostal movements are responsible for the charismatization of HMCs.[33] Through their functional ecumenism, all night prayer vigils, conferences, women's meetings, and men's meetings, they attract members from all Christian expressions in the city. Charismatic Christians are groups within HMCs which espouse characteristics of Pentecostal churches. Their worship incorporates local music and prayers which address similar concerns to Pentecostal churches. They are conscious of the need for divine provision and healing amidst the concerns of living in a fast-moving, unpredictable urban existence.

One example of charismatic Catholics are the Vincentians in Kenya. In their sermons, they aim to address their attendees' context. They conduct prayer mass every Monday and Thursday where people come for healing. Catholic charismaticism is also found in small residents (Jumuia) groups which meet in homes. Within these groups, people care for one another often sharing resources. They function like families, supporting each other through rites of passage and similar family based occasions.

The key difference between Pentecostal denominations and charismatic movements in HMCs is the latter's rootedness with the denominational connection. Charismatic Catholics, as with other HMCs, maintain fidelity to their denominational doctrine. They express the charismatic ideals within their HMC spirituality without letting these hinder their denominational connection.

Pentecostal charismatic Christians make room for diversity within the Christian experience. They welcome Christians from other traditions to their worship spaces. Much of their growth is transfer growth of attendees from other denominations. Pentecostal-charismatics exhibit a high level of double affiliation. This illustrates the permeability of denominational boundaries through the practice of functional ecumenism.[34] The movement of members between churches represent a constant negotiation where outcomes are not guaranteed. Some leave and join Pentecostal churches. Most remain and live and thrive in the tension. The dissonance is less evident among charismatic movements in Protestant denominations, which seem to have more readily accepted and incorporated charismatic elements, mainly through the youth. This keeps the charismatics' theology rooted in terms of orthodoxy. In terms of their expression, though, there might not be any real or observable difference, say in the prayer vigil. It is in the formal written liturgy that the differences emerge.

Conclusion

As the foregoing chapter illustrates, Pentecostals are at home in the city. They use their worship services, such as those described in this chapter, to navigate the rhythms of Nairobi. Aware of the demands on people's time and energy, they strive to provide answers in the form of Pentecostal charismatic worship. They meet the high volume of city life with a loud spiritual rejoinder. Just as business is dynamic so are these communities. Their potential for pathology is never far from being realized. Fraud, materialistic impulses, and deviation from orthodoxy draw much legitimate criticism against them.[35] Not all survive the vicissitudes of the city. Many fold for lack of funds to sustain rent and the cost of equipment. The Pentecostal entrepreneurial impulse inspires many more to start than shut down.

Taken together, Pentecostal Christianity in Nairobi represents the most vibrant of religious expressions in the city. Pentecostals' resilient spirit is responsible for the growth of each of the diverse forms outlined above. The movements, once marginal to Christianity in the city, have now shifted to being mainstream with a following of almost 30 percent of Nairobi's Christian population. Their presence in the residential areas, and in the wider city is testament to their resilience. With noisy, bold statements of their presence, Pentecostals challenge every aspect of secularism found in the city. The energy these communities generate in the city's residential and commercial areas, as well as within social interactions constitutes form of "charisma" that emanates from the "kiosk" and affects every institution, religious or otherwise.[36] A stark contrast to more muted historic mission expressions, they illustrate the possibilities of what a more spiritualized yet modern Christianity looks like in a city in Africa.

5

Ancient Altars Orthodoxy

Sunday at the Orthodox Patriarchal Cathedral of St. Cosmas and Damian was full of surprises. The first was the beauty of the cathedral's interior, or the nave in Orthodox architecture, where the people gather before the altar and receive the words and symbols of the gospel. Gazing around the nave at a congregation of about fifty mostly local attendees, one is struck by the "cloud of witnesses" watching as we worship. Wherever one looks, icons cover the walls. These images of Christ and the saints bridge the wood and marble-paneled "lower world" of the worshiper with the cerulean blue and white "upper world" crowned by a dome of colored glass panes and images of a triumphant Christ and his angels gazing confidently down upon us.

The second surprise was the Divine Liturgy itself. In twenty-first-century Nairobi, worshipers take part in ninety minutes of song and responsive readings using the fifth-century formulations of St. John Chrysostom, bishop of Constantinople. The Divine Liturgy is profoundly Trinitarian and unmistakably ancient. The only concessions to the local context are versions one can download from the internet giving the text of the liturgy in either Swahili or English.

The third surprise came at the end of the service. An icon was given to the church by a family. The priest received it gratefully and performed a ritual of blessing the sacred object. What was remarkable was the backstory of this icon. The family donating the icon told the congregation how they had sought to restore the aging icon using the services of a local artisan. In the process, the artisan had damaged the piece even more, sanding off the face of the Virgin. The distraught family brought the defaced icon home. Within a few days, the face of the Virgin miraculously reappeared. The congregation responded to this testimony with enthusiasm and lined up to kiss the icon while the priest touched each head with a green pine branch. Ancient liturgy and charismatic manifestation happened back-to-back. We all filed out of the nave, having connected through the liturgy with the church in time, with the miraculous icon, and with an eternal power beyond time that penetrates the present.

A final surprise came at home while examining the Cathedral's website. They belong to the African Orthodox Church of Kenya (AOCK), affiliated with the Greek Orthodox family of churches, with a half dozen churches scattered around the city and more in the rural areas. But this family of churches is not the only orthodox communion in the city. Less than a mile away in Kilimani, across from the Yaya Centre one of Nairobi's most popular malls, is the Ethiopian Orthodox Tewahedo Church (EOTC). Slightly further away is the Coptic Orthodox Church (COC) of Egypt. These three churches make up the largest members of the Orthodox family in the city. Yet the AOCK website boldly states that they and they alone are "the only legitimate Church in the country."[1] This is no doubt news to the EOTC and the COC, not to mention the leagues of Protestant, Catholic, Independent, and Pentecostal churches in Kenya. Orthodoxy in the city of Nairobi, like other Christian traditions in the city, is a story of both solidarity and separation. These themes are not new. They appear at the beginning of the Orthodox story in Kenya, a story to which we now turn.

A History of orthodoxy in Kenya and Nairobi

Orthodoxy is deeply rooted in Kenya. Writing in 2013, Orthodox deacon William Black described the Orthodox church in Kenya as "robust and growing."[2] Orthodoxy in Kenya, he reports, is a movement,

> With hundreds of parishes and hundreds of thousands of Kenyan members, the liturgy already translated into fifteen local languages, hundreds of priests trained at an Orthodox theological seminary in Nairobi, scores of primary and secondary schools providing an education for tens of thousands of Orthodox children, and several dozen clinics and even a teachers college established. It is a church with a vibrant mission outreach, planting churches from Lamu to Kisumu and, most recently, seeing Orthodox churches established among the Turkana people in the remote north of the country, led by Turkana priests and deacons.[3]

One might assume from the above that the story of orthodoxy in the city of Nairobi and the nation of Kenya follows the pattern of the historic mission churches, with foreign missionaries laboring for decades to win converts, plant churches, and gradually hand over control to highly trained and trusted indigenous leaders. That assumption would be wrong. The actual story of Kenyan Orthodoxy (Greek, Ethiopian, and Coptic) carved its own original path. We start with the AOCK.

Many African-initiated churches were characterized by a reaction against missionary control in their churches and the attempt to incorporate them into the colonial project. They established churches of protest that sought to liberate themselves from both colonialism and Western-style missionary Christianity. The African Orthodox Church (AOC) shares this pattern with the AICs. What is distinct about all branches of orthodoxy in Nairobi and in the wider nation is that instead of rejecting the "historic" churches in their attempt to be both African and Christian, African converts actually deepened their adherence to historic Christianity by embracing one of the most ancient expressions of early Christianity, Eastern Orthodoxy. Through orthodoxy many Africans would find a haven for their souls, not just by forming new movements of protest Christianity but also by returning an ancient movement of early Christianity.

Orthodoxy began officially in Kenya in 1935, but a near decade of mission-church conflict set the stage for its arrival. The female circumcision crisis among the Kikuyu was the first major crack in the eventual split. History has left us a unique firsthand account of this controversy and the role it played in the founding of the AOC.

Thomas Nganda was born in 1876 in Kigara village, Murang'a. In 1888, he and his mother left their home to find work. They made their way to Kiambu where they lived for a few years before being drawn to the newly emerging city of Nairobi. Thomas became a rickshaw driver, forced to wear bells on his ankles to alert the dense foot traffic to jump out of his way. Nganda didn't hate the work, but he realized there was little future in it. He decided he needed more education. He went back to school at the Church of Scotland Mission (CSM) in Ruthimitu. He was soon involved in the Presbyterian church the mission had planted and became a lay leader in the church. A crisis that would change his life and the life of many of his fellow Kikuyu soon broke his sense of contentment in his new spiritual home. Nganda wrote that "All was well until 1929 when the white men of Thogoto and Kambui Missions sued one man for having his daughter circumcised. I and some other coworkers in the church were not happy with those whites because they were controlling our church and school at Ruthimitu."[4]

Nganda elaborated on the crisis. The head of the CSM working in the Nairobi suburb of Thogoto, John William Arthur, wouldn't let the case drop. The colonial government intervened. The local leadership protested. Reverend Arthur withdrew his suit but devised yet another strategy for ending the condemned practice and imposing the will of the mission. He called for all church members to sign a code of conduct (which Nganda called the *Kirore*,

Kikuyu for thumbprint, showing the common way many locals signed their name). If the lawsuit created tension, the *Kirore* created a firestorm. Nganda listed the four demands as follows:

1. You solemnly swear never to circumcise female children.

2. You solemnly swear that you will never be a member of the KCA (Kikuyu Central Association) party (a political party, called the people of the Uniter).

3. You solemnly swear that you will never become a follower of the man who has been sent by the KCA to England (the Uniter, Jomo Kenyatta).

4. You solemnly swear that you will never join any party whatsoever, if it is not organized by the missionaries or the Government. You swear those things in front of the people and God.[5]

Nganda and his community were outraged. Female circumcision was clearly not the only issue. Reverend Arthur, by condemning both the KCA and Kenyatta, was striking a blow at the heart of Kikuyu political aspirations. Failure to sign each item of the *Kirore* would lead to immediate expulsion. Nganda and hundreds of others refused and were expelled. By the time the dust settled, the Kikuyu churches had lost half their membership.[6]

In the months following, thousands of Kikuyu Christians found themselves without a church and without a school for their children. To deal with the lack of schools, two associations were quickly formed. Nganda and associates joined the Kikuyu Independent School Association (KISA) while others opted for the Kikuyu Karing'a Education Association (KKEA). KISA would give birth to the AOC in Kenya. Karing'a would create the African Independent Pentecostal Church (AIPC).

Nganda was involved in both organizations. The growing number of schools under their supervision faced more than the challenge of finding a good education. For Kikuyu leaders like Nganda, feeding the souls of their children was as important as feeding their minds. In an interesting twist on the typical Western missionary pattern, these Kikuyu schools decided to plant a church to provide spiritual nurture to their schools.

After a series of failed attempts to get the help of the Anglican bishop of Mombasa and the Protestant Alliance in Nairobi, word spread of a new church in Uganda under the leadership of Reuben Spartas, freshly ordained by the South African bishop of the AOC, Daniel William Alexander.

Archbishop Alexander was primate of the AOC in South Africa, whose roots lay in a newly formed church of that name in the United States. Kikuyu leaders of both KISA and Karing'a, eager to explore this Orthodox connection, invited

Bishop Alexander to visit Kenya in 1935. Alexander's presentation of orthodoxy divided his Kikuyu hosts. He spent much of his nearly two-years stay in Kenya seeking to unite the two factions, represented by their respective school associations, under the AOC but without success. A discouraged Alexander left Kenya for his native South Africa in 1937, placing the AOC in the hands of Arthur George Gathuna (1905–87). The KISA group rejected Gathuna's leadership and started the African Independent Pentecostal Church.

In 1938, Reuben Spartas, primate of the Ugandan AOC, visited the Kenya AOC church. Spartas recognized that an immediate challenge to the new AOC was the absence of young priests. He helped four candidates receive training in Uganda and Cairo. At the same time, he became increasingly aware that Bishop Alexander's brand of orthodoxy was deeply flawed and, more seriously, that AOC ordination might not be recognized as valid in international orthodox circles. Spartas applied to the Patriarch of Alexandria for affiliation. Spartas and the fledgling AOC in Kenya had to wait until after the Second World War before Alexandria answered. By 1946, the AOC churches of Uganda and Kenya were received into the Greek Orthodox fold.[7]

Troubled Waters in the 1950s

With Alexandrian recognition, the AOC seemed well on its way to a long period of growth and expansion. By 1952, however, the AOC found itself banned by the government and its schools closed. The State of Emergency meant an open war between the British colonial administration and the Mau Mau and all who supported its insurgency. The government was convinced that independent churches like the AOC were part of that support. Their flock scattered, drifting into other churches or meeting in secret during the dark years of the Emergency.

Eight years after the banning of the AOC, the State of Emergency ended in 1960, and the AOC churches and schools reopened. After independence in 1965, President Kenyatta invited all African independent churches, formerly banned by the colonial regime, to register with the new government. On July 5, 1965, the AOCK became a legally recognized church in the new nation.[8]

John Njoroge calls the relaunching of the Orthodox church in Kenya as "the beginning of new mission encounter of Orthodox theology and African cultures."[9] A call went out to Orthodox communities in Alexandria, Greece, Cyprus, Finland, Australia, and America to engage in a missionary encounter with different parts of the African continent. The Church of Cyprus took a special interest in the work going on in Kenya. In 1971, the visit of Cypriot Archbishop Makarios helped spur fresh growth in the AOCK.

Makarios received a rapturous reception in Kenya. As the President of Cyprus, he was both the leading political and spiritual leader of the island nation. Makarios and Kenyatta had much in common. Both had struggled against British colonialism in their respective countries and had successfully brought their nations to independence. The presence of such an international figure as Makarios, liberator, president, churchman, did much to attract the attention of many Kenyans to the presence of the Orthodox church in their midst. At two open-air meetings during his visit, the archbishop baptized 5,000 people.[10] More concretely, Makarios established an Orthodox seminary in Nairobi for the training of Orthodox clergy. Over time, this seminary became the major training center for priests and catechists across the continent.[11]

Not all within the church were happy with the impact of Archbishop Makarios on the AOCK. Makarios sought to pull the Kenyan church increasingly into the orbit of Greek Orthodoxy. In 1937, Daniel Alexander's chosen successor, Bishop Gathuna, regarded as the founding father and first bishop of the Orthodox church in Kenya, sought to move the AOCK in the opposite direction. Bishop Gathuna made repeated statements about making the AOCK more independent. Additionally, money became an issue. Gathuna was accused by regional Orthodox authorities of soliciting funds from the worldwide Orthodox community without authorization. Sides were taken and the enemies of Gathuna waited for an opportunity to neutralize the aging Bishop's influence.

The opportunity came by way of Gathuna's political involvement. In 1965, after independence, Bishop Gathuna resumed his episcopal office and helped guide the church during the turbulent decades of the new government. In addition to his work as Bishop, Gathuna held a variety of political offices in Nairobi. In 1974, President Kenyatta asked for Gathuna's help in the campaign of his choice for MP for Nairobi, Dr. Njoroge Mungai.

Mungai was running against a popular candidate and an Orthodox Christian, Dr. Johnstone Muthiora. Most of the Orthodox community favored the election of Dr. Muthiora. Gathuna made several important enemies within the church by campaigning for Mungai, the non-Orthodox candidate. When Muthiora won, it appeared the controversy generated by the campaign would fade away. The opposite happened. Within weeks of his win, Muthiora died under suspicious circumstances; his death blamed on President Kenyatta and his circle which included Gathuna. Old animosities against the aging bishop, first circulated in the 1930s, resurfaced and Gathuna's enemies sent a letter to the Patriarch of Alexandria calling for the aging bishop's defrocking.

The response from Alexandria was unsurprising. Bishop Gathuna had been a thorn in his side for years, calling for the complete independence of the AOCK. The charges leveled by his enemies provided him with the opportunity to silence a radical. Gathuna was defrocked. Complicating the actual removal of Gathuna from office was his continuing popularity among the majority of Orthodox churches in the Nairobi area. On the strength of this local support, Gathuna declared himself archbishop of AOCK, receiving support for his ordination by a breakaway group within the Greek Orthodox Church. By the end of 1979, Nairobi and Kenya had two rival bishops and two churches, both claiming to be the AOCK.

For the next twenty-five years, the rival churches engaged in a struggle for power. The death of Gathuna in 1987 did little to moderate the conflict. Bishop Nipon became the leader of Gathuna's faction. A reconciliation of the divided church occurred in 2004, but a remnant loyal to the memory and positions of Bishop Gathuna remains. The effective leadership of Father Makarios Tillyrides was responsible for holding the fractured church together for almost two decades. The church has grown to over a million members with its numeric strength remaining in Nairobi and Central Province.

Challenges remain. The Russian-Ukrainian war that began in 2022 impacted the Kenyan Orthodox Church. The Nairobi Newspaper *The Star* reported that the split between the Ukrainian and Russian Orthodox churches affected Kenya. The AOCK sided with Ukraine. According to the newspaper, Russian Orthodox missionaries infiltrated AOCK congregations and were buying off Kenyan priests to support Russia in the Ukrainian conflict. What the long-term impact of this tug-of-war will be can only be imagined. What is more certain is that the AOCK, after over ninety years of conflict, will most likely weather the storm.[12]

The Coptic Church of Kenya

The story of the COC in Kenya followed a very different script than that of the AOCK. Kenyan church contact with the COC in Egypt dates to 1958 when the Coptic Orthodox Seminary in Cairo received ten Kenyans to study for the orthodox priesthood. The establishment of the COC in Kenya, however, unlike the AOCK, took place post-independence in 1976 (Figure 5.1). It was not the result of a long line of pioneers, such as Daniel Alexander, Reuben Spartas, George Gathuna, Archbishop Makarios, and a host of others but is rather associated with the unlikely partnership of an Egyptian and a Kenyan. Bishop Antonius Markos came to Kenya in 1976. His missionary work in Ethiopia had been interrupted by the military coup that ousted Haile Selassie in 1975. Markos came to Kenya accompanied by Joseph Umanyo, a deacon and graduate of the Coptic Seminary in Cairo and a native Kenyan. The call to Kenya was influenced by the desire of the Coptic Orthodox Bishop Samuel to contact Kenyans who were using the "Copt" label but had little firsthand

FIGURE 5.1 *Coptic Orthodox Church. Photo: Clara Koimett.*

knowledge of what that meant. The mandate of Markos was to find these indigenous "Copts" and instruct them in the ways of Coptic Orthodoxy.

The Coptic missionaries met with the AOCK leaders in Maseno, in Western Kenya, along the shores of Lake Victoria. They were welcomed by the AOC leaders and was invited to preach and lead worship at their gathering. The mystery of how the name "Coptic" came to be used by certain Kenyan Orthodox Christians was soon solved. During the struggle for independence, members of the Kenyan Liberation Front (KLF) were forced to flee to Egypt, where they were being sheltered by President Nasser, a vocal supporter of African nationalism. While in Egypt, these Kenyan exiles learned of the COC, about both its Apostolic and African roots. Returning to Kenya after independence, they formed the Holy Ghost Coptic Church. Using the name of a respected Orthodox church made registration with the Kenyan government easier.[13]

The leader of the Holy Ghost Coptic Church was Archbishop John Juma Pesa. Relationships with the Coptic missionaries soon degenerated. They criticized the worship of the church as a modified Roman Catholic rite. Pesa attempted to pull rank on Markos, appealing to Egypt. Pesa's application to the COC of Egypt was rejected.

Markos returned to Egypt in June 1976 and reported the Kenyan situation to Patriarch Shenouda III. He was consecrated as bishop of African Affairs and sent back to Kenya to register the COC with the government. After registration, Markos restarted his study groups on the Bible and Coptic Orthodoxy for pastors of the Holy Ghost Church as well as the AICs.[14]

Archbishop Pesa responded to the challenge posed by Markos and the new Coptic church in Kenya with savage attacks on the character of Markos and, on one occasion, assaulted Markos with a deadly weapon. On another occasion, he attempted to poison the Egyptian missionary. In 1984, after years of aggression and vitriol, Pesa was arrested. He was sentenced to three and a half years in prison. The name of his church was changed to the Holy Ghost Hermetic Church.

Unopposed by Pesa, Markos helped lead the Coptic church to flourishing. He was a gifted networker who was a founding partner of the Organization of African Independent Churches (OAIC). Today, the COC runs a well-regarded hospital in the heart of Nairobi and schools and training centers across the city and nation.

The Ethiopian Orthodox Tewahedo Church (EOTC)

The Ethiopian Orthodox Tewahedo[15] Church (EOTC) is tucked away on Tigoni Road, in the shadow of the Yaya Centre mall (Figure 5.2). Its long rectangular structure is a combination of stone and stucco, crowned with a silver and turquoise dome at one end. Each Sunday, some 600 worshipers convene to celebrate the Divine Liturgy. The vast majority are Ethiopians, mostly women, with a few Kenyan nationals. It is the youngest sibling in Nairobi's Orthodox family, having started in 1984.[16]

Sprinkled in the congregation are a few Kikuyus, Luos, and Luhyas who serve as deacons. Prominent among these Kenyan deacons is Sylvester

FIGURE 5.2 *Ethiopian Orthodox Church. Photo: Clara Koimett.*

Ndung'u, who fought against the British as a Mau Mau warrior in the 1950s. His admiration for Ethiopian Orthodoxy dates back to the Second World War when Ethiopia resisted the occupation by Mussolini's Italian fascists. By his testimony, Deacon Ndung'u planted the seeds for the EOTC in Nairobi by traveling to Addis Ababa in the early 1970s to personally appeal to the newly installed Abuna Theophilos to plant a church in Nairobi. That a church was not planted until 1984 says little about the Abuna's reluctance and more about Ethiopian church and state relations in the 1970s.[17]

Abuna Theophilos (1910–79) was consecrated as head of the EOTC in Ethiopia in 1971. He was an outward looking leader. His first few years were filled with international travel and networking, seeking to establish stronger ties with the wider Orthodox community. He sought to modernize the church and its educational system. Everything changed in 1974 with the Ethiopian Revolution. Emperor Haile Selassie was overthrown by a military junta, dying under suspicious circumstances in 1975. A Marxist-Leninist Derg (Amharic for "council") was set up to rule the country. Mengistu Haile Mariam became head of the Derg and created a totalitarian state. The EOTC lost its historic standing as the nation's state church.

In 1978, Theophilos was imprisoned. The Derg appointed a rival Abuna in his place. Theophilos was executed by order of Mengistu in 1979. The

Derg's right to replace Theophilos was widely opposed. A rival bishop was chosen by the Ethiopian church in exile in the United States. The struggle between these rival church leaders would occupy much of the next few years. The rule of the Derg began to unravel in the 1980s, triggered by the severe Ethiopian famine of 1984 as well as massive changes in the Soviet Union, its main international ally. Mengistu's loosening grip, combined with the flood of Ethiopian exiles escaping across to Nairobi, gave the new Abuna the moment he needed to support the expansion of the EOTC in Kenya's capital.

Before Nairobi had an Ethiopian Orthodox Church, it had Ethiopian Orthodox Christians. From the Ethiopian Revolution of 1974 onward, thousands of Ethiopians fled for their lives into neighboring Kenya. They found themselves inevitably drawn to the capital. They found housing and jobs. What they had more trouble finding was a church that felt like home. Some attended other Orthodox churches like the COC and the AOCK. Others tried attending the Anglican church. Justus Musya captured their dilemma:

> Attending the church became uncomfortable with what they deemed as its alien ecclesiology. For example, they complained that the services were conducted in either English or in Swahili, languages of which most of them were ignorant. The attitudes of the respondents toward the CPK were indicative of their attitude to Kenya as whole. They were refugees who had arrived in Kenya under the most inclement conditions, after the Ethiopian army, under Mengistu Haile Mariam, overthrew the Ethiopian monarchy of Haile Selassie in 1974.[18]

As strangers in a strange land, these Ethiopian exiles longed for at least one haven where they could worship in their own way and in their own language. With the birth of the EOTC on Tigoni Road, that dream was realized.

For Ethiopians in exile, the creation of the EOTC in Nairobi was a return to the "promised land." Justus Musya explains the unique place of the church in the Ethiopian soul:

> The culture, civilization, political independence, and even the basic education of Ethiopia were instituted by the EOTC. In a way, the EOTC symbolizes the cultural unity and political independence of Ethiopia. The church has served the people in Ethiopian by passing on cultural and religious beliefs, ancient relics, works of art, and even a system of education. The monasteries of the church, which are strewn across most regions in Ethiopia, are not just places of worship, but also places of learning and socialization.[19]

For most exiles, the church was an island of "Ethiopianness" in an alien sea.

There are two sides to the EOTC experience in Nairobi. The church is a deeply satisfying place to feel at home. At the same time, for many Kenyans eager to taste the Orthodox experience, the church can be a place where no one else is allowed to feel at home. The use of Amharic in worship, the dominance of Ethiopian priests, and the close-knit Amharic community have become a barrier that, unlike the AOCK, has limited the number of Kenyans in the church.

Beyond the cultural barriers, however, is the barrier of contradictory visions for the mission of the church. According to church leadership, while recognizing the cultural role the church plays for Ethiopian refugees, the mission of the church entails a desire to reach out more widely in Kenya. They encouraged members to invite their Kenyan friends and neighbors. However, not all parishioners share this sense of mission. For many church members, the EOTC exists "to satisfy the social, cultural, and religious needs of Ethiopians in the Diaspora."[20] The church enabled them to live "in Ethiopia" by preserving its character as an enclave of Ethiopian religion, language, culture, and customs. They want it to stay that way.

Orthodox Worship in Nairobi: The EOTC Experience

Before we close this chapter on orthodoxy in Nairobi, it would be good to visit the heart of the Orthodox experience, the Eucharist. Mention has already been made of the Divine Liturgy at the AOCK Cathedral with its eucharistic climax. While the Eucharist celebration varies little between the three main Orthodox churches, we want to focus on EOTC worship. It represents the most distinctive form of Orthodox worship in Nairobi.

Ethiopian dress is an important part of worship. Shoes are removed before entering the nave. Both men and women wear the *netela*, or shawls, over their clothes. Women wear white dresses, the *habash kemis*. Men also dress in white. The symbolism of purity is obvious. But beyond the religious message is a social one. By worshiping in white, worshipers declare that they are equal in status before their God and hence before one another.[21] Their distinctive dress makes Ethiopian Orthodox Christians highly visible around the city on Sundays and Holy days, especially in areas like Hurlingham, Kilimani, and Lavington.

Music plays a lively part in the service. Traditional instruments like the *washnit*, a six stringed lyre, and various drums, horns, and flutes are used to produce a celebrative atmosphere. Ethiopians move to the music as they prepare for worship.[22]

The central focus of the service is on Jesus Christ, God become man. Though this is true of most churches in Nairobi, there is a history to EOTC's Christological focus. The EOTC is a member of the Oriental Orthodox churches, along with the Coptic church. The Oriental churches represent those Orthodox churches that disputed the Creed of Chalcedon in 453 AD and its representation of Christ as existing in one person but two natures, one fully human and another fully divine. The complaint of the Oriental Orthodox was that the unity of Christ was compromised by the two-nature model (what they refer to as dyophysitism). They prefer a miaphysite model, in which Christ has one nature; fully divine and fully human, and one person. The Christological division that this caused has softened in recent decades and little of this controversy is visible in the worship service.

What is visible is a very Ethiopian Jesus. The EOTC objects to imposing an overtly white Christ in the Christian art of Africa. They argue that "Christ did not belong to a particular race; instead, he belonged to all humanity." Therefore, every ethnic group has a right to portray him in their own way, for each group is, equally before God, a reflection of humanity.[23]

More striking perhaps for a non-Orthodox observer is the prominence of Mary in the religious art of the EOTC's church interior. She is a young innocent in one instance, and a regal protector of the Ethiopian people in another. Many Orthodox and Catholic churches give Mary high honor as the Virgin mother of God, stressing her virginity. Ethiopian Orthodoxy places the emphasis elsewhere. As one parishioner put it: "In our culture, Mary the mother of Jesus is taken as the goddess of fertility."[24] This appears to be a crossover with Ethiopian traditional religion where the goddess *Atete* was responsible for fertility. Mary, over the centuries, assumed her role and it has persisted into modern times. This may also be an instance where "lived religion" departs in some ways from "textbook religion."

The climax of the two-and-a-half-hour service is the celebration of the Eucharist itself. The priest prepared the people for the wine and bread of Christ's body through the prescribed prayers traditionally attributed to St. Gregory. The priestly vestments and the elements of the Eucharist are kept in the "Holy of Holies," the most sacred of the three sections of every Ethiopian church: the narthex (for people in general), the nave (for worshipers), and the sanctuary (or altar) where the table is placed. When the priest speaks the words, "the mystery of faith," a miracle occurs. The wine and bread become in ways not visible to the human eye, the body and blood of Christ. This is the "sum and summary of our faith" for Ethiopians. The elements are shared with parishioners who make their way forward only after having fasted at home in preparation to receive the mysteries.[25]

With the taking of the Eucharist, the service comes to an end. People make their way out of the church interior, not to depart, but to join the "communal meal." Having their souls fed by God, they now receive the food for their bodies. "We eat together," one member explained. "According to our Ethiopian culture, [the] communal meal is very important. It brings us together. We fellowship together."[26]

Conclusion: Orthodoxy and Pluralism

The Orthodox churches of Nairobi are churches of surprise. From their exclusive claims and cultural nationalism to their white-cladded worshipers swaying to the music and mysteries of the Amharic Eucharist in the EOTC, the orthodox experience both mystifies and delights.

Orthodoxy in Nairobi, in its three major expressions, adds to the ever-growing and quite colorful picture of religious pluralism in Nairobi. This may not be obvious given sectarian-sounding statements like the AOCK's that they are "the only legitimate church in Kenya." Yet that statement is not the whole story when it comes to how orthodoxy relates to the broader Christian community in Nairobi.

One recurring theme of our research is that cities like Nairobi are engines of the new religious pluralism. Cities create choices. Different places to eat. Different places to work. Different places to worship. Cities multiply our choices in each of these areas. For some theorists, this religious pluralism is a serious threat to the peace and concord of a society. Choices can mean conflict. Choices can challenge cherished and sacred traditions. Choices, particularly in a heavily politicized society, can be bought and sold and even end up in violence. Yet the potential threat of urban pluralism has been exaggerated. Rural areas can be just as violent and divided. Often more so. Hand-wringing over religious and ideological divisions and competing worldviews misses the fact that enormous levels of social solidarity, altruism, and friendship take place every day among millions of people in the world's largest cities, people who belong to competing religious institutions.

Theoretically, pluralism should tear us apart. In practice, it can bring us together. Our discussion of orthodoxy in Nairobi is a good place to raise this question of the paradox of pluralism because, in certain ways, orthodoxy is a contradiction in terms. Orthodoxy, by the book, sees itself as the only true church of Christ. This sectarian position gives it solidarity, inner cohesion and creates a wall of separation from all other churches. A consistent application of this sectarian position should render African independent churches, Protestants, Pentecostals, and Catholics as pretenders and false churches to be shunned. In practice, this sectarian spirit has not dominated relations with other churches. Even though the three Orthodox churches seem to have little to do with one another institutionally, they relate amicably with each as they sometimes do with Christians outside of orthodoxy. Why is this so?

Peter Berger's definition of pluralism given earlier in this book bears repeating: "Pluralism is a social situation in which people with different ethnicities, worldviews, and moralities live together peacefully and interact with each other amicably."[27] Berger argues that religion in the modern world, often blamed for polarization and violence, may be a key ingredient in building community and social capital that holds societies and cities together. How? Berger references two ideas from the thought of German social theorist Arnold Gehlen. Gehlen argued that society depends both on human tradition and human instincts. Our institutional tradition provides the basic rules of life and thought that enable us to make everyday decisions. When our tradition doesn't have a relevant answer in particular situations, we are freer to make choices based on our individual moral reasoning and interaction with others. Gehlen called tradition, with its ideas, moral codes, creeds, and institutions, the "background" of a community. He called the act of choice, instinct, and interpersonal interaction with others the "foreground" of a community. Berger summarizes: "The background is strongly institutionalized, the foreground is de-institutionalized; the background is the realm of fate, the foreground that of choices."[28] A healthy pluralism thrives in the foreground of religious individuals and groups. It is the place of "Golden Rule" Christianity and fosters the amicable interactions that Berger includes in his definition of pluralism.

Protestantism, so dominant in the Nairobi Christian economy, has a built-in bias for "foreground" relational Christianity over "background" institutional Christianity. First, two central tenets of sixteenth-century Protestantism were the belief that no one institutional expression of Christianity could ever fully contain the mystery of Christ and his gospel, and second, the belief that the individual Christian has the right to privately interpret the Scriptures. Both are pluralizing principles that favor the foreground pluralism of the Golden Rule and limit, without abandoning, the background Christianity of institutions and creeds.

We have noted the phenomena of how urban Christianity in Nairobi is a force of re-sacralizing the secular. It meets in the city's cinemas, plays its music on the city's radio stations and social media, and proclaims its message on urban sidewalks and street corners. But that is not all. Foreground Orthodoxy, when Orthodox individuals work with, play with, befriend, and converse with those outside their tradition, is a significant player in the positive pluralism of Christianity in Nairobi, even if their background would seem to prevent it. When Orthodox Christians love like Christ in the daily interactions of life, secular space is being re-sacralized in charismatic, informal, and deeply relational ways.

Orthodoxy is exclusive in its theology and ecclesiology. Orthodoxy is equally inclusive in its relationships and everyday life. Why? Foreground Christianity, in Nairobi, Lisbon, or Los Angeles, will smooth out the rough edges of background Christianity more often than not. Urban Orthodoxy in Nairobi is yet one more striking example of this reality.

6

"Youth Arise"

Nairobi Christianity as a Youth Movement

Thousands of youth congregate at the Nairobi Chapel grounds at 10:00 p.m. on December 31. Each of the five tents on the fourteen-acre compound holds hundreds of the gathered youth, with many milling around within the spaces between. They listen, sing, and dance to the music blaring out of the public address systems in each tent. Each tent has a stage with singers or a DJ playing different genres of music. One stage plays the local version of hip-hop which mixes English, Swahili, and the local slang known as *sheng*. Another tent plays *benga* music, and another plays local congregational worship music. The young people, aged between seventeen and thirty, energetically follow along with the music. The students are from high school, college, or have just finished their tertiary studies. They are familiar with the songs, having heard them on radio, television (TV), and social media. They sing the lyrics as the singers perform to backing tracks. The young people mimic the dance routines of popular music videos. As the night rolls on, more young people find their way to the venue using public transport. They come in busloads from the city center.

Their goal: to spend the entire night out at the venue—singing, in an all-night event punctuated with prayer and short sermons—as they usher in the New Year. "Totally Souled out" is a vibrant annual event where the youthful energy of the attendees represents a vibrant Christian youth culture of overnight prayer meetings that combine music, sermons, and prayer.

As one of their evangelistic initiatives, Kubamba Krew (K-Krew) gathers these young people each year. The innovative group harnesses emerging social media platforms as evangelistic tools. They constantly originate new events as fresh ways of engaging with the youth. They look out for new genres of music and dance moves to reach the young people. Through these, they find ways of connecting with young peoples' fluid experiences that characterize the African city. Young people in schools, colleges, and churches grapple with their multiple identities as they navigate the city's pluralist context. Innovative Christian groups allow the youth to affirm and celebrate their place in society.

A Youthful Continent

Multiple measures offer demographic evidence that Kenya, like most African countries, is a young country.[1] The youth are eager to participate in religious experiences that they can relate to, in ways that historic mission-church worship and liturgy have not envisaged in the past. As Kenya's cultural center, Nairobi continues to host innovative experiences that offer alternatives for the youth. The experiences are representative of an Africa that is very young. The median age in Africa is nineteen. Africa south of the Sahara has a younger median age—eighteen.[2] If one takes individual countries—Tanzania is eighteen, Burundi is seventeen, Uganda is sixteen. Malawi and Zambia are seventeen. Benin is seventeen and Niger is fifteen. Kenya's median age is nineteen.[3]

Different definitions of youth exist.[4] The UN considers the age of youth as fifteen to twenty-four years of age. The UK's Department for International Aid (DFID) uses the range of ten to twenty-four to define the youth, while USAID includes those between the ages of ten and twenty-nine. The African Union's African Youth Charter defines the youth as those between the ages of fifteen and thirty-five.[5] In this chapter, we will use African Union's definition.

The most significant population of social, cultural, and religious agents in Kenya are the youth. As such, Christianity in Nairobi is representative of the youthful Christianity found in Africa. Forty-five percent of Nairobi's 4.3 million comprises residents between the ages of fifteen and thirty-five.[6] These demographics show that reflections on Christianity in Nairobi, and potentially all of urban Africa, are, in effect, conversations about the youth. This chapter is about the ways the youth express Christianity in Nairobi. The youth are present, both in urban and rural churches, where they are active. One study found that teenage youth in Kenya consider the church one of the most important parts of their lives.[7] It follows therefore that youth participation in Nairobi's religious life reveals a vibrant attempt to express divine activity in both the secular and the sacred spheres. Youth involvement secures the place of Christianity in the religious landscape of cosmopolitan spaces such as schools and urban centers. Historic mission churches were slow to give voice to the emerging youth population in the 1980s and 1990s.[8]

The youth are at the forefront of negotiating urban pluralism. As city residents, they navigate diversity within Christianity and the multiplicity of religions, as pluralism broadens the scope of what members of the society see as conceivable within religious experience. They demonstrate the ways young people negotiate religious diversity. We consider the different ways youth define their role in negotiating diversity.

We must note here that Pentecostal churches are largely a youth occurrence. Whether in schools, colleges, or churches, young people are highly involved in Christian activities.[9] Youth pastors in their twenties and thirties bring together young people and from them, new ministries begin. This is true of denominations such as Deliverance Church and Gospel Outreach ministries. The kind of youth ministry we address in this chapter concerns targeted initiatives for high school and college-age people. The youth age bracket also includes young adults in the first decade of their lives after college.

Youth conceptualize themselves as cosmopolitan residents with multiple identities.[10] The young African urban resident is at once—a member of a family, has an ethnic identity, a national identity, a regional identity, and a continental African identity. This person also carries a religious identity and is part of a global world. Each of these identities presents its ideas about culture and faith. These ideas factor into the collective social, political, and religious experience in the society.

The urban African youth come from a family which might be first, second, or third-generation urban residents. They retain their African surnames, which echo their ethnic identity, whether they speak their ethnic language or not.

First-generation urban residents are more in touch with their cultural identity and are more likely to speak the native languages of their families. The later generation of urban residents are less acquainted with their language but retain an ethnic identity. Youth are also conscious of their national identity. They consider themselves as members of "the 254."[11]

Urban youth celebrate their national identity through their language, sporting events, and even through music. Kenyan residents are more inclined to use English, Swahili, and *Sheng*. *Sheng* is a local language that combines elements of Swahili, English, and local languages. Embedded within this national identity is a regional identity which comes out of increasing interaction, particularly in media and the arts. Liberalized mass media channels create opportunities for musicians and artists to travel across the East Africa region. Social media enables such artists to curate their public image in ways that endear them across the region without losing their national appeal.

Urban African youth, as found in Nairobi, also see themselves as part of the wider African community. They are conscious of their African identity. They refer to it often in their engagement with one another on social media. Once again, musicians are at the forefront of this discourse. Pieces of music have gained continent-wide appeal through TV, radio, and online channels.[12]

The religious identity of the youth forms a significant part of their self-understanding.[13] They see themselves in terms of their religious identity—as Christians.[14] They are also citizens of a global community, viewing themselves as active participants within a broad-based worldwide social discourse. As youth navigate urban cosmopolitan realities in their lives, they express them through the arts, music, and language.[15] Each of these identities presents nuanced ways of perceiving the world. These viewpoints factor into the young people's collective social, political, and religious experience. Their art and music express their creativity not just in art form but also in the development of language.

Sheng is a unique Kenyan language through which youth express themselves in the street, in music, and in the arts.[16] This language is a medium of expressing identity as well as communication. *Sheng* is always evolving to reflect the changing realities of the city. This aspect of Nairobi culture originates largely from Eastlands and flows to the rest of the city. These neighborhoods of Jericho, Jerusalem, Maringo, Umoja, and the expansive Buruburu area were originally designated in colonial Kenya for African settlement.[17]

The contiguous areas where these neighborhoods are found were known in the 1950s as the labor lines. After independence, the areas housed the lower middle-income African families who worked for the national and city government agencies. Today, these areas are home to second- and third-generation urban residents. The youth in these areas internalized their urban identity and created linguistic and artistic cultural expressions, of which *Sheng* is an important part.[18]

Two streams of youth experiences illustrate the diversity and versatility of Christian youth engagement in the African city. One comes out of the educational infrastructure, and the other from media, entertainment, and the arts. Both streams of youth engagement demonstrate that Christianity, especially the Pentecostal charismatic form, has the power to capture the imagination and inspire innovation among young people.

Student Movements in Educational Institutions

Christian student movements, especially Protestant ones, are a significantly visible force in the education system. Youth participation in educational institutions represents youth religious engagement with the establishment—the "cathedral." High schools and colleges form part of the secular instruments of society instituted to distribute knowledge. Nairobi has 1.5 million young people in high schools and colleges.[19] The national education system was built on a framework—reminiscent of modern Western models—that sought to separate religion from society. In this way, they became an instrument of the secularization process, though far from being secular. The institutions provide education based on Western models, which idealized the development of secular society. Such models idealized the separation of religion from the "secular" functions of society. However, given the holistic worldview of the African context, the schools are, in fact, religious spaces where young people express their faith.

The missionary heritage of schools in Kenya is, in part, responsible for the widespread Christian influence in schools. In pre-independence Kenya, these schools emerged out of missionary efforts. As a result, the school as a religious place is less contested. Inclusion of Islamic religious instruction within the national curriculum in the 1980s expanded religious diversity beyond Christianity. Such an open approach to religious pluralism is enshrined in the constitutionally mandated freedom of worship.[20]

Under this constitutional cover, mission schools and government schools are open to and encourage religious activities. Several Christian umbrella organizations are active. In colleges, students organize themselves into vibrant Christian groups known as the Christian Union (CU). They facilitate a Christian vitality that contributes to the Christian landscape among the youth. CUs use existing educational administrative infrastructure to catalyze student involvement. CU groups are largely Protestant. The Catholic equivalent is the Kenya Young Catholic Students.

Students in schools are free to congregate and relate around religious themes. CUs use their presence in schools to conduct student outreach by organizing activities on campus. The national education structure supplies knowledge and, in some aspects, represents the institutional ethos of the Cathedral. Here students articulate their religious expression within an established, national structure.

The Fellowship of Christian Unions (FOCUS) provides institutional support for youth in colleges. Their Nairobi "parish" constitutes over half a million youth in academic and technical skills training colleges.[21] The FOCUS was originally affiliated with the International Fellowship of Evangelical Students (IFES). FOCUS began its work in the 1960s and gained formal registration in 1973.[22] Their headquarters are in the Kasarani area on the eastern side of Nairobi.

CUs are entrepreneurial gatherings that emerge spontaneously. Students found CUs in new educational institutions. CUs serve as revival movements in form and function. They are student-led, organizing services which draw from the students' leadership and creative capabilities. CUs are also very active in evangelism and discipleship activities. They mount vibrant gatherings in the schools. Active preaching, evangelism, and discipleship initiatives occur throughout the school calendar.

CUs receive two layers of support. FOCUS provides institutional backing. They guide discipleship activities, often providing discipleship materials written locally. CUs also operate under the chaplaincy structure of the school. CUs consider the school chaplain a part of their movement. Chaplains have theological training, and many are ordained in one of the historic mission churches. In addition to their chaplaincy responsibility, they serve as teachers within the school system. They usually teach religious classes and oversee the spiritual life in the schools. Most schools use their large halls for their Sunday services. The choice of Christian liturgy for the school services is often influenced by the school's missionary heritage.

These Christian student movements are a notably visible force in the education system. They nurture a vitality that contributes highly to the vibrant Christian landscape. The Christian movements use the school's existing educational and administrative infrastructure to manage student involvement. The students use classrooms and halls of residence before or after classes. The groups function within the school's weekly and annual academic schedules.

Within CUs, students engage in charismatic expressions of Christianity. They use music found in charismatic churches and often engage pastors from Pentecostal churches to speak. Their charismatic leaning is also very evident in the way they carry out prayer. The prayers are energetic and loud. It is not unusual to hear glossolalia in these sessions.

The gatherings are cosmopolitan bringing together people from multiple ethnic, cultural, and geographic backgrounds. This is because the schools themselves are melting pots of ethnic and regional diversity. The schools become microcosms of the cosmopolitanism found in cities. This in turn is a forerunner to the multi-ethnic experience found in urban Pentecostal churches.

Schools and colleges bring people from different parts of the country. Students in colleges encounter similar forms of pluralism found in urban centers. Secondary schools and colleges are spread throughout the country. Only 10 percent or less of the students who complete high school make it to colleges. As a result, schools and colleges draw students from a wide area. This produces pluralistic communities that are microcosms of African urban centers. The university CU experience season of learning serves as a forerunner of the urban multiethnic experience of city churches.[23]

The CU in Kenyatta University (KUCU) is the largest in the country. Its gatherings bring together 3,000 students every Sunday. That constitutes a megachurch, in terms of size and organizational infrastructure. The students organize themselves, run, and fund it. All its operations are run from within the existing student infrastructure, but its expression is highly charismatic. The

University of Nairobi (UoN) CU meets at the Taifa Hall in the main campus. The campus, which houses Taifa Hall, is next to Nairobi's central business district.

CUs informally use kinship language found in some charismatic churches in Kenya. In this way, these student groups draw from their socio-cultural context to find categories to express aspects of their faith. Not only does this help them remain relevant to their audience, but it prepares them for urban Christian life beyond their studies.[24] The chairperson and/or leader(s) of the movement is informally given the title of dad (for males) and mum (for females). This assignment of a parent or kinship term to a peer is unusual in African socio-cultural settings. This is because the age gap between the youngest and the oldest is between three and five years. This communal kinship language found its way into CUs and has entrenched itself over the course of fifteen years.[25] It is unusual in African culture to assign a parental kinship term to a colleague who is only three years older than the younger members of the community.[26]

Students in CUs congregate in various types of prayer meetings. The overnight prayer culture of *keshas* is a popular variation of the prayer culture. *Keshas* are found in many charismatic churches. The term refers to an entire night of prayer. The format of the service includes two or three sermons and lengthy sessions of congregational singing mingled with prayer. The sessions are not easy to regulate. While most meetings maintain Orthodox Christian doctrine, some may go out of line, often as a result of guest preachers who wander off the beaten path. Areas of deviance include issues of extra-biblical revelation, excessive focus on demonology, unorthodox interpretations of apocalyptic texts, and cultic practices surrounding prophecy and healing. In most cases, schools and college chaplaincies rein in the incidents, sometimes with the help of interventions of FOCUS and Kenya Students Christian Fellowship (KSCF).

As a subset of the ethnically mixed school and college context, CUs are a microcosm of the cosmopolitan context of urban churches. The multicultural, multi-ethnic experience proliferates through interschool gatherings regularly held regionally and nationally. Here many students get a foretaste of the scale and diversity they find in large churches in the cities where they seek employment after studies.

Youth in Media and the Performing Arts

Kenyans most acutely feel secularization forces through mass and social media. The youth are proficient and use social media to navigate their social and religious heritage. In Nairobi, 1.7 million youth own phones.[27] This group is the most prolific in their use of internet and online commerce.[28] Through their aptitude in using the media, the youth negotiate the implications of matters of public interest, especially in the area of social relations, politics, culture, and religion.[29] For the Christians among them, God is at work in the city, in the different sectors of youth activity. Here, the urban youth express their multiple identities, integrating the shared modernities that abound in the modern African city. They are at home both in the kiosk of religious innovation and the cathedral of Christian institutions.

An integral part of youth engagement is music.

The 1990s were important for youth and the performing arts. Young leaders such as Mwaniki Mageria, Bob Nyanja, and others catalyzed Christian drama events for young people.[30] In the same period, pioneer Christian music groups like Hart Ministries, led by Kenyan Pete Odera and the Ugandan trio Limit X, demonstrated that modern popular music could be produced within East African soil.[31] This music held a wide youth appeal as the media spaces liberalized. The groups' blending of African beats with American hip-hop music reached a generation that was becoming increasingly globalized. Young people in urban centers flocked to a handful of church venues where the group performed. During these days, Christian music beyond hymns and choir music did not have a wide reception.

Since those days, Christian music among the youth went through several iterations within the church. Musicians such as Mercy Masika and Kanjii Mbugua demonstrated that music could be used within the church in the late 1990s. They combined local music genres and languages with a strong Christian message. In the early 2000s, musicians such as Daddy Owen and Rufftone created larger-than-life personas while still maintaining a Christian missional perspective in their music.[32] Some Christian artists went on to have crossover appeal, developing a huge platform built from their Christian message, crossing over into social issues. These include Juliani, whose official name is Julius Owino.[33]

The music industry in Kenya is challenging for artists. Revenues from music play are low, and many artists report being taken advantage of by promoters.[34] Artists who produced Christian music in the 1990s felt that the church leadership did not affirm their work. They also felt underappreciated within Christian circles, where they expected more support.[35] The music industry expanded in the 2000s when the quality of music production improved. It was also during this time that producers of Christian music reached wider audiences through the efforts of Christian youth ministries that focused on the arts.

Building on youth affinity for music, itinerant youth ministries of preachers, and DJs integrate the entrepreneurial ethos of the kiosk. Ministries such as K-Krew create outreach events tailor-made for the youth. They carve out a niche for religious expression, interpreting mission as evangelism. These ministries create events of varying sizes, mobilizing resources to bring together young people for mission. These ministries have no official umbrella organizational oversight. For the most part, the groups run without any large administrative bureaucracy. They rely on internal expertise, entrepreneurial acumen, and the charisma of their leaders.

Moses Mathenge (whose stage name is DJ Moz) and John Njuguna Waiguru (popularly known as Njugush) founded K-Krew in 2000.[36] Their vision was to engage in evangelism initiatives optimized for Kenyan youth. Initially, they used the medium of music, traveling as itinerant DJ units with sound equipment and a preacher to high schools.[37] They eventually expanded these to include colleges. Their traveling mission programs reach 200,000 students annually.

Their effectiveness with youth caught the interest of liberalized commercial radio and TV stations. The students respond positively to K-Krew's extraverted approach to evangelism through music.[38] Their energetic meetings with musicians, dancers, and DJs provide the school and college students with avenues to celebrate their faith in a youth affirming environment. This is, for many, Kubamba affirms the fact that Christian faith is an opportunity for rejoicing. "Kubamba" is a *Sheng* word used to refer to moments "to enjoy."

They began gospel Sunday TV programming aimed at young people in their late teens and early twenties.[39] In the process, developed a Bible study program.[40] They initially intended this as a resource for their leaders, but then expanded it to reach young adults within their orbit. K-Krew eventually began to harness their media power to put together large gatherings for Totally Souled Out, the annual overnight New Year's Eve event they founded in 2005.[41]

Their affiliation with churches such as Nairobi Chapel and CITAM remains "loose." Their autonomy retains the entrepreneurial innovation of a kiosk. Through their relationship with media, K-Krew augments their itinerant ministry approach with the national reach of large media institutions. A symbiotic relationship with the media allows youth ministers like K-Krew to accomplish their evangelism goals. In turn, the media gets the youth viewership which it needs for its business goals.

The unique draw of K-Krew is their understanding of, and relationship with Christian pop culture icons. K-Krew community has defined themselves as a key contributors to youth Christian activities. Their wide reach gave them a unique relationship with young and upcoming artists who want to reach the youth. In this way, Kubamba raised the profile of gospel-themed music in Kenyan mass media. K-Krew engages with various art forms, but music and, to some extent, dance are the main forms of pop culture. Members of dance groups such as Allover who had found faith in Pentecostal churches found a place to express their art in K-Krew's outreach initiatives. Much of K-Krew's activity is in the grassroots, with youth groups in Pentecostal churches and increasingly with historic mission churches. A few movement leaders mobilize resources from companies and from the youth themselves to mount big gatherings in different cities.

Mass media is both institutional and transient. TV and radio is institutional because it depends on economic incentives and national communication infrastructure. It is also transient because it is ephemeral; its content is for use at a particular moment in time. Youth ministers can co-opt the institutional structure of media for use in mission.

Other smaller media-oriented initiatives include the Clean the Airwaves (CTA) initiative. CTA emerged from a group of artists who came together in 2008. Their goal was to accomplish the mission by raising the quality of Christian music and taking advantage of existing mass media channels to communicate the Christian message. Richard Njau, a former music artist, spearheaded the initiative. He sought to "to create content that will positively impact the society."[42] At the core of CTA was music. Njau used CTA as a discipleship avenue for upcoming artists. He also used the platform to encourage Christian artists to counter the materialistic, secular trends in music videos. At the time, the hyper-materialistic culture had found its way among the youth, through both secular and Christian music videos. Njau later expanded the scope of CTA activities to video-log interviews containing historical content on the development of the music industry in Kenya.

The proliferation of social media channels accelerated the impact of these trends on the youth. Social media provides an easy way for young people to participate. This widespread phenomenon is responsible for the Kenyans on Twitter (#KOT) phenomenon. Young people in the 2010s and 2020s forged a Kenyan sense of identity which fiercely criticizes failures in government. The group acts as a commentator for uniquely Kenyan social trends.[43] The group also defends Kenya in instances where they feel the national pride is under attack.

Youth Ministries in Churches

The other way Nairobi youth engaged with the vibrant Christian spirituality was through trailblazing youth ministries led by charismatic individuals. Youth work as a formal category of ministry within churches is a recent development. Before 2000, there were very few dedicated youth ministries within churches. Youth ministers were essentially young people who coordinated youth mission and discipleship activities within churches that did not have structures for them.

Trailblazing youth ministries within churches began to take shape within the city in 2000 with leaders like Gowi Odera (Nairobi Baptist), Toni Kiamah (Kenya Assemblies of God), Joel Chola (Nairobi Lighthouse), Patrick Kuchio (Christ is the Answer Ministries), and Oscar Amisi (Deliverance Church). These leaders began meeting in 2000 after an overnight youth gathering at the City Stadium in December 31, 1999.[44]

Kiamah, a converted formerly deviant youth from Eastlands popularized youth ministry through Angaza, a local TV show on the national public channel. He built on the small foundation that radio preachers laid in the late 1980s and early 1990s. Using *Sheng*, he was one of the early leaders to integrate youth work within churches.[45] Gowi Odera worked with Youth For Christ, an international youth evangelism organization. Through his work with leaders in Nairobi, he helped catalyze indigenously led forums for youth ministers to provide training and connections.

These efforts bore fruit in the birth of a group of workers that in 2001 came to be known as the Nairobi Youth Network (NAYNET). The group organized regular meetings which shaped the leadership of youth ministries in Nairobi's Protestant churches. The meetings were the first to organize youth leaders toward the common goal of outreach to young people. Until then, youth ministries happened on an ad hoc basis.

Non-denominational churches and Pentecostal churches worked with volunteer youth ministers, who were young people with a vocation trying to do mission and discipleship within churches. These structures did not exist within historic mission churches until the mid-1990s. Independent Protestant churches began formally hiring youth pastors in the 2000s as the profile of youth ministry began rising within the city.

More recently, historic mission churches began to invest heavily in youth work. All Saints' Cathedral is the largest Anglican church in Nairobi, and its parish is at the center of the city, serving members from all over the city. The Cathedral in Nairobi runs an extensive youth ministry program with multiple Bible studies, meetings, and activities in arts. Up to 1,500 young people come to these ministries from within an Anglican denominational support.[46]

The challenge that remains is giving young people higher levels of education and keeping them gainfully employed. Kenya continues to struggle with low employment rates for young people. Youth employment is higher in urban areas than it is in rural areas.[47] These realities present a constant challenge for ministers of all denominations who work with the youth.

Catholic churches also run youth ministries to address these needs. The Don Bosco Shrine, run by the Salesians of Don Bosco, is a Catholic church located 2.5 kilometers north of All Saints' Cathedral. The church is home to a vibrant Catholic youth group which, like the Anglican church, has multiple study and arts activities for young people. Don Bosco runs vocational training centers in Karen, on the outskirts of Nairobi, to train young people in trade skills. These centers are an effort to address the youth unemployment in the country.

Conclusion

Nairobi's nearly 2 million youth are a part of the story of Christianity. Not only are the church congregations young, they are also founded by young adults. It is in Christian initiatives for high school and college-age Nairobi residents, that we see the youth wrestle with their cultural, ethnic, national, and religious identities. Through this struggle, the youth present diverse approaches to the pluralism of the African city.

While the initiatives are the work of individuals with immense entrepreneurial capacities, the youth assert their voice by their participation in them. The youth initiatives display the nimble agility of the "kiosk" in their innovative vigor. Through the school and the media outlet, these youth initiatives also demonstrate a familiarity with the institutional mechanisms of influence.

The large youth population in Nairobi is the result of Kenya's high population growth rate. At 2.2 percent, the country's population will produce a steady supply of young people into the middle of the twenty-first century. In the meantime, the rural-urban migration which began in the 1960s continues to support Nairobi's growth, as it does in major African cities. The devolution of power and resources into counties in 2010 slowed down the migration into Nairobi but has not stopped it altogether. These factors of growth account for the large youth population in the cities. Through their active participation in the churches, and in their diverse initiatives, the youth enact the vision of God at work among them in the cosmopolitan spaces within the city. Here, these young people contend with their multiple identities emerging from their heritage in a modern African city. They populate smaller groups and congregate in large gatherings. These varied expressions illustrate multiple ways young people live out their Christianity. The youth initiatives also demonstrate the centrality of youth to the story of Christianity in the African city.

7

"Your Daughters Shall Prophesy"

Women's Role in Shaping Christianity in Nairobi

A group of fourteen women gather in the living room of a small two-bedroom house in Kayole on a Sunday at 5:00 p.m. This sprawling residential area is on the furthest eastern limits of Nairobi metropolis. The women sing a Swahili song, "*Ametenda maajabu*" (He has performed wonders), their singing is slow and fervent, with closed eyes. After five minutes of the song, they spontaneously break out into prayers, each one voicing their own petitions. For several minutes, a third pray in glossolalia, another section say their prayers in Swahili, and the rest pray in indigenous languages. Mama John closes the session in Swahili, with a loud, passionate expression of God's goodness, mercy, and provision. Loise doesn't go by her first name. The culture accords honor to mothers by the title "*Mama*," followed by the name of the child best known to the group. Thirteen-year-old John is her last-born son whom everyone in the group knows. Loise, aged fifty, runs a small grocery shop built at the front of her house, just a block away.

The meeting ends and they bring out large flasks of tea. The tea is brewed in the characteristic Kenyan way with milk, sugar, and ginger added to the tea leaves. It is served very hot in big mugs, with slices of buttered white bread to go with it.

This marks the end of a long day for the women. Most attend the same Pentecostal church in the neighborhood. Two attend a local Catholic church, another attends a nearby Presbyterian church, and one goes to the Anglican church. They are all involved in different ways in their churches, which is the reason for beginning their meeting at 2:30 p.m. for their *chama* (an informal savings group). The unfamiliar observer might mistake this for a Bible study. The prayers at the beginning, the singing of choruses, and the sermonette bear all the marks of a church small group.

After the sermonette, the group then turns to the business of the day. The *chama* has an empowerment agenda that extends beyond the spiritual well-being of the members. At each monthly meeting, the women pool money. Each contributes the equivalent of US$20. The group retains 20 percent of each month's collection and gives the rest to one of the women in rotation (also "merry-go-round"). The women use the money for various things. Many use it to run their businesses or pay fees for their children. The money retained by the group is used for emergency loans for members of the group during times of need.

Two months prior, Mama Wangui, the host of this meeting, took out an emergency loan to pay medical expenses for her teenage daughter's pregnancy. Earlier that year, Mama Otieno took out an emergency loan to cover the costs of Otieno's traditional wedding event. The financial empowerment extends to social needs within this microcommunity.

The group rotates their leadership on an ad hoc basis. Mama John has been the leader for two years. The previous year was difficult for her, but with the support of the women and her exceptional leadership gifts, she skillfully led the group. Her first-born daughter was about to finish a college course in education at the University of Nairobi (UoN). Mama John lost her husband to cancer in her first year leading the group. The women cherish the memories of their shared experiences gathered over the two decades the group has been in existence. Their faith is the glue that holds them together as they navigate the challenges of life.

Mama John's *chama* is typical of hundreds of similar groups scattered around the city's 1.5 million households.[1] This *chama* embodies the many dimensions of women's role in Nairobi's Christianity. Women are central to the spiritual life of the city.

In spite of the challenges of the secularizing forces evident in the challenging urban life, the women's spirituality strives to illustrate God's sustaining presence. Their narratives try to portray divine interventions in their everyday lives. Through the multitude of challenges in every aspect of their lives, the women root their responses in religion. Their belief, nurtured in their groups, is the essential truth that fortifies their resolve to overcome.

The groups come together in churches while others meet in residential areas. While there are men who form their own *chamas*, and some women's *chamas* allow men as well, most *chamas* are women-only groups. The predominance of women in these groups mirrors the higher attendance of women in churches.

Leadership in business and politics has been patriarchal in Kenya's recent history.[2] As a result, women's societal influence has been less visible. However, their influence is present and emerges not only through their leadership at the micro level in small groups but also in churches. In a society where women were initially relegated to the backseat of political, economic, and social spheres, the prominence of women in Christianity is remarkable.

For Christian women in Nairobi, God is at work in the secular city. Evident in their gatherings is the ardent belief that divine encounters manifest in both the secular and sacred spheres. Though they experience a myriad challenges in their social, economic, and religious background, the women ground their responses in their spirituality. Their Christian faith remains the core influence that shapes how they navigate their urban realities.

The presence of women in Kenya's Christianity cannot be overstated. As is typical in many parts of the Global South, there are more women than men in church services.[3] More women volunteer in church activities, and more women attend church small groups than men. In charismatic churches, Kenyan women defy the odds to show remarkable leadership resilience in the dynamic urban environment. In this chapter, we explore how Nairobi's diversity manifests in the various dimensions of Christian women's involvement. Through their varied participation, women in Nairobi bring the Cathedral and Kiosk Christian priorities together in functional ways that contribute to spiritual life in the city.

Women and Christianity in Kenyan History

The history of women's engagement in Christianity begins with evangelism through the education of women in pre-independence mission stations. Women did not take part as leaders in the mission except under the leadership of men. In a departure from the norm, the Church Mission Society (CMS) put together concerted efforts to raise the profile of women's education in Africa.[4] They set out initiatives to train women who could then participate and become leaders within the Christian society that was envisioned.

Though historic mission churches (HMCs) devoted effort to women's education, they did not envision women in religious leadership. The goal of women's education through missionary schools in the colonial era aimed at producing Christians whose contribution to society did not include religious leadership. Educated women could serve society at home or in basic clerical roles.[5]

This was a break from women's religious participation in traditional society. Communities in Kenya allowed the possibility of women's participation in religious activities. Women could engage in divination or healing, both of which had religious dimensions within holistic African worldviews. Religion and other spheres of life were integrated. Gender role separation in the practice of traditional religion was more fluid than in missionary Christianity. There are multiple examples of women who functioned in traditional society as religious leaders.[6]

Indigenous Christian movements allowed more space for women's participation than Christian missions did. Early African Initiatives in Christianity (AICs) kept patterns of religious engagement similar to those of traditional society. For example, there were women singers and prophets in these early indigenous Christian expressions.[7] These groups came about in the 1920s and 1930s and can still be found today.[8] Women in AICs served as prophets, prayer leaders, and singers.[9] Their participation was welcomed in the oral liturgies of AIC meetings. Though the top church leadership was predominantly male, women's leadership influence was evident in the diverse AIC groups.

From the 1940s to 1980s, East Africa revival's egalitarian ethos made room for women's participation in gatherings.[10] Women and men sat in fellowships together and had equal opportunities to share their testimonies. Revivalists, as they came to be known, retained their membership of HMCs. In their HMC churches, leadership remained male. It was through their fellowships, however, that a different model of participation emerged.

Revivalists made space for women to speak by sharing their testimonies. The fellowships are precursors to church small groups. The fellowships allowed women to engage with Christian reflection in much the same way as a priest would in a Sunday sermon. In these small groups, the giving of "testimonies" became a broad narrative genre of group participation which incorporated elements of storytelling, theological reflection, evangelism in the practice of Christian faith.

Women and Christian Leadership in Modern Kenya

More recently, women's senior-most leadership in male-led Pentecostal charismatic churches came in the title of the pastor's wife. This informal office of the pastor's wife provided a new legitimate avenue for women's influence in the church structure.[11] As a highly visible, though unofficial position, it reassured laywomen in the church of their place in the community.

The position of pastor's wife enabled women's contribution to be visible through the church community through the kinship relationship with their husbands. While many churches have not institutionalized this office in their constitutions, the pastor's wife held a significant position of influence and authority within the church. Pastors' wives often lead women's ministries and ministry to the children. It was also not uncommon for the pastor's wife to teach in Sunday church services, especially in Pentecostal charismatic communities. Women's participation in this way reveals a new feature of pluralism in urban contexts.

Charismatic Christianity in its diverse forms breaks historic gender stereotypes previously entrenched in HMCs by unraveling gender monopolies of power found there.[12] Though women were not initially envisaged in the "cathedral's" hierarchy of power, recent indigenous expressions have brought women from the periphery of religious leadership.

Pentecostal charismatic Christianity leads the charge for women to have considerable influence in the religious sphere. They also play a central role in other ways. Women, especially in the Pentecostal charismatic churches, draw from their small groups the entrepreneurial value characteristic of the "kiosk." They innovate new ways of expressing themselves as Christians using these entrepreneurial impulses. Women combine this innovative spirit with institutional structures which emerge from their work.

The impetus for women in leadership comes from charismatic theology lived within the indigenous cultural worldview. These two forces come together to create an environment where women became active participants in religious activity. Charismatic theology and the cultural license for religious leadership. These forces shaped society's expectations, making room for women's participation in religious activities and even leadership. Pentecostal charismatic Christianity began confronting the secularizing forces of modernity that seemed in the colonial era to relegate women to the periphery in religious, political, and economic activities.[13]

Women in HMCs

The rise of prominent women church leaders in twenty-first-century Nairobi is a striking feature considering the patriarchal nature of HMCs. As mentioned earlier, until the 1990s, most HMCs limited women clerical leadership. Roman Catholics' educational work with women began in Nairobi with schools for European girls.[14] Later, these schools began to contribute to women's religious orders. It was through their women's religious orders that Catholic missions provided for women's participation in Christian leadership. This was in some ways a peripheral engagement which followed the missionaries' context in Europe. While Catholic women might have participated fully in religious life, they could not join clerical ministry. Until recently, training of women for lay leadership in Roman Catholic churches was rare.

Protestant missionary initiatives made efforts to educate women.[15] Within that framework, the training included opportunities for women to learn how to be active participants in society.

Historical sources show initial reluctance among Protestant missionaries and the government to invest more heavily in the education of women. One source, for example, cites lukewarm government officers' response in 1943 to the spirited efforts of female Anglican missionaries to rally support for more engagement with women's education.[16] The local designated authorities did not oppose these women's initiatives, but neither were they keen. The lack of enthusiasm frustrated what might have been a growth trajectory for the empowerment of women for the purposes of Christian mission.

The cathedral, as represented by HMC structures, thus offered limited provisions for women at apex leadership. The Anglican Church of Kenya (ACK), whose archbishop sits in Nairobi, had no female bishop until January 2021. Until then, there were no women representatives to the house of bishops in the Kenyan provincial synod.[17] The ordination of women in the Anglican church in the 1990s opened the door for women to live out their call within the institutional church. Even then, women at that level were underrepresented in the key leadership organs.[18]

While one might consider Nairobi a broad-minded religious center with a higher disposition toward women leadership, there were no Anglican, Presbyterian, Methodist, or Lutheran bishops before 2020. In January 2021, the ACK consecrated Emily Onyango as the first woman assistant bishop in Kenya. Rose Okeno became the first female Anglican bishop in September 2021.[19] These women leaders come from long personal histories of distinguished service in the church.

Protestant HMCs host groups which encourage women's participation. Mothers' Union and Woman's Guild movements have long been organizations driving volunteerism within the Anglican and Presbyterian churches respectively.[20] Their stated goals were to promote family ideals of marriage and parenthood through women's active participation. Mothers' Union was initially a women's movement among Europeans. Africans first enrolled in March 1956 encouraged by Gladys Beecher, the wife of the first Anglican bishop, of the province of East Africa.[21] With the exit of British women in the 1960s, the movement is now indigenously led. The organization incorporates a broad range of initiatives which deal with contextual issues women face. These include women's empowerment groups, prayer groups, micro-finance, and agri-business. Their work also involves active campaigns against child marriage, domestic violence, and gender-based violence.[22]

The women's groups organize themselves into fellowships and play a prominent role, creating a sense of belonging and relationship, particularly for older women, within the HMC setting. Increasingly, the groupings are finding ways to integrate younger women to enroll. These women lead prayer in the church. They also take the initiative to give leadership in community and social initiatives.

Theology and Practice of Women in Church Leadership

The role of women in society is the subject of important theological reflection which takes place in Nairobi's academic centers. Here, theologians contend with the challenges Christian women face in the church and in society. While women did not experience full participation in HMCs, they found expression in Nairobi's universities and women's caucuses. University of Nairobi and Kenyatta University (KU) nurtured important intellectuals who wrote widely and incisively about the plight of women in society.

Kenyan Christian women academics such as Musimbi Kanyoro, Esther Mombo, Nyambura Njoroge, Teresia Hinga, Mary Getui, Anne Wasike, Philomena Mwaura, Damaris Parsitau, and Loreen Maseno have made important theological contributions to discourse on women in African society.[23] Though the Circle of Concerned African Women Theologians began in Accra, Ghana, the group convened many meetings in Nairobi over the years to deliberate and publish material on the subject.[24] This group's intellectual pursuits represent an important dimension of women's leadership that has a global impact.[25] The group has also laid the foundation for developing women intellectual leaders in the male-dominated field of African theology. Up-and-coming theologians include Telesia Musili, Fancy Cheronoh, Edith Kayeli, Mary Kihuha, Wanjiru Gitau, and others who are carrying on the legacy of academic reflection on women in church and society.[26]

At the ecclesial level, Pentecostal churches have more readily incorporated women in their formal structures of leadership. Their theologies democratize charisma and carry forward the reformation notion of "every member a minister." Challenging clericalism, they expect that congregation members can also participate in church leadership. The theology of the gifts of the Spirit and their distribution among Christians enables women to find a place in Christian leadership. This vibrant volunteerism animates Christian life during the week and adds to the vivacity of the church in the weekend. Here women can influence society unbridled by societal constraints. Their influence impacts the city in ways that were not previously possible in other spheres, such as business or politics.

The East African Revival from the 1940s, with its culture of orality through testimonies, did much to bring about opportunities for women to express their Christian faith in the context of gatherings of men and women.[27] Raising in the aftermath of the East Africa Revival, the charismatic communities that emerged in the 1970s broadened the possibilities for women's participation.

Building on the Revivalist precedent (where women emerged as religious leaders), Pentecostal charismatic churches invited women to participate in religious leadership in Nairobi. Teresia Wairimu is one example of women at the apex leadership of churches. She is an important spiritual leader in Kenyan society.[28] Her church, FEM Family Church, in the Karen suburb west of Nairobi, often hosts senior government officials. She is frequently seen in the presence of influential members of society and high-ranking government officials. The New Year Prophetic services in her church receive broad viewership online and in the mass media.[29] Her approach to ministry resembles leading televangelists. She speaks about current issues facing society, drawing inspiration from scripture.

Teresia Wairimu's leadership illustrates Pentecostalism's preference for spiritual calling over gender stereotypes.[30] Her story, as presented in her autobiography, illustrates Pentecostalism's acceptance of women in leadership. As a single parent who divorced in the early 1990s, Wairimu's example offers insights about how Pentecostalism reframes unwritten, potentially limiting, societal, cultural, and religious norms for women in leadership. Wairimu offers herself as a model of a successful, productive life in faith. Wairimu, like other women leaders, upholds conservative ideas of personal piety. Pentecostals ability to revisit and even revise rules of social engagement allows women to play an active part. This Christian expression provided a redemptive narrative of a divorced mother to assume a place of influence in the church. Wairimu teaches about marriage, abstinence, and the broader issues facing the country. Pentecostal theology of redemptive grace stresses that past personal life issues are not a drawback to the (preacher's) ability to lead in ministry. Past difficulties are, in fact, illustrations of God's salvific work in the individual.

Pentecostals also take seriously the idea that grace and charisma work together to redeem and empower women for their role in society. In this way, Wairimu's example affirms women who otherwise would face societal condemnation but can now be influential leaders. Women leaders within this framework can teach about marriage, parenting, and abstinence despite the challenges or stigma they might have previously faced.

Pentecostal pneumatology promotes the notion of democratized charisma, where everyone has the potential to have the gifts of the Holy Spirit. Such a theological framework envisions women as recipients of the power of the Holy Spirit who can, and do, influence religion in society. Such influence grows in ways not represented in business or politics. Pentecostal charismatic Christianity rewrites the rules of acceptability for women in leadership.

It provides for women to participate actively at all levels of Christian religious expression. It invites women to lead the liturgy, as well as in the life of the church, outside the confines of a Sunday worship experience.

Kathy Kiuna is another example of women in leadership. She writes about how early in life, she had a child out of wedlock.[31] In her writings, she is honest about the ways in which this piece was a drawback. However, she narrates her story as one of personal triumph and the redemptive grace of God. She often tells the story of how she overcame this seeming obstacle. Her story shows how she got married and rose to a place of influence. She contrasts her early life with her present status as a leader—who is successful and leads a highly visible ministry.

Motivation and Kinship

Motivational empowerment plays a critical role in these gatherings of women. The women attend gatherings within which they are empowered. This is a case with Esther Obasi-ike and Kathy Kiuna.[32] These social groupings allow women to empower one another. They also take part in social action at the micro and regional levels.

The promise of mentorship through the pulpit and interpersonal interaction supplies avenues for younger women to aspire for greater things in the ever-changing life of urban Kenya. One of the ways they activate this mentorship is through the "kin" role of motherhood. Kinship is an important dimension of Pentecostal expression. Christians in Nairobi frame their communities as families. They use familial terms to frame the relationships within the groups. Their spiritual "families" have patriarchs and matriarchs and offspring.

Allan Kiuna and his wife Kathy present themselves as the spiritual parents of their church. It is against this "church family" backdrop where Teresia Wairimu is viewed as their spiritual mother. This kinship relational perspective of religious kinship works as a framework of engagement with community in urban settings. Here, Teresia Wairimu and Kathy Kiuna are not separated from their gender-specific responsibility as mothers. Instead, their motherhood becomes an integrated aspect of their leadership. The function of women in mentorship and nurture is highly treasured in women such as Kathy Kiuna and the preacher-turned-politician Margaret Wanjiru. They are highly sought after as mentors for younger women.

The women leaders' input in the lives of younger women forms the basis for relationships with networks of leaders around them. The women prove the powerful role of mentorship in overcoming life challenges to bring about great achievement. This is especially the case when the mentors are women who have faced and successfully overcome social stigma. Testimonies from lay members of the groups often emphasize the inspirational role of the leaders play. The narratives highlight the powerful influence women leaders use to shape the lives of their "spiritual" progeny. Such power, though inspirational, has the potential to also be manipulative and exploitative.

Beyond the Church

The religious influence of women also supplies opportunities for women to be involved in politics. Margaret Wanjiru is a unique example of a prominent Christian woman leader in elective politics.[33] Wanjiru founded Jesus is Alive Ministries in 1992 after sensing a call into evangelistic ministry. She credits Reinhard Bonnke's catalytic role in the formation of her ministry.[34] A Nairobi resident, Wanjiru built a political platform in the city, drawing from her reputation as a minister. Wanjiru cut the image as religious agent of change engaging the highest powers in the country's capital city. Her blend of religion in politics offered yet another response to the city's secularizing impulses.

The women leaders expand their leadership reach through the media, as in the case of Lucy Natasha, Teresia Wairimu, Kathy Kiuna, and others. They use media for their evangelistic initiatives. Wairimu's proximity to power structures shows the level of influence she wielded in political circles in the 2010s. Before this, the public already held a high view of Wairimu's mission from her evangelistic outreach in the mass media from the early 1990s. Through their engagement with the media, women leaders build their institutions and appeal to youth, especially young women.

Social justice and community care initiatives also find a place among women in Nairobi. Not only do they participate in small groups, but prominent women leaders founded community care initiatives that make important contributions to the city of Nairobi. Judy Mbugua began Homecare Spiritual Fellowship (HSF) in 1980.[35] A Pentecostal, Mbugua founded the group from her experiences at CITAM. Her aim was to cater to the needs of married women whose husbands were not practicing Christians. In 2021, the ministry had women groups in four of Kenya's forty-seven counties. Over a period of forty years, the group morphed into a holistic ministry to hundreds of women. At its inception, the group initially met for fellowship and prayer. In 2021, HSF ran a retreat house, Bethel School of tailoring (a women's skills training school), Fadhili Women Group (a HIV/AIDS support community for women), and a program for orphaned and vulnerable children.[36] A gifted mobilizer, Judy Mbugua was the founding executive director of the Pan African Christian Women Alliance (PACWA) in 1989. PACWA is affiliated with the Association of Evangelicals in Africa. PACWA's mission in Africa is to "mobilize and empower women through prayer, evangelism, discipleship, and capacity-building to be all that God made them to be in the home, church, and society."[37]

Linda Ochola-Adolwa, an ordained clergywoman, has long engaged in civic education in the rural areas. Working from her base in Nairobi, she has orchestrated civic education initiatives. Using written material and her foundation, she has taken part in a wide range of community and social activities to empower women in the areas of civic duty.[38] Hatua Trust "is a civil society organization that uniquely engages and catalyzes Christian organizations and individuals to actively participate in social accountability processes towards their local or national governments."[39] Her work harnesses the potential of women groups to organize women and provide sustainable structures after her training interventions have ended.

As a testament to its globality, Pentecostalism encourages speakers from outside Kenya into their gatherings. Women's Christianity in Nairobi is connected to the rest of Africa. As a testament to its globality, Pentecostalism allows women from outside the country to speak into the Kenyan situation. Nairobi's central geographic location and the well developed infrastructure makes it an ideal locality for this. Through women's ministries such as Daughters of Zion and Queen Esther's Generation, continental and global diversity is encouraged through a long list of Christian ministers who have had an impact on the Kenyan Christian scene.[40] Some of the influential voices in these gatherings are from West Africa.[41]

Some are from within the country, such as Esther Obasi-ike, who is a senior leader at the Redeemed Christian Church of God (RCCG).[42] As a highly sought-after women's leader, she is a regular speaker in Christian gatherings. It is also common for Kenyan women leaders to invite ministers from outside Kenya. Sinach and Victoria Orenze are female Nigerian singers frequently welcomed into Kenyan gatherings.[43] Lesley Osei gets regular invitations to speak at Jubilee Christian Church (JCC). She is Nigerian pastor who co-leads a vibrant Nigerian church in Connecticut, United States.[44]

Through their gatherings and grassroots work, women leaders extend their social networks to harness relational power within society. This they use to bring women together into their religious fold. They teach the women to negotiate the complexities of urban life while keeping their Christianity at the center of their lives. Frequent sermon references to marriage, family, and the workplace ground the discourse in the women's lived experiences in Nairobi. The gospel is, in their view, the solution available to all to counter the challenges the women face. Christian networks formed in the church provide the framework within which faith acts to support the women. Storytelling in the form of testimonies from the women reinforces the perceived value of Christian witness in the women's lives.

Conclusion

Though women's participation can be seen in many places, it is in small groups that the impact of women in the church is most powerfully felt. In the *chama*, the message of religious fervor mingled with practical empowerment situates the woman's foundational role in the family, the church, in the neighborhood, and in the city. The *chama* has become an important vehicle for women to challenge the secularity of the city. In Nairobi, women's groups rehearse in their homes, the truths they consider important in addressing the challenges of urban life. The pooling of spiritual, emotional, and financial resources helps women address the challenging environment of urban centers.

The *chama* offers opportunity for women to meaningfully participate in the life of Nairobi. The *chama* is family. A social innovation that allows urbanites to expand their circle of relationships to meet the challenges of living in the city. This social configuration is the meeting point of Nairobi's pluralism. It brings women from different Christian denominations, and even religions into a functional space. Here, they suspend the potential ethnic or religious conflict to exercise their interdependence. They bring their diversity into the space, celebrating each other's devotion to their own religious tradition while meaningfully participating in each other's lives.

The small group is a microcosm of the expansive range of women's contributions to the city. Here, women's participation in Christian life in the city and their vital role in keeping the vibrancy of the Christian faith becomes evident. As an overwhelming majority of 89 percent of Nairobi's 2.2 million women, they seamlessly weave their spirituality into every aspect of their lives.[45] Keeping prayer, scripture reading, and preaching a central part of their activities, both in the church and at home within their small groups. Nairobi's women illustrate one way the cathedral Christianity and kiosk Christianity coexist in the urban African city. Each form benefits from the other while mutually promoting the resilience of the faith in the city.

8

Rival Cities
Nairobi Christianity and Public Life

The Parliament buildings in Nairobi's city center are a highlight of any tour of the city. They are a monument not only to political life in Kenya but also to architectural modernism. Amyas Douglas Connell, a New Zealand native, found his modernistic designs too radical for London in the 1930s. He moved to Kenya, where he served as the principal architect for a new complex of government buildings to fill the heart of the city. He dreamed of a design that would embody the modern architectural concepts of "sun, light, and air." [1]

After the interruption of the Second World War, Connell and city planner Harold Thornley Dyer resumed work on the government project. They were told to include an English-style clock tower that would echo London's Big Ben. In 1954, they completed the construction with the 165-foot clock tower, then the highest structure in Nairobi. With independence in 1963, the buildings became the new Parliament (Figure 8.1). Soon after, a new assembly chamber was added. Inside, artistic murals reflecting Kenya's wildlife brightened the building's halls and chambers. Most Kenyans are justly proud of their legislature's home.

But some are not. In 2003, the Reverend Dr. David Githii, moderator of the Presbyterian Church of East Africa (PCEA), attacked the decor as being more demonic than democratic. Githii was from a humble background yet, by the time of his appointment, had earned two advanced degrees from American universities. Soon after becoming moderator, Githii joined other clergy in attending a prayer service for the nation in Parliament. Githii came away disturbed by what he saw. Everywhere he looked, he saw the painted

FIGURE 8.1 *Nairobi Parliament by dreamstime, commercial and editorial licence obtained.*

and carved symbols of snakes, crocodiles, tortoises, and wild beasts. These artistic symbols were not merely decorative. The moderator sensed each symbol exerted a secret and sinister influence. Githii claimed that the colonial architects were members of the Masonic order. Could these occult objects help explain the endemic corruption infesting parliament? He further claimed that they intentionally placed symbols in the buildings to corrupt Christianity. He began a one-man campaign to liberate parliament. In 2007, Githii self-published a book attempting to prove his claims, *Exposing and Conquering the Satanic Forces over Kenya*.[2] His campaign to exorcise Kenyan politics continued after being defrocked by the PCEA in 2012. Facing opposition to his message about demonic influence in Kenyan politics, he founded a new church called El-Gibbor (Mighty God) in 2014. The church aimed to combat homosexuality and Satan worship. In 2022, at seventy-one years of age, he unsuccessfully ran for president of the country. His declared aim was to help the poor and rid Kenyan politics of corruption.

Githii was not alone in seeing radical evil at the heart of both church and state in Kenyan politics. Others saw the powers of evil not in demonic influence but in a church culture that refused to speak out against political corruption. Paul Gifford has accused the Nairobi churches of promoting a culture of impunity by staying silent on government corruption. Gifford has succinctly described the church in Kenya as "Christianity co-copted."[3] Gifford's argument is that

Christianity is indeed domesticated in Kenya. The prominence of individual churchmen in the early 1990s in the struggle for political liberalization cannot disguise the fact that Christianity has become an integral part of the dysfunctional system. . . . Christianity helps further the general ethos of unaccountability. The entire political elite benefits from this Christianity-induced impunity.[4]

The Nairobi churches' relationship with the state has been a wild *matatu* ride, careening from the extremes of veneration to demonization and back. In this chapter, we seek to document that "ride" by sketching the history of this troubled relationship. We begin our story with Jomo Kenyatta, Kenya's founding president.

Church and State under Kenyatta

On December 12, 1964, Jomo Kenyatta became Kenya's first president (Figure 8.2). Released from prison in 1961, Kenyatta's rise to the top of Kenya's political elite was swift. He wasted no time in making clear his intentions about the church and its role in the new nation. In a speech just a few months before his inauguration, he declared that "the Churches and missions have done a great deal to help our progress and our independent government will welcome their continued help and cooperation in the years to come . . . . I hope that over the years the churches will also play their full part in bringing us together in a true and everlasting unity." [5]

There were clear limits, however, to the role he wished the churches to play. One of the most important limits was education. The Kenya African National Union (KANU), his party, issued a manifesto on education expressing gratitude for missionary schools but declaring that "the government . . . is bound to provide education and cannot delegate this responsibility to any other bodies."[6]

By 1964, Kenyatta's political policies were taking a marked turn toward centralization. Kenyatta embraced the local practice of *Harambee* ("let us pull together"), which originally meant family or village-level fundraising. For Kenyatta, *Harambee* became another term for nation-building. He politicized *Harambees* and sought to align them with his political purposes. Opposition or dissent meant undermining the *Harambee* spirit and threatening unity and progress. For Kenyatta, *Harambee* evolved into an entire political philosophy of development through government centralization. The president promoted the benefits of a one-party state which alone could guarantee unity and began to speak of the threat of "opposition for opposition's sake." He called multiple parties a threat to democracy.[7]

FIGURE 8.2 *Jomo Kenyatta statue by dreamstime, commercial, and editorial license obtained.*

Galia Sabar observes how Kenyatta used state bureaucracy as the main tool to centralize his power. "Kenyatta turned the state bureaucracy into a source of patronage," she writes, "The bureaucratic apparatus, from the course through local government mechanisms and down to the state-owned enterprises, burgeoned. By the end of the 1960s, the state bureaucracy employed the majority of wage-earners."[8]

Political opponents faced disappearance, detention, or death. The government barred the opposition party, Kenya African Democratic Union (KADU), from participating in elections. By 1969, Kenya was functioning as a one-party state. Kenyatta's consolidation of power was all but complete. Standing outside his control was the church.

How did the church respond to these centralizing tendencies? The Anglicans reflected the general attitude of the church in the early years of independence. "During the first years of Kenya's independence, the Anglican Church avoided public confrontation and did not establish a clear policy on fundamental issues concerning the structure of power and its own relationship with the ruling elite and the state," Sabar summarizes. "Under both the British occupation and the new government, the Church offered its services and the support of its hierarchy to those in power."[9]

The church knew its place and that place was national unity. Church leaders praised the new government and pledged their full support. They took part fully in government-driven *Harambee* projects. The leadership of the NCCK was largely Kikuyu, and they sought to show their ethnic loyalty with almost every chance they could get. Churches resisted whatever temptations they felt to confront the government over its growing abuses of power. The exception to this silence was the oathing crisis of 1969.

Shortly after 11:00 a.m. on June 9, 1969, PCEA pastor Reverend John Gatu and the PCEA moderator, Crispus Kiongo, were summoned to Gatundu, President Kenyatta's personal residence just outside of Nairobi. Kenyatta had a warm relationship with the PCEA, which was widely seen as the "Kikuyu church." Whatever questions the two pastors had about the purpose of the meeting soon became clear. Kenyatta had called them to Gatundu to take an oath. Gatu had heard rumors of a GEMA (the coalition of Gikuyu, Embu, and Meru peoples) oathing ritual similar to the Mau Mau oath in the 1950s. Gatu himself had participated in the Mau Mau oathing movement before his conversion. The pastors probed deeper. What kind of oath they asked? Kenyatta's answer was unequivocal. The church must pledge to support Kikuyu control of power in the country forever. All church leaders were expected to take the oath. Many already had, the president claimed. He was willing to make concessions for the clergy. They would not have to drink blood but could drink milk if they preferred. A refusal to take the oath would be seen as an act of betrayal against the president. Consequences could be expected.

Gatu and Kiongo were "lost for words" and requested time to think and pray about a matter so serious. Kenyatta's response was terse. The sooner the better.[10]

Over the days that followed, the oathing campaign intensified. Gatu's wife was stopped on her way home by an angry mob and was forced to take the oath. Other clergy reported beatings and threats to themselves and their congregation. The oath was known locally as *Chai* (an euphemistic use of the Swahili word for tea). As Gatu wrote in his memoir, "It was no longer secret that the perpetrators of the *Chai* oath had declared war on the PCEA church."[11] It was during this time that the assassination of Tom Mboya, a Luo politician, by a Kikuyu supporter of Kenyatta increased political tension in the country and strengthened the *Chai* oathing movement.

Many churches spoke openly against the murder and oathing campaign. At the heart of the protest, however, were the Anglican, African Inland, and PCEA churches. In a confidential memo to Kenyatta on July 22, 1969, signed by the heads of the above churches, they made their position clear. The tone of the letter was respectful, quoting Romans 13 on the need to obey rulers (although referencing it as Romans 15). Even so, "above all, we declare our loyalty to Jesus Christ as King and Lord, who is the sure foundation of all that is honorable as well as [of] the government of just men where protection of fundamental rights and freedoms of the individual are respected and protected."[12] The letter listed political, theological, and constitutional objections to the oath, ultimately calling on Kenyatta "to act now and save Kenya before the historians write a new chapter and a tragic page of a Kenya that once was the envy of many."[13]

The church's letter of protest had little impact and oathing continued to divide the nation. The churches continued their protest and held more meetings with the president. Matters reached a climax with the murder of Samuel Gathinji, a member of both the PCEA and the Revival Brethren, who was beaten to death by an oathing gang for refusing to participate. Media coverage of this tragedy, combined with his widow's heart-rending testimony, touched the nation. Parliament called for action. The government eventually issued a public statement which condemned oathing and promised to prosecute those involved. Behind the scenes, however, Kenyatta's support for the oath continued. On September 30, 1969, Gatu and the PCEA moderator were once again summoned by an angry president. For two hours, they presented their evidence of oathing abuse. Kenyatta finally relented. Oathing ended.

The oathing crisis of 1969 marked a change in the relationship between church and state in Kenya. It ended the honeymoon of unquestioned support for the government by the church. It also taught the church an important lesson on confronting the state. Instead of publicly debating political differences, church leaders opted for behind-the-scenes negotiations with those in power. This "backdoor" approach would be severely tested by the next regime.

Church and State under Daniel arap Moi

The death of Kenyatta in 1978 shook the young nation. In the scramble for power that ensued, Daniel arap Moi, Kenyatta's vice-president, emerged victorious. In November 1978, three months after the death of "Mzee" (the popular nickname for Kenyatta: literally "elder" in Swahili), Moi took the oath of office as Kenya's second president. He was subsequently elected president in 1979. In the early years of his presidency, Moi appeared to veer away from the dictatorial style of his mentor and predecessor. His true colors, however, were revealed in June 1982 when parliament, pressured by the president, made an overnight amendment to the constitution and officially declared Kenya a one-party state. On August 1, lower-rank officers in the Kenya Air Force attempted a coup to overthrow Moi. Nairobi, the epicenter of the coup, was in turmoil as the army crushed the revolt. Hundreds were killed. Stores were looted. The city was locked down. Moi's promising reconciliatory beginning ended as he joined the ranks of dictators across the continent.

The church reacted to Moi's one-party state, issuing a new prophetic call. It was a call for democratization, a call echoing across the continent. As Wanjiru Gitau writes:

> In the late 1980s and early 1990s, a slow and often brutal series of transitions out of one-party, military regimes or the rule of "big men," began to occur throughout the continent. By June 2003, 44 out of 48 Sub-Saharan Africa's states had conducted a first round of elections, 33 had gone through a second election cycle, 20 had completed three uninterrupted cycles, 7 had held four more consecutive elections. [A] majority of these countries had become more democratic with each election cycle.[14]

In Kenya, during the late 1980s and 1990s, there were influential voices advocating for justice and democracy. These included Anglican bishops Alexander Muge and David Gitari of PCEA, Pastor Timothy Njoya, and Nairobi Baptist Pastor Mutava Musyimi, who also served as the NCCK General Secretary. John Lonsdale captures the thrust of their message: "that liberty, and not just for clerics, could be assured only with the rebirth of multiparty democracy and, when that was thwarted by the state-sponsored violence prior to the elections of 1992 and 1997, by constitutional reform that would drastically reduce the power of the executive, give more independence to Parliament, decentralize much administrative power and financial responsibility."[15]

This prophetic message was less about political technicalities and more about people. In 1996, a sermon by Bishop Gitari captured the highly relational element of the church's critique of the state and its practices:

We must work to remove all that which divides us if we want to lay a deserved claim to shalom. Where there is division we need to work for reconciliation. True reconciliation does not come by sweeping problems under the carpet or by a mere shaking of hands in public places. We must find the root cause of our divisions and deal with it. The Christian must labor to produce right relationships between people . . . Christian reconciliation means reconciling people to God and reconciling people to each other. A reconciler must not take sides except when it is the side of the truth.[16]

Church and State in the Post-Moi Years

Moi and KANU won the first two multi-party elections in 1992 and 1997, but the 2002 elections brought a new face to Kenyan politics—Mwai Kibaki, Kenya's third president and leader of the new party, National Rainbow Coalition (NARC). Kibaki was an economist whose policies helped revive the economic sector by 2006. Kibaki also announced plans to abolish secondary school fees. But despite these areas of progress, NARC showed little improvement over KANU in fighting corruption. Constitutional change was needed.

No account of the role of church and state since independence would be complete without mention of the *Ufungamano* House Initiative. This movement helped lay the groundwork for the revised constitution of 2010. In the late 1990s, religious leaders from the NCCK, Catholic bishops, Muslims, and Hindus convened at the Ufungamano House near Nairobi University to talk about constitutional reform. Bishop David Gitari was the initial chair of the council. The council sent commissioners around the country to gather the views of ordinary Kenyans (then coined "*Wanjiku*'") about the changes that were needed. The council then compiled these reports as the basis of proposed constitutional changes. The council enjoyed widespread support across the country. The KANU government, however, viewed this church initiative with suspicion. The Ufungamano House initiative, despite government opposition, paved the way for the 2002 multi-party elections that ended the KANU era of political dominance. While it continued to meet in the years after Kibaki's election, the initiative was eventually overtaken by a parliament-established constitutional committee and by growing internal dissent.

According to John Karanja, the *Ufungamano* initiative failed mainly because of the divide between mainstream evangelicals and conservative evangelicals, not because of Christian and non-Christian tensions. This latter group was represented by the new Pentecostal churches and more fundamentalist churches like the Africa Inland Church (AIC).[17] By the middle of Kibaki's first term, it was a spent force. The Ufungamano House initiative, nonetheless, was the boldest example of church involvement in the state in Kenya's history.

The next elections in 2007 were a major blow to the promise of democratization in Kenya. The charges of rigging were rife, and ethnic violence erupted across the country. Thousands lost their lives, and many more thousands were displaced. As a result of the public upheaval, Kibaki was forced to form a coalition government, creating the position of Prime Minister, to be held by the chief thorn in his side, Raila Odinga.

It was clear to all that the ad hoc changes to the constitution necessitated by the aftermath of 2007 required more than piecemeal constitutional reform. A new constitutional beginning was needed.

On August 4, 2010, Kenyans went to the polls to vote on a new constitution for the country. In many ways, the new document gave Christian churches the very changes they had called for over the previous decades. Presidential power was limited. Power would devolve from Nairobi to the rural areas. Multi-party democracy was established. Human rights were expanded. Religious freedom was guaranteed. Yet many Christian leaders, both Catholic and Protestant, opposed the new constitution and advised their followers to vote no. What was the problem?

Oliver Kisaka, an official with the NCCK, was blunt. "We believe the constitution doesn't meet religious, moral, economic, and justice concerns." In what ways did it fall short? "It privileges one religion over another. It allows abortion on demand. It has strong socialist tendencies." The NCCK also disliked the provision that made Kenyan law answerable to international law.[18] The Anglican Church issued a similar statement. "We say NO to the proposed constitution as it is." They insisted on amendments that would ensure "justice and equality for all religions, the limitation of the fundamental rights based on religion, the protection of the right to life, and the supremacy of our constitution in the light of international conventions and treaties."[19] The Catholics were in agreement with their Protestant counterparts. They issued fliers across the country featuring a red traffic light and the words "Stop!!! Think . . . Choose life."[20]

The two most controversial issues for church leaders were abortion and Kadhi Courts. While the constitution outlawed abortion, the document allowed exceptions in cases of rape, incest, or saving the life of the mother. For a nation that prized children, any concession to the practice was an outrage.

The recognition of special Muslim courts, called Kadhi Courts, was regarded as preferential treatment of a religion. From colonial days, Muslims on the coast could handle matters related to marriage, divorce, and inheritance in their own courts. The new constitution not only enshrined these special courts as the law of the land but extended the Muslim court system across the country.

When an overwhelmingly Christian electorate went to the polls, however, some 67 percent voted "yes" to the new constitution. The "yes" vote revealed that church leaders were out of step with their congregations. Political fatigue was a factor in accepting the new constitution, but more was involved. In church life, Kenyans were deeply conservative. In public life, however, the golden rule of "doing to others what you would want them to do to you" made more sense. In this clash between denominational Christianity and "Golden rule" Christianity, the latter won the day. In 2010, the new constitution became the law of the land and, as of 2023, had yet to be amended.

Church and State under Uhuru Kenyatta and William Ruto

The election of Uhuru Kenyatta in 2013 as Kenya's forth president returned the Kenyatta's, one of Africa's wealthiest families, to power. Despite Kenyatta's pledge to end corruption, financial scandals haunted his two terms in office. Kenyatta was also Kenya's second Roman Catholic president and enjoyed firm support from the Catholic bishops during his years in office. The rise of Muslim terrorism in the country during Kenyatta's presidency, most notably the Westgate Mall attack in 2013, which left 50 dead, and the Garissa campus attack of 2015 with 170 dead, further polarized the religious community. The country's growing religious divide meant Kenyatta's government did not face the same kind of Christian protest that marked the Moi regime. The Center for Strategic and International Studies described Kenya's church and state relationship under Uhuru Kenyatta as mixed.

The government of Uhuru Kenyatta found that controlling religious groups was a harder task than ever before because of Kenya's increasingly diverse, fragmented religious landscape. The government followed the practice of its predecessors, adopting a strategy of divide and rule, rather than trying to promote cohesion among its religious communities. It favored the Christian majority over the Muslim minority, a stance that had become more pronounced in response to a terrorist threat that had attracted support from a small number of Muslims. Arguably, religious polarization helped the government consolidate control in the short term but carried long-term risks for social peace and Kenya's stability.[21] The election of 2022, which saw William Ruto become Kenya's fifth president, revealed a new twist in the story of church and state in Kenya. To curb corruption in Kenya's elections, Parliament passed a bill in 2013, "The Election Campaign Financing Act," which limited the amount that could be spent on political campaigns.[22] Politicians found a way around this law, however, by "donating" money to churches for speaking opportunities. The COVID-19 lockdown in 2020–21 made the churches an attractive campaign platform because of internet streaming and more government flexibility in allowing in-person meetings for churches. The donations flowed. According to one report, William Ruto donated $600,000 to churches during his campaign in 2021.[23] Ruto openly aligned himself with Pentecostal churches. Kenyatta's second inauguration as president included the participation of David Oginde, the then presiding CITAM Bishop. Ruto's involved a more elaborate ceremony with more extensive prayers led by a Deliverance Church bishop—Mark Kariuki.[24]

Other politicians sought to exploit this campaign financing loophole. The churches' response was not uniform. Three distinct positions emerged, according to research by Allan Muchiri.[25] Some churches, such as the Methodist Church of Kenya and the Redeemed Gospel Church, practiced full accommodation. The Catholics, Anglicans, PCEA, and the NCCK practiced critical accommodation. Most of the independent churches were silent on the matter. Most churches allowed donations, but the key difference was whether they allowed politicians to speak in the pulpit. The Anglicans and Presbyterians mostly allowed donations but were hesitant to let others speak at their pulpits. The AIC had some flexibility in letting local churches decide. On the local church level, there was much confusion about what the actual denominational guidelines were and how they were to be applied. The church was implicated in financial corruption, where politicians looted public funds and used them to buy influence. The lack of a clear political theology by the churches left them, once again, ill-prepared to navigate the space between church and state.

Facing the Future

As the churches of Kenya face the future, central on the agenda is the question of how to be "in" the political system without being "of" it. The challenge remains daunting, but there are several opportunities for constructive Church-State interaction as we see them.

The first opportunity has to do with Kenya's Millennial Goals and Kenya Vision 2030. In the year 2000, Kenya joined much of the rest of the global community in following the United Nations Millennial Goals initiative. For Kenya, that meant a new commitment to see the country grow in key ways including eradicating extreme poverty, achieving universal primary education, promoting gender equality and women empowerment, reducing child mortality, improving maternal health, combating HIV and AIDS, Malaria and other communicable diseases, ensuring environmental sustainability, and developing a global Partnership for Development. Faith-based organizations (FBOs) and NGOs have historically played a key role in education and health care and are natural partners in working alongside the state in these areas. Churches can get behind such projects, which are consistent with a broad understanding of Christian mission. Though these goals ended officially in 2015, Kenya Vision 2030 has extended its pursuit for the next few years. The church's role in the state has evolved from focusing on "nation-building" to prioritizing "human flourishing" in different aspects of development.

The second opportunity for the church in the nation has to do with Kenya's shift toward China. This new political reality reflects a wider pan-African trend. Over 1 million Chinese have migrated to the African continent in the twenty-first century.[26] Kenya has about 40,000 Chinese working in both private and public sectors. For many Kenyans, Chinese workers represent foreigners stealing jobs and driving up prices. Resentment has grown. Chinese workers have been deported for overt racism. The churches of Kenya have helped to ease some of the tension by spiritually ministering to the new wave of Eastern workers. New Chinese churches are springing up as well, many of them offering services in both English and Mandarin. Intermarriage is increasing, fueled by new conversions. For a country that is 80 percent Christian and actively so, bridging the faith gap is, for many, more important than bridging the ethnic gap. The government can only do so much in building social and cultural bridges between Kenyans and the new immigrants. The church possesses the "faith card" which has great potential to bridge such divides and provide a path of unity and cohesion between all Kenyans.

A third opportunity for the church to partner with the government in the flourishing of its citizens is in the area of the environment. Kenyan environmental pioneers, such as the late Nobel Peace Prize winner Wangari Maathai, have made "creation care" high on the agenda of the rising generation. Faith-based organizations, in partnership with local churches, are a central part of the environmental thrust. "FBOs contribute significantly to this work," write Moyer, Sinclair, and Spaling. "Organizations such as World Vision, Catholic Relief Services, and World Concern, for example, are listed among the top NGOs working in Kenya."[27]

African Heads of State are taking the issue seriously. In September 2023, Nairobi hosted the first Africa Climate Summit. Kenya's newly elected president, William Ruto, addressed the international gathering. He admitted it was high time for African governments to make climate change a political priority. World leaders gathered at the Kenyatta International Conference Center (KICC), while faith leaders from different traditions met nearby. They pledged to work together with the government to achieve sustainable development in Kenya.

We urge our governments and all those represented in the Africa Climate Summit and Week to be guided by the wisdom of our faith traditions and the undeniable urgency of the moment. The faith constituency is deeply concerned by actions that fall short of the required ambition in tackling the climate emergency which threatens life on earth. We must leverage this momentum to deliver concrete actions that will help the continent address the challenges of the Climate crisis. It is now more than ever before that our governments must prioritize policies that honor our planet and its biodiversity, that promote sustainable land practices, that mitigate the effects of climate change on the most vulnerable among us, and that deliver adequate and predictable climate finance to where it is most needed.[28]

A fourth opportunity for cooperation is in regulating churches in Kenya. In June 2023, news reports shocked Kenyans with the discovery of mass graves linked to a "Christian" church in Malindi, formerly known as the Good News International Church, now called the *Shakahola* cult (named after the forest where the bodies were found). The pastor, Paul Mackenzie, declared that the end of the world had come. He called upon his estimated 1,000 followers to fast themselves to death to escape the destruction to come. Three hundred dead were discovered, many young people, with speculation that the number was much higher.[29]

This extreme case of unauthorized religious activity highlights the growing challenge of regulating churches in Kenya. Previous attempts by the government to regulate new churches have met with fierce opposition by the churches, old and new. Opposition from independent churches eventually scuttled an attempt by the mainline denominations to create a self-regulating body.[30] The *Shakahola* massacre has renewed the debate. Whether the churches will seize this opportunity to find just and fair ways to prevent rogue pastors and churches from preying on the nation's citizens remains to be seen.

New church coalitions are a fifth and final opportunity for church and state cooperation. Over the course of the twentieth century, the cast of characters leading the drama of church and state in Nairobi's city and the nation stayed stable. Anglicans, PCEA, Methodists, Catholics, and the AIC played the leading roles. In twenty-first-century Kenya, the lead characters are changing. In 2000, Evangelical churches in Kenya sought, without success, to speak with a unified voice to the government of Daniel arap Moi. Mainstream evangelicals and Conservative evangelicals ended up on different sides of the democracy debate. The PCEA's David Githii saw ancient demons behind these divisions and within the political system. Paul Gifford saw modern ones still fueling a culture of corruption and impunity.

In the 2020s, a slow but significant shift took place. A new coalition of churches was forming under a broad charismatic umbrella. The event announcing this new coalition was the 2021 Church and Politics convention. While the nation was still reeling from the COVID-19 pandemic, a virtual conference on the broad theme of Christian political engagement drew a virtual crowd of over 3,000 participants from fifty countries. Speakers included Dr. Samuel Kobia, former general secretary of the World Council of Churches and head of the Kenyan government's National Cohesion and Integration Commission, Catholic Archbishop Anthony Muheria, the President of Malawi, Lazarus Chakwera, Reverend Canon Chris Kinyanjui, General Secretary of the NCCK, Presiding Bishop of CITAM, Kenya's largest Pentecostal denomination, Calisto Odede, the late Ron Sider, Executive Director of the US-based Christians for Social Action, as well as university presidents/vice-chancellors, deliverance church pastors, and leaders of Christian NGOs. This broad coalition was very different from the past.

The organizer of the Kenyan-based conference was Dr. David Oginde, Bishop Emeritus of CITAM. Oginde was motivated partly by the divisions within the churches that marked the 2007 election in Kenya, but more recently by the 2020 US presidential election, which divided American evangelicals and revealed their severe lack of a coherent political theology. Though no manifesto was issued by the conference, they produced a study guide signaling that this broad coalition of Pentecostals, Mainline denominations, Catholics, and Christian laymen is still on the way, responding to a need but not yet settled on an answer they can unite behind. A quick survey of the study guide makes clear the directions this movement hopes to pursue in the years ahead. In relation to the state, the church must take on a wider variety of roles than it has had in the past. The study guide, significantly entitled "The Church in Politics," calls the church to be a participant in the political arena, an advocate for the powerless, a mediator for the common good, a custodian of society's morals, and responsible servants willing to suffer for justice. Behind these calls is the conviction that "beginning with repentance of the sin of neglect of its God-given mandate, the church needs to recover its lost identity as God's holy people, reclaim its neglected spaces of influencing the political narrative in Kenya, and lastly, renew its prophetic and transformative mandate as the salt of the earth and light of the world."[31]

The Voice of the People as the Voice of God

However promising these new opportunities for church and state cooperation may be, they do not replace the overwhelming need to address corruption and tribalism in Kenyan politics and governance. Whether the forces of evil are working through the artistic symbols of Parliament, as Reverend Githii claimed, or through the Church's silence in a culture of impunity, as Professor Gifford asserts, or both, corruption and kleptocracy remain an endemic problem in Kenya's politics. But how then can the church regain its moral authority and prophetic voice?

Oginde's call for a new church engagement with politics is one answer to this question. Yet his call need not be answered only by the clergy. People in the pew are rising up. Boniface Mwangi is Kenya's best-known anti-corruption activist. His outspoken tweets and blogs attack corruption in both the church and state. Mwangi's story is a journey from grinding poverty to high purpose. He moved to Nairobi with his mother as a boy, dropping out of school to help make money selling books on the street. Mwangi's mother's death when he was seventeen years old, shook his world and led to a search for God and a profound religious encounter. He attended Bible school intending to become a pastor, but his discovery of photography changed his career trajectory. He became an award-winning photographer and journalist. His coverage of the post-election violence of 2007 had a radicalizing impact on his life. His photographic exhibit of that event, with its graphic depiction of violence and suffering, toured the nation and was seen by an estimated 600,000 people.[32] In 2008, he left photojournalism to focus full time on his anti-corruption work. Mwangi describes himself as a "firm believer in Christ" and insists that his faith is his "first identity."[33] Like the Christ he seeks to follow, Mwangi's attack on religious corruption is as unrelenting as his call for public justice. He has organized Kenya's Creatives into a movement called PAWA254, promoting what he calls "artivism," the use of art for social change. His unsuccessful run for Parliament has only deepened his commitment to become a political change agent. Paul Gifford's search for a prophetic Christian voice to oppose the culture of impunity stopped with the clergy. Perhaps the prophetic voice of the future will more likely wear a t-shirt than a clerical collar and write tweets rather than sermons.

One of Boniface Mwangi's mantras is that "We cannot change the world as individuals. We can only change the world together."[34] Urban historians Anders and Kristin Ese would agree. Their book, *City Makers of Nairobi*, makes the case that the city was built as much from the bottom up as from the top down.

"What the history of cities like Nairobi has shown us is that for . . . changes to take place in ways that are meaningful, urban development issues cannot be left to colonial masters, the elite, the industrialists, or the international community. It has to be owned and driven by its citizens."[35]

In the wild ride that is church and state in Kenya, it may well be the Mwangi-like masses of Kiosk Christianity more than the Njoya's, Gatu's, and Oginde's of the Cathedral, who determine whether that ride moves Nairobi closer to the city of God or further away.

9

The Kiosk, the Cathedral, and the Mosque

Christians and Muslims

Kibera is Nairobi's largest slum and one of the largest in Africa. Religious tensions between diverse faith traditions among the impoverished of this informal settlement have at times spilled over into violence. The "Colour in Faith Project," which launched in 2015, encouraged places of worship to paint their exteriors yellow, the color of tolerance. As of 2016, two structures, the Holy Trinity Anglican Church and the Jeddah Mosque Kambi, were painted yellow. Muslims painted the church and Christians painted the mosque. Six more churches and four mosques were primed and ready for a similar repainting. This project was inspired as a response to the April 2015 Garissa University College attack, in which 148 people, mostly Christian students, were killed.[1]

The "Colour in Faith project" and the Garissa terror attack represent two ends of the volatile spectrum of Muslim-Christian relations in Nairobi. We have focused on Christian diversity in this book. What about religious diversity? Is religious diversity a blessing that generates social capital and bridges differences between the two faiths? Or is it a curse that threatens the national project and the peace of the city?

Nairobi is a good place to explore these questions. This diversity is at the heart of the debate about Kenya's future. Some observers fear that religious diversity, not only within Christianity itself but also between the Christian majority and competing religions, may undermine the future development of the nation. That concern is reflected in the United Nations's Sustainable Development Goal (SDG) 16, adopted by Kenya, with its call to "Promote peaceful and inclusive societies for sustainable development."[2] Will rival religions behave themselves and support the national agenda, or will their competition produce levels of discord, confusion, and violence that derail the journey to 2030? Can the Christianity of the Cathedral and the Kiosk coexist with the religion of the mosque?

To answer the religious diversity question, smaller questions must be answered. Who are Nairobi's Muslims and where do they live? How has the history of Muslim-Christian relations in Kenya contributed to the growing sense of marginalization and alienation of the Muslim community? What do Christians think about Muslims? What do scholarly and popular statements by Christians reveal about attitudes toward Muslims? Finally, is religious diversity a blessing, a curse, or something in between?

Who Are Nairobi's Muslims?

Islam has been in Africa since the ninth century. Some 30 percent of the world's Muslim population, or about 248 million, live in sub-Saharan Africa. In many places across the continent, Islam is growing faster than Christianity, largely through a higher birthrate. The number of Muslims in Africa south of the Sahara is expected to rise to 670 million by 2050. Christianity will continue to be the dominant religion on the continent, but the religious gap will narrow.[3]

Across the continent, Islam has grown over the course of the twentieth century from approximately 11 million in 1900 to about 234 million in 2010. Muslims in sub-Saharan African make up one in seven of the Muslims around the world. African Christians make up one in four. Muslims in Kenya make up approximately 11 percent of the population.[4] Other religions add to the spiritual diversity of the country but are statistically much smaller than Muslims or Christians. Muslims, once the majority faith of Nairobi, are no longer that today. While accurate numbers are scarce, the best estimates point to Muslims as less than 10 percent of the city's population, a smaller ratio than in the nation at large.[5] More visible evidence of Muslim presence in Nairobi are the over eighty-four mosques that dot the urban landscape and the ever-present *bui bui*, the long flowing robe worn by Muslim women.[6]

Most of the major branches and subbranches of Islam are found in Nairobi. Sunnis and Shias represent the major divisions. Most urban Muslims align with Sunni Islam. Other minor branches are also present. The Khariji are an early secessionist group that refused to identify with either Shia or Sunni Islam. A heretical sect, the Ahmadiyya, has at least one mosque in the city, built in 1923. Their distinctive approach to the faith includes the vernacular translation of the Koran and an aggressive missionary commitment to grow the faith through preaching and conversion.

Of the major Sunni schools of thought, most Nairobi Muslims are Shafii, accepting the principle that rational interpretation of the Koran and the Sunnah (the sayings and acts of Muhammed) is preferred over traditional or mystical interpretations. The three Shia groups in Nairobi are the Bohra, the Ithnasheri, and the Ismailis. The latter group has had a large impact on city life through the Aga Khan Hospital, the Aga Khan Foundation, various schools, the Nation media group, and the Serena hotels.[7]

Sufism is not so much a branch of Islam but a kind of spirituality that exists within both the Sunni and Shia worlds. Sufism believes God can be known directly outside formal rituals and revealed texts. This kind of mysticism and subjectivity is much more accepting of African traditional religious practices and sentiments. Sufism "stresses local saints and leaders and provides a certain syncretism with local pre-Islamic belief."[8]

Muslims are scattered widely throughout the city, but certain sections host larger concentrations than others. While Eastleigh is home to an equal number of Muslims, largely of Somali extraction, Kibera was Islam's first home in the city. In 1902, the Jamia Makini Mosque was built. The Nubi, descendants of Sudanese settlers in Nairobi, along with converted Luos, account for most Kibera Muslims. Indo-Pakistani communities can be found in Parklands and Westlands.[9]

Some of the poorest areas of the city—Pumwani, Kibera, Riruta Village, Eastleigh—are also areas with high concentrations of Muslims. There are few public services, almost no Muslim representation on the city council, and frequent official questioning of their Kenyan nationality. The government, and not the Muslim community, appoints judges for the Kadhi courts (Islamic courts dealing with marriage and family matters), and teachers for Koranic schools, as well as controlling of academic programs.[10]

Nairobi Muslims are divided by their faith. Sunnis, represented by the Supreme Council of Kenyan Muslims (SUPKEM), stand in opposition to the Iranian Cultural Centre which organizes the Shia community. There is little interaction or communication between the two sides. There is also a political dimension to the divide. Saudi Arabia backs the Sunni community and SUPKEM. Iran backs the Shia and its cultural center. There is a constant jockeying for control and influence.[11]

Another tension within Nairobi's Muslim community pits reformers against fundamentalists. Reformist Islam longs for a unified Islam, rational interpretation, and the purifying of some local traditions. Fundamentalist Islam, or Wahhabism, with its literal and traditional interpretation of the Koran, rejects both modernity and reform.[12]

Despite these deep divisions, Muslims have a surprising source of unity in the city of Nairobi. What brings many of these diverse expressions of Islam together is their common feeling of isolation, marginalization, and alienation. To help explain this, some historical background is needed.

The History of Muslims in Kenya

Islam in Kenya is older than Nairobi. Shia refugees arrived in East Africa in the eighth century from Southern Arabia. A century later, Sunnis arrived from Persia and over the subsequent centuries became the majority in the region.[13]

The Muslim community waxed and waned over the centuries, content with its foothold along the Kenyan coast in the cities of Mombasa, Lamu, and Malindi. The building of the East African Railroad by the British would change all that and open new possibilities for Muslims in the country's heart. Somali, Sudanese, and Swahili soldiers and porters settled in the new city of Nairobi, formed as a depot by the railway engineers. Indian laborers joined these predominantly Muslim settlers. By 1920, despite the growing number of colonial administrators, coffee farmers, and Indian entrepreneurs, most of the city was Muslim.[14]

While British authorities depended upon Muslim translators and administrators in the early days of the colony, the influx of Christian settlers and missionaries after the First World War tipped the religious scales in favor of the new faith. William Patterson writes that the coming of Christianity "split Muslims from the larger Society." Christian expansion and influence came through schools. "Christianity came to predominate in Kenya, and Western culture generally developed preeminence through the school system," Patterson continued. "Kenya's Muslims became culturally isolated as the Christian Church and Western educational system became established in the rest of the country."[15]

Christianity continued to dominate Colonial Kenya up to and beyond independence in 1963. Muslims in Nairobi became united in a shared sense of marginalization by the dominant Christian culture of the city and the nation. Though Muslims dominated the city in the first few decades and shared in the call for the end of colonial rule, independence in the 1960s brought little progress to Muslims, politically or economically.

Muslims hoped that the "Independence Constitution" of 1963 would level the political playing field politically. Constitutionally, the new nation declared itself "pro-religion" without being partial to any religion. Ndzovu observes that Article 78 particularly gave hope to Muslims:

As indicated in Article 78, the Independence Constitution provides for freedom of religion to all citizens. In terms of this article, the state is not allowed to interfere in or control religious affairs. The policy of the state is to accord equal treatment to all religious denominations. The objective of Kenya's constitution is not to promote one religion at the expense of other religions, but to provide an enabling environment to all religions.[16]

Yet the new constitution did little to change the status of Muslims. Jomo Kenyatta and his victorious political party, KANU, was "strongly linked to Christian ethnic groups, [and] was perceived as benefiting those groups disproportionately while largely ignoring problems specific to Muslims."[17]

Kenyatta's attitude toward the Muslim community was not helped when the Somali-dominated northeast along with areas along the coast called for succession. It was not an accident that positions of influence in his new Kenyan government passed over the Muslim community and went to a Christianized elite educated in Christian mission schools. Muslim feelings of alienation from the new government deepened.[18]

The 1970s began as a decade of hope for Kenyan Muslims. As Ndzovu observes, "Muslims came to the realization that their efforts in uplifting their welfare had been weakened by the prevailing fragmentation along ethnic and racial lines."[19] They realized they needed an umbrella organization that could represent their common concerns. In 1973, after years of discussion and negotiation, the SUPKEM was born. From the beginning, though, SUPKEM was limited by government restrictions on its membership, leadership, and focus. It could only guide Muslims on secular matters and did not influence theological issues. SUPKEM, initially a sign of unity and hope for a divided and discouraged Muslim community, became an increasing disappointment.

One response to the failure of SUPKEM has been the rise of "Salafism, which advocates strict interpretations of Islamic scriptures, rejects esotericism, and seeks to emulate the early Muslim community as a corrective to the corrupt and decadent modern world."[20] This turn toward Salafism was seen in Muslim schooling. Muslims often complained of restricted access to government-run schools. Many families turned to madrasas dominated by Wahhabism. Patterson describes this development: "Since the late 1970s, Kenya's madrasas have been dominated by wealthy Wahhabi charities and foundations. Madrasas at the primary and secondary level have . . . frequently focused on teaching Arabic and Wahhabi theology. In fact, religious inculcation rather than an employable education has often been the primary aim of these institutions."[21]

In the 1980s, Muslims continued to seek their political voice, but the one-party rule of Daniel arap Moi permitted little opportunity. All that changed in 1992 when Kenya took its first few steps toward multi-party elections. While most of the new parties were dominated by Christians, Muslims on the coast sought to register the Islamic Party of Kenya (IPK). The government arrest of the firebrand Muslim preacher Khalid Balala led coastal intellectuals such as Omar Mwinyi and Abdulrahman Wandati to call for a new political party to represent the political needs of Kenya's Muslims. According to Ndzovu, the IPK was careful not to "propagate a narrow ethnic agenda . . . [but] focused on Muslim grievances that stemmed from perceived marginalization, discrimination, and injustice by the various postcolonial regimes."[22]

The attempt to register the IPK failed. Moi's government, though allowing new parties after a change in the constitution, still controlled new party registrations by the office of the Register of Societies. The IPK was denied registration "on the grounds that it was discriminatory, requiring specific religious beliefs of its members." Months of riots followed the government's decision but the end result was the death of the IPK and the added of yet one more grievance against "Christian" Kenya.[23]

With the failure of the IPK, Kenyan Muslims felt adrift politically. The influence of transnational Islamic groups, like al-Qaeda and al-Shabaab, disrupted Kenyan politics after 1992. In 1998, Al-Qaeda bombed the US embassies in Nairobi and Tanzania. Al-Shabaab, an affiliated group, engaged in many terror attacks. This "radicalization of Muslim faith has caused significant polarization and fears, and led other others, particularly Christians, to feel threatened."[24]

The rise of terrorism in Kenya prompted government action. In 2003, the Kenyan Parliament debated the Suppression of Terrorism Bill. The bill allowed arrests based on mere suspicion and the detention of people without the judicial process. The bill even suggested that Muslim appearance and dress were sufficient reasons for arrests and detention. While the bill was formally withdrawn in 2004, the bias of the government against Muslims was difficult to miss.[25]

While the Parliament sought to find new ways to exclude Muslims, the faith-based Ufungamano Initiative sought new ways to include them. SUPKEM was invited to join the working group drafting a new constitution for Kenya. As time went on, conservative Christian members of the Initiative pushed back against the role of Muslim (Kadhi) courts in the new constitution. John Chesworth recounts the clash over Kadhi courts, a clash that led to the withdrawal of the Muslim delegation and the ultimate decline of the Ufungamano Initiative:

> Christian leaders had become increasingly uneasy about the place of Kadhi's Courts within the constitution, and one group comprising largely of Pentecostal churches, calling themselves the Kenya Church, published a statement in 2003 attacking the place of the Kadhi's Courts in the constitution and making their recommendation to the Kenya government on this issue. At one point, they said that although these courts were in existence in

the current constitution, they could no longer be accommodated, as the draft clearly states the relationship between the state and religion, that there is no state religion (Kanyoni 2004:21). Christian leaders' opposition to Kadhi's courts resulted in the members of SUPKEM resigning from the Ufungamano Steering Committee and withdrawing from the Ufungamano Initiative.[26]

A major step forward for Muslim legal and political recognition took place during the constitutional debates of the early 2000s. After the government took over the constitutional process with the formation of the Constitution of the Kenya Review Commission (CKRC), Muslims were invited to take part. In 2004, after resolving the Kadhi court issue, Abida Ali Aroni, a Muslim lawyer, was appointed as chairperson of the commission. Her appointment marked a significant change in public attitudes toward Muslims in politics.[27]

While Muslim political participation seemed to grow, the realities of Muslim daily survival showed little sign of change. In 2005, Muslims in Nairobi, the Coast, and the Northeast "had the highest levels of unemployment in the country." More troubling was the fact that by 2008, Muslim young people had the highest rates of youth unemployment in the nation.[28]

Unemployed youth, particularly in Nairobi, turned to the internet. Patterson added that "Rapid internet diffusion has led to a mushrooming of cyber-cafes charging users less than a dollar per hour." These new cafes became "crucial sites of Kenyan Muslims' engagement with the global Muslim ummah [community], enhancing their knowledge of Islam through cyber-literacy, and networking within and between (cyber)-communities with shared interests."[29]

Through the internet, a new narrative was forming in the minds of a new generation of Muslim youths. "While some Muslims present Muslim concerns as synonymous with broader agendas of human rights and democracy" others identified Kenyan Muslim suffering with the "wider global narratives of Muslim persecution, locating the solution to Muslim grievances in Islamist strategies that seek an overthrow of the current international system."[30] Groomed by the extremism found on the internet, a new generation of urban Muslims denied a legitimate political path to address the needs of their communities, listened to more radical voices calling for more violent action. Patterson describes a 2010 lecture at a Muslim Youth Center (affiliated with al-Shabaab) that implored Kenyan Muslims to stop engaging in national politics and urged them instead to "'Chinja' (cut), 'Chonga' (peel) and 'Fiyeka' (slash) the throats of the [Kenyan] infidels and 'to hit back and cause blasts [in Kenya]'." [31]

It was only a matter of time before the calls for violence were acted upon. Al-Shabaab attackers, in September 2013, killed more than sixty-five people at the Westgate Shopping Mall in Nairobi. "All four of the known assailants were Somalis who had been living in the Nairobi suburb of Eastleigh, known for its large Somali ex-patriot population." A host of others, several with Kenyan citizenship were arrested for assisting the terrorists.[32] Most Muslims were horrified by the violence, even if they were not surprised that the simmering pot of resentment had boiled over. The Garissa Attack in 2015 made even more Muslims horrified but also deeply concerned about what Christians might be thinking.

How Christians See Muslims

Looking back on the long history of Muslims and Christians in Kenya, we can only agree with Oseje on the various negative ways that the former view the latter.

> Many Muslims in Kenya see Christians as ethically and ritually unclean. They fail to recognize the truth of the Koran and therefore do not follow the required practices. Christians are seen as gluttons who cannot restrain their appetites. Ramadan, the month-long mandatory fast demonstrates the restraint of Muslims. No similar fast is found in the Christian world. Similarly, Muslims look at Christians in the Kenyan government and understandably blame them for the corruption that seems to run unchecked in the system.[33]

What, meanwhile, were Christians thinking? What has been the Christian response to the rise of more aggressive forms of Islam in the current century? Kenyan Christian attitudes toward Muslims in the 1960s were marked by avoidance and indifference. The NCCK sought to break through the apathy by appointing Reverend James Ritchie, who worked with the Islam for Africa Project. While his work aimed to present the gospel to Muslims, it did so first by creating a "spirit of love towards Muslims in Christian Hearts." The *Kenya Church's Handbook* of 1973, looking back on this project commented, "The number of Muslims who do become Christians is any case small, and very few Christians have any taste for the unrewarding work of evangelizing Muslims." Consequently, both sides seemed "content with the status quo." While little impact seems to have been made, there was at least a desire on the part of some Christian leaders to cross the religious divide.[34]

In the last few decades, this attitude has changed. Indifference and avoidance are still there but new understanding, new hostility, and new cooperation characterize the range of current Christian attitudes. By many Christian academics, there has been a new attempt to understand and appreciate Islam. Pentecostal voices have been raised expressing fear and hostility to Islam. Interfaith Christian leaders see the current situation as an opportunity for new cooperation.

Encountering Islam

Most Christian academics approach Islam with a desire to create mutual understanding. One representative Kenyan Christian scholar who has written extensively on Islam in Kenya is Dr. Newton Maina. A member of the Presbyterian Church of East Africa (PCEA) Maina, as of 2015, was a senior lecturer in Islamic studies at Kenyatta University, Kenya's largest university. The basic conflict between Christianity and Islam, according to Maina, is not theology but history. Maina wrote in 2009 that

> Since the first interaction between Christianity and Islam in Kenya, the former enjoyed a position of power while the latter was presumably reduced to an underdog status. This was the situation during the colonial period, a situation that created competition between Christianity and Islam. This competition has engendered conflict between Christians and Muslims. It is concluded that the causes of conflicts between Christians and Muslims in the contemporary period are a product of historical antecedents.[35]

Maina is aware of other factors like the growing economic competition between Muslims and Christians given the infusion of funds from the Middle East in the early twentieth century and the frequency of *mihadhara* (public debates) which have sometimes led to physical confrontation. More significant, however, is Christian Islamophobia often fueled by acts of terrorism. "Kenyan Christians," he writes, "have an inherent phobia for Islam and Muslims."[36]

Despite the many tensions between them, Maina remains optimistic that "Christians and Muslims can work together for the common good."[37]

Joseph Wandera, an Anglican pastor, agrees with Maina that Christian-Muslim relations have been shaped more by historical injustices than theological differences. He adopts an older pluralist paradigm associated with John Hick to argue that both religions are limited window into the fuller picture of God and his will:

> What possibilities are there for both Muslims and Christians to lay claim to the complete revelation of truth from the One Almighty God? Although, there are conflicting claims in the Qur'an and the Bible, is it not possible to witness to that truth without conflicting with one another? For example, is it not possible to come to an understanding of how God shows us His holy will in revelation in a way acceptable both to the Muslims and the Christians? That indeed God has not left himself without a witness, the witness even of a fully saving knowledge in other faith traditions? I have a sense that perhaps such a pluralistic theology would save both Muslims

and Christians from imperialistic tendencies that tend to pit them against each other.[38]

For Wandera, mutual understanding between Christians and Muslims can be built on the foundation that both sides have only a partial view of truth. Such humility should lower the volume of violent rhetoric and produce a new space for peace.

Dr. Stephen Sesi, a former lecturer in Islamic studies at Africa International University from 2003 until he died in 2011, offered a slightly different take on Islam than did Newton Maina and Joseph Wandera. Sesi affirmed certain commonalities between Islamic practice and Biblical teaching in matters such as monotheism, prostration in prayer, Abrahamic roots, and certain acts of worship. The stress in his writing, however, was more on discontinuity. At the end of the day, "Though Muslims and Christians have a lot in common, they adhere to two different religions with different sets of beliefs and views about cardinal theological issues, like the nature of God and the ultimate solution to the human problem of sin."

For Sesi and many evangelical scholars like him, authentic understanding between Muslims and Christians must be marked by an understanding of differences and commonalities. There needs to be an honest recognition of both the absolute truth claims and the missionary impulse of both Muslims and Christians. To build mutual understanding by relativizing the Muslim's or the Christian's claim for absolute truth is an insult to both religions and a non-starter in genuine engagement. Positing a secular absolute, such as Maina's pluralist paradigm in which only the scholar of religious pluralism occupies the heights of religious truth, is a non-starter. Islam and Christianity derive their missionary mandate from their monotheism. There is only one God, and he has spoken. This impulse involves mutual witness but not with a desire to "conquer" the other. Christ's golden rule of doing to others what you would have them do to you invites the Muslims to be free to speak their truth to the Christian and similarly, the Christians to be free to speak their truth to the Muslim.[39]

Competing with Islam

Pentecostalism has a more complicated relationship with Islam than does some of the more historic churches. Margaret Wanjiru is a major figure in Nairobi Pentecostalism, the presiding bishop of Jesus Is Alive Ministries (JIAM). She served as a Member of Parliament from 2007 to 2013. She has been vocal in her opposition to Muslim influence in the country. She was influential in the draft's constitution defeat in 2002 for its equality for gays, the legalization of abortion, and extension of the Muslim Kahdi courts. When challenged about her opposition to the draft constitution, she defended her views as pushing back against a Muslim conspiracy. "We need to understand," she declared, "that what is happening here is part of a well-orchestrated drive to Islamize Africa. . . . [and have them] entrenched in the constitutions of the African states." She concluded that the battle for the constitution is a spiritual battle.[40]

Wanjiru's political views seem to be shaped by the paradigm of Spiritual Warfare, where every issue is a battle between Christianity and Satan, and whatever would benefit Christianity is automatically seen as on the side of God.

The rhetoric of spiritual warfare is even more pronounced in other Pentecostal churches. A teacher associated with Chrisco New Life Church in Nairobi stresses fear as a motive to evangelize Muslims:

> Nairobi has been invaded by Islam from all the four gates. The heart of the town has been invaded and bought too. Not to mention Eastleigh. Christians have been in their comfort zones, but they are now realizing what is happening. If we don't wake up and not only pray, but also evangelize, it will be very difficult in future to preach the Gospel. Unless we act now, it may take people's lives to take back what we've lost. Islam is using technology, craftiness, anything it can use, to spread the religion. People have testified how they were being offered money in order to join Islam; some Shs 70,000, others Shs 40,000,175 etc. This is in a bid to increase the numbers of Muslims in case Sharia law, which can be effected because of numbers, can be applicable in future. It is a trick of the enemy. In this hard economic time, some people are falling victim to this. While the church is busy preaching prosperity gospel, Muslims are busy "buying" people into Islam. The government is also embracing Islam in the name of wooing investors to the country.[41]

Michael Brislen argues that Christians view Islam in terms of a kind of spiritual capitalism:

> While the popular view of spiritual power sees it as a mystical power that can affect material change in the world through healing, prosperity, etc., spiritual power can also be understood as a form of symbolic power. Those who are understood to possess the mystical-form of spiritual power accumulate spiritual capital. There is then the possibility of exchange with other forms of capital, such as economic capital and political capital. Examples would be of well-known Neo-Pentecostal (and mainline) pastors pursuing political careers or gaining economic wealth due to their position.

This can also help explain the hidden mechanism behind the naïve theocratic vision. Christianity in Kenya is understood to have accumulated a sufficient amount of spiritual capital to transform some of it into political capital (i.e. the theocratic vision). However, if spiritual capital can be converted into economic and political capital, then the reverse must also be true. Therefore, when Islam accumulates considerable economic capital and political capital, this may be transformed into spiritual capital (increasing spiritual power) and thus enhance the likelihood that some Christians may convert to Islam.[42]

Religious plurality seen in terms of aggressive competition may be one explanation for why Christian-Muslim relations remain tense and may continue to do so for the foreseeable future.

Cooperating with Muslims

A third response to Muslim-Christian relations is that of the leaders of interfaith initiatives. Most prominent in Nairobi is the Inter-Religious Council of Kenya (IRCK). According to their website, the IRCK is composed of a wide variety of religious organizations, including:

1. The Kenya Conference of Catholic Bishops (KCCB)
2. The National Council of Churches of Kenya (NCCK)
3. The Evangelical Alliance of Kenya (EAK)
4. The Organization of African Instituted Churches (OAIC)
5. Seventh Day Adventist Church (SDA)
6. The Supreme Council of Kenyan Muslims (SUPKEM)
7. The National Muslim Leaders Forum (NAMLEF)
8. Shia Ithnasharia Muslim Association
9. The Hindu Council of Kenya (HCK).[43]

What ties the council together is cooperation in nation-building. Founded in 1983, the IRCK's stated purpose is "to deepen inter-faith dialogue and collaboration among members for a common endeavor and mobilize the unique moral and social resources of religious people and address shared concerns." What that means in practice has been spelled out in a series of strategic plans that have focused the "unique moral and social resources of religious people" toward several issues critical to civil society. IRCK's motto is "Mobilizing Faith Communities for Common Action."

The involvement of IRCK with the issue of slavery is an example of using its moral and social resources for "common action."[44] In 2022, the IRCK joined a host of other nations in signing the Declaration of Religious Leaders to fight Modern Slavery. This declaration was originally signed in 2014 by Pope Francis and Grand Ayatollah Taqi al-Modarresi. The declaration has gained momentum in many countries around the world, mobilizing faith communities against all forms of modern slavery, defined as "an umbrella term, which includes human trafficking, domestic servitude, the worst forms of child labor and forced and child marriages." Abdirahman Ismael, the IRCK Executive Director, pledges to "use our connections and resources to address the root causes of this vice and ensure that it is completely eradicated from our society and perpetrators brought to book."[45] In a press release, IRCK announced the *Faith For Freedom* smartphone app, which "explains what modern slavery is, how to detect it, how to respond to people affected by it, and how and where to find help to address it."

How effective has IRCK been as an agent of peace and religious harmony in Kenya? Ismael's predecessor, Dr. Francis Kuria, who directed IRCK for over ten years from 2008 to 2020, acknowledged that the Al-Shabaab's Garissa massacre of 148 university students in 2014 was a major destabilizing event for the nation and for the cause of religious harmony. In an interview with the Berkely Center at Georgetown University in 2015, Kuria addressed the state of interreligious relations in Kenya:

> They are very dynamic. If you asked that question before October or November 2014, I'd have said interfaith relations were strengthening. But, after the massacre in Mandera and the killings in Mombasa, I would say that there is a lot of tension for interfaith in Kenya. So, right now, I wouldn't say that we are at the best point we have ever been. There is a lot of bridge-building we still have to do. But I would say that over the years there has been better appreciation of interfaith, and therefore, the need for it and commitment to it. The various religious leaders have recognized that they can't go alone on some of these issues.[46]

For religious leaders like Kuria and Ismail, the key to Christian-Muslim relations is action, cooperative action in dealing with disease, slavery, economic development, and education. They may both agreed with the divine command spoken by the Prophet Jeremiah to "seek the welfare of the city where I have sent you into exile, and pray to the LORD on its behalf, for in its welfare you will find your welfare."[47]

Blessing, Curse, or Something Else?

Is religious diversity a blessing, a curse, or something in between? Nairobi is a laboratory of religious pluralism. The newly formed National Cohesion and Integration Commission (NCIC) is testimony to the government's anxiety about disunity in the nation. Some regard religions with exclusive truth claims, such as Christianity and Islam, as threats to peace and unity across Africa and the world. While Islamist terrorist groups are real threats to peace, most Muslims and Christians have coexisted peacefully for generations. The percentage of Muslims in the total population (10 percent) may be part of the explanation.

Peter Berger's work, as we have argued throughout this book, suggests that religious pluralism can be a force for cohesion. This new pluralist paradigm calls for combining "two pluralisms." By separating church and state (no state church and no religious requirements for public office), religion is freed from abuse by politicians and abuse by religionists seeking to add power to faith. The separation of church and state thus encourages two pluralisms. The first is the pluralism of the secular public square, in which the law or violence cannot enforce religious claims. In this public space, the common good must be determined by rational arguments and not religious edicts or private revelation. The second pluralism is that of allowing different religions to believe whatever they wish if violence is avoided. When these two pluralisms work together in a nation, they can help both the state and the religious institutions thrive. But can this work in practice? Muslim and Christian fundamentalism can be strident in their respective claims of absolute truth. They may insist on imposing their deeply held convictions on one another and on the public. But where the new pluralism exists, a pluriformity of mutual respect and cooperation flourishes.

According to Nancy Ammerman's research, when the two pluralisms coexist, there is minimal violence or fragmentation. Part of the reason for this is built into Christianity. Religions have a "background" and a "foreground." The background is the institutional side of the faith community where deep convictions and customs are held, and absolutes about God and righteousness adhere. Religions, however, also have a foreground, a way of relating to others outside the background community of doctrine and codes of conduct. This is true of Christianity. Ammerman calls this foreground "Golden Rule Christianity" where Christians can easily develop friendship networks with people of other faith or no faith by applying a central command of the founder of their movement—"Do to others what you would want them to do to you." Combining a soul-satisfying background faith that permits deep and absolute convictions, with a foreground faith that seeks to serve others with kindness and fairness—whatever their belief or ethical system—can lead to high degrees of interfaith cooperation and tolerance. Her extensive research documents the workability of the two pluralisms. The Kenyan churches can be a force for social and political cohesion not by becoming less Christian but by becoming more Christian, deepening their background convictions even as they practice their foreground convictions.

Supporting Ammerman is Robert Dowd, associate professor of political science and fellow of the Kellogg Center for International Studies at Notre Dame. In a paper presented to the American Political Science Association in 2003, presented his research on the religious factors affecting democratization in sub-Saharan Africa. His seventy-five-page paper concluded that "there is a strong relationship between the extent to which there is religious diversity in a country and democratization."[48] Countries that had both Christians and Muslims were more democratic than countries that had only one of the two groups. The reason for this, Dowd proposed, was the "limits of power" argument, where religious leaders would seek to limit the power of other religious groups in society from becoming the privileged group by promoting civil liberties and political rights for all. His extensive statistical research in Nigeria and Uganda coupled with earlier work on public education in Kenya gave a strong scientific grounding to his analysis. Dowd later published the results of his research in 2015 in *Christianity, Islam and Liberal Democracy: Lessons from sub-Saharan Africa*.[49]

What is the color of the future? The peaceful yellow of Kibera or the violent red of Garissa? Which event is the most predictive of Kenya's future? For believers, God most certainly guides the future, but he does so through the actions of his people. Under the guiding grace of God, the destiny of Kenya and its capital lies largely with the Christian majority. It is they who must decide if Muslims are an enemy to be feared or a neighbor to be loved.

Conclusion

People congregate around a wide courtyard on a Friday lunch hour in Nairobi's Aga Khan Walk. On the southern end of this walkway is the city's main railway station at the edge of the central business district (CBD). It is next to a bustling transport hub for minibuses known as *Matatus*. The northern end of the walkway is Kencom, another transport hub at the heart of the city. Minibuses going to the western side of the city draw their passengers from there. Kencom gets its name from the large headquarters of the Kenya Commercial Bank, one of Kenya's largest banks.

At the paved walkway lined with a few trees and patches of greenery, people eat or take a lunchtime break, basking in the midday sun. A preacher (or two) bellows his sermon to the mixed audience. The sermon will likely expound from scriptures and personal stories on the virtues of Christian living, amidst national and personal challenges. The preacher's voice sounds hoarse from months of shouting aloud in the street, without a public address system.

The "audience" sits along a low stone that walls around the space and silently listens to the preacher. At times, they laugh at his dry humor, at other times, they nod in acknowledgment of his depiction of the life trials urbanites face. Nearby, at the Nairobi Cinema, a Pentecostal church meets for lunchtime prayer. Their worship service format is typical of Pentecostal services and comprises music, a sermon, and prayer session, with a call for conversion at the end.

The Aga Khan walkway represents Nairobi's multiple dimensions of diversity. It is lined by commercial offices and shops. It has large corporations such as Kenya Commercial Bank (now KCB Bank Kenya), Kenya Reinsurance Corporation and Cooperative Bank. The street also hosts the state-owned electricity company. One can spot the Supreme Court, the National Education building, and the Treasury from the street. Aga Khan Walk also hosts food and shoeshine kiosks and commercial stalls. It has two cinema halls next to each other. It has two transport hubs. The street hosts different preachers during the day. The cinema halls host prayer meetings in the morning, revival meetings in the evening, and church services on weekends. Jamia mosque's Muslim call for prayer, faintly heard from here on Fridays, reminds of the Islamic provenance of the street's name, Aga Khan.[1] The rest of the week, the religious space on the walk is dominated by Christian voices.

FIGURE *Aga Khan walkway. Photo: Kyama Mugambi.*

This street brings together the complex pluralist nature of Nairobi's spiritual existence. Those who walk this street or sit by the pavement enact in their private lives the broad diversity that the street represents. They navigate the multiple identities that characterize the complex composition of the city's residents. Religion is the core which seems to hold these identities together and a somewhat stable equilibrium. Religion is in the home, in the street, in the office, in the school, and in the college. Men and women, young and old, participate in it to various degrees.

Christianity is as highly visible in Nairobi's central business as it is in the Estates (the residential areas). When the city center's energy quietens down on a Friday evening, Christian faith finds expression in churches within the estates, in overnight prayer meetings, weekend evangelistic meetings, and Sunday worship services.

Christian spirituality has not always been as dominant in the public space. Nairobi's motto before independence was *Concilio, Fide, Vigilantia* (Council, faith, and vigilance).[2] "Council" found expression in the British monarchy

CONCLUSION

through the city and national legislative chambers. "Vigilance" found its expression in the military might of British rule. The coat of arms, in use since 1923, was modeled after European coats of arms.[3] In 1950, a lion was included holding a Maasai shield the land represented the purported peace-bringing character of British rule.[4]

Faith, however, was only visible in the life of the city through historic mission-church buildings. It hardly received any mention in the colonial era narratives except when it had to do with official engagements. This institutional dimension of Christianity expressed itself in formal government functions, in the buildings, and in the private lives of the colonial residents. African religious agency was left out of the colonial memory.

After the end of British rule in 1963, the visible marks of historic mission Christianity remained, as did the city plan. The structure of the city continued to reflect the initial priorities of colonial rule. Out of this heritage grew a new future for the city. Nairobi's twentieth century reality represents a future different from what colonialists anticipated in 1950. The colonial community at the time imagined that "somewhere in this territory a new race would quickened into life, be tolerant, generous, retaining in its new culture that which was best in the old."[5] The 50th Jubilee Memorial book talked about how "on threshold of a new age Nairobi has within its grasp the leadership of that new civilization worthy of those who in the beginning came from the White Queen to give the country peace."[6]

Nairobi was indeed on the threshold of a new age. Seventy years later, Nairobi developed a new pluralist existence. As predicted, it retained in its new culture elements of both its African and colonial heritage. African Christian agency emerged from the shadows and is evident in the sights and sounds that inundate every corner. This faith is not just a silent, private experience. It is a visible, vocal, public aspect of Nairobi's life.

The entry of historic mission Christianity preceded the colonial enterprise. The unexpected success of various expressions of Christianity in post-colonial Kenya—after the exit of missionaries—illustrates the extent to which Christianity finds its home among indigenous peoples. The Christianity found here challenges the secularizing forces found in modern cities of the world. It asserts its identity through innovative ways. In this book, we have shown how the process of translation in history affects historic mission Christianity in profound ways that promote its resilience. Protestant HMCs cannot resist the charismatizing forces of indigenous forms. Yet they retain their liturgical forms.

The numeric strength of Catholicism and its visible presence in the city demonstrates that historic mission Christianity still has an important place in the spiritual landscape of the city. The institutional fortitude of these established forms of Christianity provides a base from which the prophetic voices of clergy challenge the maladies that mar Kenya's political history.

Orthodox Christianity maintains its connection with ancient African expressions. This form bypasses the Western missionary history, illustrating an alternative path of provenance. Though few in number, these Christians demonstrate the translatability of Christianity in different contexts.

African initiatives in Christianity remind the keen observer of the role of culture and indigenous leadership in the translation process. Though less equipped to speak to the globalizing impulses, AICs emphasize the importance of rootedness in the context. They were the "spiritual home" which signaled the emergence of other more recent initiatives in Christianity.

Pentecostal charismatic Christianity encompasses a broad spectrum of initiatives bound by their commitment to the immanence of the Holy Spirit in the life of the believer. Their diversity bears testimony to the varied ways the Christian message can incarnate in pluralist society. Pentecostals present the most visible rebuttal to the secularizing forces. Their entrepreneurial acumen creates a prolific Christianity which proposes a response to the challenges of an African urban society in transition. Pentecostal innovation affords opportunities for failures in leadership and religious extremes. These are evident in Nairobi side by side with the powerful examples of hope and resilience.

Pentecostal Christianity leads the way in affirming the place of women and youth in the grassroots development of Nairobi's spirituality. The youth represent the future potential of Christianity in the city. Their energy and passion shines through their varied responses to Nairobi's pluralism. It is in the women's initiatives that one sees the different ways in which Christian spirituality is grounded in the fabric of society.

In sum, vivacious expressions of Christian faith exist side by side with other religious expressions which have been a part of the city's history. On Fridays, the Jamia mosque complex gathers hundreds of Muslim faithful in the middle of Nairobi. A large Hindu temple stands out from among the commercial buildings on the congested eastern side of the CBD. The city's 38,000 Hindus constitute two-thirds of the nation's total number. They are served by a number of temples scattered around the city. Some of these have since been converted to churches to serve the growing needs of Pentecostal churches for space.

The expressions we have explored in this book are by no means static. New questions continue to arise about how the Christian message will be relevant to a city that is grappling with various issues. One such tension involves sexual ethics and the definition of family. Mainstream Christian groups described in this book have been vocal about their opposition to the registration of LGBTIQ organizations and the legalization of same-sex marriage. They have expressed themselves in street demonstrations at various points. At the same time, members of the LGBTIQ community explore their Christian faith as they meet in small groups in less public spaces.[7] They are a small marginalized group who have to contend with the legal and social implications of their perspectives. Their position finds little accommodation within mainstream Christianity in Nairobi. These tensions illustrate the constant negotiation inherent in navigating the multiple identities in a pluralist Nairobi.

As the different churches service their networks with the church globally, they are also expanding their internal reach to constituencies not previously addressed before. Church ministry to the deaf is one area that has seen vast growth in the 2010s and 2020s.[8] HMCs and Pentecostals now include sign language interpreters in their services. They extend these services to their broadcasts on the mass media and social media platforms. Children's ministry is now taking a more prominent role in HMCs and other churches as well. These efforts illustrate that Christian mission in a dynamic Nairobi is not static. Christian engagement is constantly trying to keep in step with the rapidly changing social context in Nairobi.

Commercial governance institutions, with their branches dotted all over the city, intermingle with market stalls that rent space there. The kiosk culture of Nairobi meets with the institutional expressions of politics and economics. In a comparable way, religion finds its expression in the institution and the kiosk. More than the other religious expressions, Christianity facilitates a vital interrelationship between the economic, political, and social life of the city. This Christianity straddles the institutional dimension through its cathedrals and the kiosk spirituality in its newer expressions.

Notes

Introduction

1 "2019 Kenya Population and Housing Census," https://www.knbs.or.ke/download/2019-kenya-population-and-housing-census-volume-i-population-by-county-and-sub-county/.
2 "Kenya Religious Affiliation," https://s3-eu-west-1.amazonaws.com/s3.sourceafrica.net/documents/119795/VOLUME-IV-KPHC-2019.pdf.
3 "Kenya Religious Affiliation."

Chapter 1

1 See the entry on Temple Moore in the *Dictionary of National Biography*, https://www.oxforddnb.com/.
2 Kyama Mugambi, *The Spirit of Revitalization: Urban Pentecostalism in Kenya* (Waco: Baylor University Press, 2020), 30.
3 David Barrett, George Mambo, Jancie McLaughlin, and Malcolm McVeigh, eds., *Kenya Churches Handbook* (Nairobi: Evangel, 1974), 22.
4 Barrett, Mambo, McLaughlin, and McVeigh, *Kenya Churches Handbook*, 23.
5 H. Strachan, *The First World War in Africa* (Oxford: Oxford University Press, 2004), 115.
6 Barrett, Mambo, McLaughlin, and McVeigh, *Kenya Churches Handbook*, 23.
7 Barrett, Mambo, McLaughlin, and McVeigh, *Kenya Churches Handbook*, 24.
8 For a good discussion of Harry Leakey's role as missionary and advocate for native rights, see Mugambi, *Spirit of Revitalization*, 30–1.
9 Barrett, Mambo, McLaughlin, and McVeigh, *Kenya Churches Handbook*, 24.
10 Barrett, Mambo, McLaughlin, and McVeigh, *Kenya Churches Handbook*, 26.
11 Barrett, Mambo, McLaughlin, and McVeigh, *Kenya Churches Handbook*, 25.
12 Barrett, Mambo, McLaughlin, and McVeigh, *Kenya Churches Handbook*, 26.
13 Barrett, Mambo, McLaughlin, and McVeigh, *Kenya Churches Handbook*, 26.
14 Anders Ese and Kristin Ese, *The City Makers of Nairobi: An African Urban History* (London: Routledge, 2020), Part II, paragraph 1.
15 Ese and Ese, *The City Makers of Nairobi*, Part II paragraph 4.

16 Paul Kollman and Smedley, *Understanding World Christianity: Eastern Africa* (Minneapolis, Fortress, 2018), Chapter 3 chronological, section: Christian churches in the Nation States.
17 Bruce Nichols, "Nairobi 1975: A Crisis of Faith for the WCC," *Themelios* 1, no. 3. https://www.thegospelcoalition.org/themelios/article/nairobi-1975-a-crisis-of-faith-for-the-wcc/ (accessed January 2024).
18 Todd M. Johnson and Gina A. Zurlo, eds., *World Christian Encyclopedia*, 3rd ed. (Edinburgh: Edinburgh University Press, 2020), 450–1 record that the number of Anglicans in 2015 were 6 milliion.
19 "Wellington Mulwa" Dictionary of African Christian Biography, https://dacb.org/search.html?query=Mulwa%2C+Wellington (accessed November 2023).
20 Ian Shaw, "What Has Glasgow to do with Nairobi? The Churches and Rapid Church Growth in Twentieth Century Nairobi," *Studies in World Christianity* 20, no. 2 (2014): 169.
21 Philip Jenkins, news, *Christian Century*, https://www.christiancentury.org/article/notes-global-church/christianity-s-explosive-growth-kenya (accessed July 1, 2022).
22 Julie Hearn, "The 'Invisible' NGO: US Evangelical Missions in Kenya," *Journal of Religion in Africa* 32, no. 1 (2002): 32–60. JSTOR, http://www.jstor.org/stable/1581671 (accessed July 1 2022).
23 Interview with Reverend Fred Nyabera, Nairobi, Kenya, August 2023. Interview by Mark Shaw.
24 Ian Shaw, "Glasgow," 166–86, 175.
25 Shaw, "Glasgow," 179.
26 Shaw, "Glasgow," 172–3.
27 Shaw, "Glasgow," 176–7.
28 Shaw, "Glasgow," 176–7.
29 Johnson and Zurlo, *World Christian Encyclopedia*, 445.
30 https://www.christianstudylibrary.org/article/worldview-abraham-kuyper
31 Interview with Bishop Rose Okeno, Nairobi, August 2023. Interview by Mark Shaw.
32 Historian of Religion David Lindenfeld points to an apparent paradox with Protestantism when it comes to power and authority. He distinguishes between "concentrated spirituality" and "diffuse spirituality." African religion is an example of diffuse spirituality in that it does not require centralized clergy, houses of worship, or written scriptures. This Protestantism, flowing from the Reformation in the sixteenth century, with all of its centering of theological truth (think of the various "solas") pioneered a new approach to the decentering of institutional power. "In these cases, concentration of experiential and theoretical spirituality went hand in hand with the diffusion of religious authority—precisely the opposite pattern from Roman Catholicism." See David Lindenfeld, *World Christianity and Indigenous Experience* (New York: Cambridge University Press, 2021), 300.
33 Peter Berger, *De-secularization of the World* (Grand Rapids: Eerdmans, 1999), 3.

NOTES

34 Peter L. Berger, "Secularism in Retreat," *The National Interest*, No. 46 (Winter 1996/97): 5.

35 See Shaw, "Glasgow," 180.

Chapter 2

1. Dorothy Hughes, a Kenyan architect of British descent, designed various other iconic buildings in Kenya, including the National Theatre, the Nakuru War Memorial Hospital, and Princess Elizabeth Women's Hospital, which became Nairobi Hospital.

2. Cothrai Gogan, *H.G.M., Holy Ghost Mission : The Spiritans in Nairobi, 1899-1999*, 1998, 13, http://archive.org/details/hgmholyghostmiss00goga.

3. Gogan, *H.G.M., Holy Ghost Mission*.

4. Gogan, *H.G.M., Holy Ghost Mission*, 42–3.

5. Kenya National Bureau of Statistics, *2019 Kenya Population and Housing Census: Volume IV* (Nairobi: Government Printer, 2019), 422.

6. Catholic populations have been in decline in traditionally Catholic Europe. See Philip Jenkins, *The Next Christendom: The Coming of Global Christianity* (Oxford and New York: Oxford University Press, 2011); Hugh McLeod and Werner Ustorf, *The Decline of Christendom in Western Europe, 1750–2000* (Cambridge: Cambridge University Press, 2003); Eli Berman, Laurence R. Iannaccone, and Giuseppe Ragusa, "From Empty Pews to Empty Cradles: Fertility Decline among European Catholics," *Journal of Demographic Economics* 84, no. 2 (2018): 149–87.

7. Paul Gifford outlines his objections in his work Paul Gifford, *Christianity, Development and Modernity in Africa* (London: C Hurst & Co Publishers Ltd., 2015).

8. "Who We Are- Pacis Insurance," May 13, 2023, https://www.pacisinsurance.com/about-us/who-we-are/.

9. "Who We Are- Pacis Insurance."

10. Three out of the five images showing religious buildings in Nairobi's colonial era Jubilee publication are depictions of All Saints' Cathedral. Very little text is devoted to religion, but the prominence of Anglican Christianity is very clear. See James Smart, *Nairobi: A Jubilee History 1900-1950* (Nairobi: The East African Standard, 1950).

11. Little mention is made in the archival documents about Catholic missions, except when transactions were made involving the state and land or education. See, for example, "KNA/Secretariat/2/1" (Kenya National Archives, 1940); "KNA/PC /RVP/6A/15/10" (Kenya National Archives, 1942).

12. Rodrigo Mejia, *The Conscience of Society: The Social Teaching of the Catholic Bishops of Kenya: 1960-1995* (Nairobi: Paulines Publications Africa, 1995).

13 Mejia, *The Conscience of Society*.

14 RS Ndingi Mwana'a Nzeki, "People for Peace in Africa," *Wajibu* 5, no. 1 (1990): 2–3; Waithaka Waihenya and Ndikaru wa Teresia, *A Voice Unstilled: Archbishop Ndingi Mwana A Nzeki* (Nairobi, Kenya: Sasa Sema Publications, 2009).

15 Beth Griffin, "Kenyan Bishops Keep up Campaign against Vaccine," *National Catholic Reporter* 51, no. 12 (2015): 6–7; Nzwili, "Some Kenyan Catholic Bishops Urge Caution on COVID-19 Clinical Trials," *Crux* (blog), May 7, 2020, https://cruxnow.com/church-in-africa/2020/05/some-kenyan-catholic-bishops-urge-caution-on-covid-19-clinical-trials/; Ian Njeru et al., "Did the Call for Boycott by the Catholic Bishops Affect the Polio Vaccination Coverage in Kenya in 2015? A Cross-Sectional Study," *Pan African Medical Journal* 24, no. 1 (2016).https://doi.org/DOI:10.11604/pamj.2016.24.120.8986

16 "About—OLQP South B," http://www.olqpsouthb.org/index.php/about/ (accessed July 29, 2019).

17 "Muslim and Christian Youths Clash in Kenyan Capital- December 1, 2000," https://www.cnn.com/2000/WORLD/africa/12/01/kenya.riot.reut/index.html (accessed December 9, 2023).

18 Muriithi Muriuki, "Kenya: Torched Catholic Church Reopened," *The Nation*, March 31, 2003, sec. News, https://allafrica.com/stories/200303310163.html.

19 P. Mark Fackler et al., "Media and Post-Election Violence in Kenya," in *The Handbook of Global Communication and Media Ethics*, ed. Robert S. Fortner and P. Mark Fackler (Malden, MA: Wiley-Blackwell, 2011), 626–54, http://onlinelibrary.wiley.com.ezproxy.aiu.ac.ke:2048/doi/10.1002/9781444390629.ch33/summary; Mara J. Roberts, *Conflict Analysis of the 2007 Post-Election Violence in Kenya* in *Managing Conflicts in Africa's Democratic Transitions,* ed. Akanmu Adebayo (New York: Lexington Books, 2012), 141–54. (September 2009).

20 "About—OLQP South B."

21 "KNA/AV/12/329" (Kenya National Archives, 1928).

22 "History: Strathmore University," *Strathmore University* (blog), April 5, 2023, https://strathmore.edu/history/.

23 "Opus Dei: Strathmore University," *Strathmore University* (blog), April 5, 2023, https://strathmore.edu/opus-dei/.

24 This body comprises the episcopal conferences in Eritrea, Ethiopia, Kenya, Malawi, Sudan, Tanzania, Uganda, and Zambia. See "Brief History- Catholic University of Eastern Africa," September 14, 2020, https://www.cuea.edu/?page_id=6827.

25 See, for example, Laurenti Magesa, *African Religion in the Dialogue Debate: From Intolerance to Coexistence*, vol. 3 (Hamburg: LIT Verlag Münster, 2010).

26 Charles Nyamiti, *Christ as Our Ancestor: Christology from an African Perspective*, 11 (Gweru: Mambo Press, 1984); Charles Nyamiti, "African Christologies Today," in *Jesus in African Christianity: Experimentation and Diversity in African Christology*, ed. J. N. K Mugambi and Laurenti Magesa (Nairobi: Acton Publishers, 1998), 17–40; Magesa, *African Religion in the Dialogue Debate*; Laurenti Magesa, *What Is Not Sacred? African Spirituality* (Nairobi: Acton Publishers, 2014).

27 J. N. K Mugambi and Laurenti Magesa, eds., *The Church in African Christianity : Innovative Essays in Ecclesiology*, 1 (Nairobi: Initiatives, 1990); J. N. K Mugambi and Laurenti Magesa, eds., *Jesus in African Christianity: Experimentation and Diversity in African Christology* (Nairobi: Acton Publishers, 1998).

28 "Mater Heart Run | Mater Misericordiae Hospital," https://www.materkenya.com/heart-run (accessed December 9, 2023).

29 Plans for these areas began in the 1960s and were actualized in the 1970s and 1980s. The houses in the developments were designed in neighborhoods with ample recreational and green space. The plans, however, were implemented with a higher density than the plans allowed for, resulting in large numbers of residents. The education infrastructure was adequate, but the medical services were not enough. "KNA/RN/6/5" (Kenya National Archives, 1971); "KNA/RN/6/6" (Kenya National Archives, 1973); "KNA/RN/6/7" (Kenya National Archives, 1977).

30 Thomas Koonammakkal, *Elements of Syro-Malabar History* (Kerala, India: Beth Aprem Nazrani Dayra, 2012); George Joseph Nedumparambil, "A Search of the Roots of Syro-Malabar Church in Kerala" (PhD Thesis, Würzburg, Universität Würzburg, Diss., 2013, 2015).

31 "Vincentian Congregation – VPH Nairobi," https://www.vphnairobi.org/about-us/vincentian-congregation/ (accessed December 9, 2023).

32 In 2023, the Vincentians had fourteen mission stations in East Africa. Five of these are in Kenya.

33 "Vincentian Congregation – VPH Nairobi."

34 Jumuia is Swahili for "the community." For more, see Joseph Healey, "Small Christian Communities (SCCs) Promote Family Ministry in Eastern Africa," *Hekima Review*, 2013; Agbonkhianmeghe E. Orobator, "Small Christian Communities as a New Way of Becoming Church: Practice, Progress and Prospects," in *Small Christian Communities: Fresh Stimulus for a Forward-Looking Church*, ed. Klaus Krämer and Klaus Vellguth (Phillippines: Claretian Communications Foundation, 2013), 113–25.

35 Catholic populations have been in decline in traditionally Catholic Europe. See Jenkins, *The next Christendom*; McLeod and Ustorf, *The Decline of Christendom in Western Europe, 1750–2000*; Berman, Iannaccone, and Ragusa, "From Empty Pews to Empty Cradles: Fertility Decline among European Catholics."

Chapter 3

1 Sherlyne Omangi, "An Assessment of Residential Neighborhood Satisfaction: A Case of Bahati Estate, Eastlands, Nairobi, Kenya" (unpublished PhD dissertation, University of Nairobi, 2016), 60. For population estimates, see the report of Slum Dwellers International, https://static1.squarespace.com/static/58d4504db8a79b27eb388c91/t/5e98b22ea1a43026aaf89f71

NOTES

/1587065404163/Nairobi+Informal+Settlements+profiling-+SDI-K.pdf (accessed August 24, 2023).

2   Omangi, "A Case of Bahati Estate, Eastlands, Nairobi, Kenya," 65–6.

3   See Ogbu Kalu, *African Pentecostalism: An Introduction* (Oxford: Oxford University Press, 2008).

4   Francis Githieya, *The Freedom of the Spirit: African Indigenous Churches in Kenya* (Atlanta: Scholars Press, 1997), 123–4.

5   Githieya *The Freedom of the Spirit*, 124.

6   Nahashon W. Ndungu, *Akurinu Churches in Kenya: Background, Development and Theology* (Nairobi: University of Nairobi Press, 2019), 46.

7   Githieya, *The Freedom of the Spirit*, 124–5.

8   Githieya, *The Freedom of the Spirit*, 125

9   Githieya, *The Freedom of the Spirit*, 129.

10 Githieya, *The Freedom of the Spirit*, 132.

11 Githieya, *The Freedom of the Spirit*, 145.

12 See Appendix C in Githieya, *The Freedom of the Spirit*, 261.

13 David Barrett, *Schism and Renewal in Africa: An Analysis of Six thousand Contemporary Religious Movements* (Nairobi: Oxford, 1968), 8.

14 Philomena Mwaura, "Paul David Zakayo Kivuli and the Founding of the Africa Israel Church Nineveh," *Journal of African Christian Biography* 3, no. 4 (October 2018): 6.

15 Nomiya means "God has given me a revelation."

16 Barrett, *Schism and Renewal in Africa*, 11.

17 Mwaura, "Founding of the Africa Israel Church Nineveh," 8.

18 Mwaura, "Founding of the Africa Israel Church Nineveh," 8–9.

19 Mwaura, "Founding of the Africa Israel Church Nineveh," 10.

20 Mwaura, "Founding of the Africa Israel Church Nineveh," 10.

21 Mwaura, "Founding of the Africa Israel Church Nineveh," 11–12.

22 George Mambo, "The Revival Fellowship (Brethren) in Kenya," in David Barrett, et al., *The Kenya Churches Handbook* (Nairobi: Evangel House, 1973), 110–11.

23 F. B. Welbourn and B. A. Ogot, *A Place to Feel at Home: A Study of Two Independent Churches in Western Kenya* (London: Oxford University Press, 1966), 46.

24 https://dacb.org/stories/kenya/ajuoga-abednego1/ (accessed August 28, 2023).

25 https://christianhistoryinstitute.org/it-happened-today/1/8 (accessed August 28, 2023).

26 John G. Gatu, *Fan into Flame: An Autobiography* (Nairobi: Moran, 2017), 2–3.

27 Gatu, *Fan into Flame*, 57.

28 Gatu, *Fan into Flame*, 59.

29 Gatu, *Fan into Flame*, 135.
30 Gatu, *Fan into Flame*, 147
31 Gatu, *Fan into Flame*, 147.
32 See Richard Gray, *Black Christians, White Missionaries* (New Haven: Yale, 1990).

Chapter 4

1 The 2019 Census lists them as evangelical churches and other Christian denominations. See Kenya National Bureau of Statistics, *2019 Kenya Population and Housing Census: Volume IV* (Nairobi: Government Printer, 2019), 422.
2 N. Wariboko, *The Charismatic City and the Public Resurgence of Religion: A Pentecostal Social Ethics of Cosmopolitan Urban Life*, 2014 edition (New York: Palgrave Macmillan, 2014), xiii.
3 John Gichinga, interview by Kyama Mugambi, August 18, 2018. David Gitari, *Troubled but Not Destroyed: Autobiography of Dr. David M. Gitari* (Nairobi: BookBaby, 2014), 297.
4 Gitari, *Troubled but Not Destroyed*, 24–5.
5 Political speeches are known to be given in HMCs, especially during the electioneering period. In the 1990s, Njoya and Gitari's sermons challenged the political elite on issues of corruption and authoritarian governance. Politicians increasingly used church services for electioneering. Historic mission churches challenged this. Rodrigo Mejia, *The Conscience of Society: The Social Teaching of the Catholic Bishops of Kenya: 1960-1995* (Nairobi: Paulines Publications Africa, 1995).
6 For a discussion on this, see Joshua Robert Barron, "Is the Prosperity Gospel, Gospel? An Examination of the Prosperity and Productivity Gospels in African Christianity," *Conspectus: The Journal of the South African Theological Seminary* 33, no. 1 (2022): 88–103.
7 One particularly tragic example is the exposure in 2022 of the Shokahola Christian cult was responsible for the death of hundreds through extremely ascetic fasting.
8 See Paul Gifford, *Christianity, Development and Modernity in Africa* (London: C Hurst & Co Publishers Ltd., 2015).
9 See the discussion in Ebenezer Obadare, *Pentecostal Republic: Religion and the Struggle for State Power in Nigeria* (London: Zed Books, 2018).
10 See Chapter 3 for more about these communities.
11 Kyama M. Mugambi, *A Spirit of Revitalization: Urban Pentecostalism in Kenya* (Waco: Baylor University Press, 2020), 39.
12 Kibera is also known as Kibra. It a large informal settlement West of the CBD.

13 Kiswahili is the lingua franca. Luo and other languages are not used for public gatherings except in rural areas where the communities are more linguistically homogeneous.

14 For a book-length discussion on this, see Allan H. Anderson, *Spirit-Filled World: Religious Dis/Continuity in African Pentecostalism* (Cham: Springer, 2018).

15 "Home- Kenya Assemblies of God," https://kag.ke/ (accessed December 22, 2023).

16 See Mugambi, *A Spirit of Revitalization*.

17 See, for example, "Kathy Kiuna Followers Trolled for Wishing Their 'mum' a Happy Birthday," *TV47*, July 29, 2019, https://tv47.co.ke/2019/07/29/kathy-kiuna-followers-trolled-for-wishing-their-mum-a-happy-birthday/; "Ati Mum? Kathy Kiuna's Birthday Celebrations Spark Debate," *Standard Entertainment and Lifestyle*, https://www.standardmedia.co.ke/entertainment/local-news/2001335854/ati-mum-kathy-kiunas-birthday-celebrations-spark-debate (accessed August 8, 2020).

18 See Chapter 6 for more on Wanjiru and Wairimu.

19 Harvey Cox, *The Secular City: Secularization and Urbanization in Theological Perspective*, Revised edition (Princeton: Princeton University Press, 2013).

20 This was true of these churches even prior to COVID-19 pandemic, which forced churches to adopt media strategies.

21 Kathy Kiuna and Allan Kiuna, *Appointment with Destiny: A Moving Testimony of God's Love and Faithfulness* (Nairobi: Jubilee Publishers, 2006).

22 Kiuna and Kiuna, *Appointment with Destiny: A Moving Testimony of God's Love and Faithfulness*.

23 See, for example, Allan Kiuna, *Anointed for the Marketplace* (Nairobi: Aura Publishers, 2012); Niyi Morakinyo, *The Seven Professional Nations (Full Version): Reconciling Them Back To God* (Nairobi: The Joshua Generation Trust, 2013).

24 Kiuna and Kiuna, *Appointment with Destiny: A Moving Testimony of God's Love and Faithfulness*.

25 Miller and Yamamori use the term "progressive" here to refer not to the theology but to the church's approach to social issues. They contrast this approach with other Pentecostal churches. See Donald E. Miller and Tetsunao Yamamori, *Global Pentecostalism: The New Face of Christian Social Engagement*, First Edition, Includes DVD edition (Berkeley: University of California Press, 2007).

26 Yamamori and Miller made this observation in their assessment of global Pentecostalism. Miller and Yamamori, *Global Pentecostalism*.

27 For the history of CITAM, see Justus Mugambi, *Five Decades of God's Faithfulness: The Amazing Story of Christ Is the Answer Ministries* (Nairobi: Evangel Publishing House, 2009).

28 See, for example, Nairobi Chapel, "Our Financials," *Nairobi Chapel Ngong Road*, https://nairobichapelngongroad.org/our-financials/ (accessed

December 22, 2023); CITAM, "Financial Reports—CITAM::Christ Is The Answer Ministries," https://citam.org/financial-reports/ (accessed December 22, 2023).
29. CITAM, "CITAM Financial Report 2022" (Christ is the Answer Ministries, March 2023).
30. CITAM, "The Church and Politics Archives," *CITAM Valley Road*, https://valleyroad.citam.org/?wpv_sermons_category=the-church-and-politics (accessed December 22, 2023).
31. Mavuno Church, "About Fearless Summit- Fearless Summit," October 22, 2018, https://fearlesssummit.org/about-fearless-summit/.
32. CITAM, "CITAM Business Forum (CBF) Conference 2022," *CITAM Valley Road*, November 13, 2021, https://valleyroad.citam.org/event/citam-business-forum-cbf-conference-2022/.
33. Cephas N. Omenyo, "Charismatization of the Mainline Churches in Ghana," in *Charismatic Renewal in Africa: A Challenge for African Christianity*, ed. Mika Vahakangas and Andrew Kyomo (Nairobi: Acton Publishers, 2003), 5–26.
34. For more on this, see Dale Irvin's engagement with post-denominationalism in global cities. Dale T. Irvin, "The Church, the Urban, and the Global: Mission in an Age of Global Cities," *International Bulletin of Missionary Research* 33, no. 4 (October 2009): 177–82.
35. See a broad treatment of these issues in Paul Gifford, *Christianity, Politics and Public Life in Kenya* (London: C Hurst & Co Publishers Ltd., 2009); Gifford, *Christianity, Development and Modernity in Africa*.
36. Wariboko uses this term to reflect on the proliferation of charismatic spirituality in African cities. See Wariboko, *The Charismatic City and the Public Resurgence of Religion*.

Chapter 5

1. https://orthodox-church-kenya.org/ (accessed August 19, 2023).
2. William Black, "Offended Christians, Anti-Mission Churches and Colonial Politics: One Man's Story of the Messy Birth of the African Orthodox Church in Kenya," *Journal of Religion in Africa* 43 (2013): 261.
3. Black, "Offended Christians," 261–2.
4. Quoted in Black, "Offended Christians," 265.
5. Quoted in Black, "Offended Christians," 266.
6. Quoted in Black, "Offended Christians," 266.
7. Black, "Offended Christians," 280.
8. John N. Njoroge, "Missiological Context of the Eastern Churches," *International Review of Mission* 106, no. 2 (December 2017): 360.
9. Njoroge, "Missional Context of the Eastern Churches," 361.

10 Francis Githieya, *The Freedom of the Spirit: African Indigenous Churches in Kenya* (Atlanta: Scholars Press, 1997), 112.

11 Njoroge, "Missiological Context of the Eastern Churches," 364.

12 https://www.the-star.co.ke/news/2022-02-18-russia-ukraine-conflict-splits-kenyan-orthodox-church/ (accessed August 18, 2023).

13 Hiroko Miyokawa, "The Coptic Orthodox Mission in Kenya: An African Search for Identity and the Coptic Encounter with Africa," *Sophia Journal of Asian, African and Middle Eastern Studies,* No 39 (2021): 80.

14 Miyokawa, "The Coptic Orthodox Mission in Kenya," 81.

15 *Tewahedo* is an Amharic word meaning "united."

16 Justus Musya, *Inculturating the Eucharist in Africa* (Mauritius: Lambert Academic Publishing, 2011), 37.

17 Musya, *Inculturating the Eucharist in Africa*, 39.

18 Musya, *Inculturating the Eucharist in Africa*, 38.

19 Musya, *Inculturating the Eucharist in Africa*, 40.

20 Musya, *Inculturating the Eucharist in Africa*, 38.

21 Musya, *Inculturating the Eucharist in Africa*, 53.

22 Musya, *Inculturating the Eucharist in Africa*, 53.

23 Musya, *Inculturating the Eucharist in Africa*, 44.

24 Musya, *Inculturating the Eucharist in Africa*, 44.

25 Musya, *Inculturating the Eucharist in Africa*, 56.

26 Musya, *Inculturating the Eucharist in Africa*, 57.

27 Peter Berger, *The Many Altars of Modernity: Toward a Paradigm for Religion in a Pluralist Age* (Saarbrueken: De Gruyter, 2014), 1.

28 Berger, *The Many Altars of Modernity*, 5.

Chapter 6

1 "Kenya Data," World Bank Data, http://data.worldbank.org/country/kenya (accessed March 27, 2017).

2 For comparison's sake, North American median age is thirty-five. Europe's is forty-two.

3 United Nations, "Median Age in Africa 2000-2030," https://www.statista.com/statistics/1226158/median-age-of-the-population-of-africa/ (accessed November 3, 2023).

4 For example, African Union, *African Youth Charter* (Addis Ababa, Ethiopia: African Union, 2006); Katindi Sivi, *Youth Fact Book: Infinite Possibility or Definite Disaster?* (Institute of Economic Affairs (IEA) and Friedrich-Ebert-Stiftung (FES), 2010); United Nations, "Definition of Youth: United Nations Youth," United Nations Department of Economic and Social Affairs (UNDESA), 2013.

5   African Union, *African Youth Charter*, 3.
6   Kenya National Bureau of Statistics, *2019 Kenya Population and Housing Census: Volume III* (Nairobi: Government Printer, 2019), 501.
7   Sivi, *Youth Fact Book*.
8   Historic Mission Church leaders like David Gitari, archbishop of the Anglican Church of Kenya (1997–2002) were aware of this. David Gitari, *Troubled but Not Destroyed: Autobiography of Dr. David M. Gitari* (BookBaby, 2014), 297–8.
9   Sivi, *Youth Fact Book*.
10 For more on this, see Wanjiru M. Gitau, *Megachurch Christianity Reconsidered: Millennials and Social Change in African Perspective* (Downers Grove: IVP Academic, 2018); Kyama M. Mugambi, "Student Movements and Spiritual Identity in the Growth of Pentecostalism in Kenya," in *The Pentecostal World*, ed. Michael Wilkinson and Jörg Haustein (London: Routledge, 2023), 82–93.
11 Kenya's telephone cell phone code, which has become one of the national identity markers for Kenyan youth. One example of this collective identity as Kenyans is Boniface Mwangi's Pawa 254, which would translate to Power to the Kenyans. This is a social and political activist forum for young people founded in Nairobi. "Pawa254," https://pawa254.org/ (accessed December 23, 2023).
12 See, for example, the case of the Kenyan pop music group Sauti Sol in Akello A. Odundo, Joyce A. Akach, and Collins S. Makunda, "The Impact of Sauti Sol in The Globalization of Contemporary East African Culture," *Africa Design Review Journal* 1, no. 2 (2022): 228–33.
13 For more on this, see Mwenda Ntarangwi, *East African Hip Hop: Youth Culture and Globalization* (Urbana: University of Illinois Press, 2009).
14 Muslims are a significant minority comprising about 8 percent of the population, concentrated mostly in the coastal region. Their youth also identify with their religious identity.
15 David Arthur Samper, "Talking Sheng: The Role of a Hybrid Language in the Construction of Identity and Youth Culture in Nairobi, Kenya" (PhD, Philadelphia, University of Pennsylvania, 2002).
16 Samper, "Talking Sheng."
17 See "KNA/RN/6/6" (Kenya National Archives, 1973); "KNA/TR/8/1733" (Kenya National Archives, 1966); "KNA/NAT/ADM/3A/111" (Kenya National Archives, 1950).
18 Mokaya Bosire, "Hybrid Languages: The Case of Sheng," in *36th Annual Conference on African Linguistics* (36th Annual Conference on African Linguistics, Somerville: Cascadilla Proceedings Project, 2006), 185–93.
19 Kenya National Bureau of Statistics, *2019 Kenya Population and Housing Census: Volume IV* (Nairobi: Government Printer, 2019), 44.
20 The independence constitution envisioned Kenya as a secular state but with a recognition of the religious heritage. This was further reinforced with the new constitution enacted in 2010. *The Constitution of Kenya* (Nairobi: Government of Kenya, 2010).

21 Kenya National Bureau of Statistics, *2019 Kenya Population and Housing Census: Volume IV*, 44.

22 Other ministry organizations which serve college students are life ministry and the navigators. KSCF supports CUs and chaplaincy work in high schools.

23 For more on this, see Mugambi, "Student Movements and Spiritual Identity in the Growth of Pentecostalism in Kenya."

24 Mugambi, "Student Movements and Spiritual Identity in the Growth of Pentecostalism in Kenya."

25 Joshua Wathang'a, interview by Kyama Mugambi, December 16, 2022.

26 This unique application of kinship is the subject of a research project. See Nagel Institute grant, out of Calvin University. "Engaging African Realities," *Nagel Institute* (blog), https://nagelinstitute.org/project/engaging-african-realities/ (accessed February 25, 2023).

27 Kenya National Bureau of Statistics, *2019 Kenya Population and Housing Census: Volume IV*, 461.

28 Kenya National Bureau of Statistics, *2019 Kenya Population and Housing Census: Volume IV*, 461.

29 Kenyan urban youth are familiar with the, largely western, secularizing forces in the media which are felt around the world. Engagement of the youth in some of these discourses illustrates the level of exposure and diversity of Kenyan youth.

30 The Mavuno drama festival came out of these efforts. Mwaniki Mageria came from St. Andrews Presbyterian church and Bob Nyanja was from Parklands Baptist. Gowi Odera, interview by Kyama Mugambi, December 21, 2023.

31 *114. The Early Days- Tedd Josiah (The Play House)*, The Play House (Nairobi: CTA- Cleaning The Airwaves, 2021), https://www.youtube.com/watch?v=6eYVNjBdG58; *584. Starting Hart With Tedd Josiah- Pete Odera (The Play House)*, The Play House (Nairobi, 2021), https://www.youtube.com/watch?v=zjnPnUB4Kew.

32 *721. The Evolution Of The Kenyan Music Industry- Rufftone (The Play House)*, The Play House (Nairobi: CTA- Cleaning The Airwaves, 2021), https://www.youtube.com/watch?v=fREmEuLwyvw.

33 For more about this, see Mwenda Ntarangwi, *The Street Is My Pulpit: Hip Hop and Christianity in Kenya*, Illustrated edition (Urbana: University of Illinois Press, 2016).

34 Teddy Odira, "The Caged Bird Sings: The Impediments Faced by the Kenyan Music Industry," Available at SSRN 4424233, 2022, https://papers.ssrn.com/sol3/papers.cfm?abstract_id=4424233; Marisella Ouma, "Copyright and the Music Industry in Africa," *Journal of World Intellectual Property* 7 (2004): 919.

35 *586. How The Church Lost 5 Alive And Shut Out Hart- Pete Odera (The Play House)*, The Play House, 2021, https://www.youtube.com/watch?v=5qaEa7OIwHc.

36 *344. Kenya's First Gospel DJ & Getting On Family Radio- DJ Moz (The Play House)*, The Play House (Nairobi: CTA- Cleaning The Airwaves, 2021), https://www.youtube.com/watch?v=fleh9tY0j2o.

37 Odera, interview.
38 See, for example, "Kubash School Life- Moi Girls Isinya. Kubamba TV Youtube," https://www.youtube.com/ (accessed April 30, 2024).
39 *345. Kubamba On Family FM, Ollovar Dance Crew, Missions & Much More! - DJ Moz (The Play House)*, The Play House (Nairobi: CTA- Cleaning The Airwaves, 2021), https://www.youtube.com/watch?v=wtGWDwjaJrA.
40 In 2023, this Bible study program had 850 youth meeting weekly in various locations around the country. Moses Mathenge, interview by Kyama Mugambi, December 28, 2023.
41 *348. The First Ever TSO (Totally Sold Out) Kubamba Event- DJ Moz (The Play House)*, The Play House (Nairobi: CTA- Cleaning The Airwaves, 2021), https://www.youtube.com/watch?v=ADD13EIMcug.
42 *CTA Cleaning the Airwaves: How It Started; Richard Astar Njau. Part 5* (Nairobi: The Kenyan Entrepreneur, 2020), https://www.youtube.com/watch?v=ISGi3VLxu2Q.
43 Grace Brenda W. Okoth, "How Kenyans on Twitter Use Visuals as a Form of Political Protest," *Journal Kommunikation. Medien* (2020): 1–27; Anne Wangari Munuku, "Influence of Twitter Hashtags on the Formation of Public Opinion on Socio-Political Issues in Kenya" (PhD Thesis, JKUAT-COHRED, 2019), http://ir.jkuat.ac.ke/handle/123456789/4899.
44 Odera, interview.
45 For more of his story, see Kyama M. Mugambi, *A Spirit of Revitalization: Urban Pentecostalism in Kenya* (Waco: Baylor University Press, 2020), 195–6.
46 "All Saints' Cathedral- Nairobi, Kenya," https://www.allsaintsnairobi.org/Youth/ (accessed November 3, 2023).
47 Samuel Hall, *Youth Employment in Kenya* (Nairobi: British Council, 2017), 21.

Chapter 7

1 Kenya National Bureau of Statistics, *2019 Kenya Population and Housing Census: Volume I* (Nairobi: Government Printer, 2019), 9.
2 This is a major area of reflection for the Circle of Concerned Women Theologians which we discuss later in the chapter.
3 For a full discussion, see Gina A. Zurlo, *Women in World Christianity: Building and Sustaining a Global Movement*, 1st edition (Hoboken: Wiley-Blackwell, 2023).
4 See, for example, "Kenya Mission: CMS CRL Annual Report 1923-1924 01 42-61" (UK: Church Missionary Society, 1924), 42, 44.
5 See, for example, a women's education report from 1943 "KNA/MSS/61/2/113" (Kenya National Archives, 1943), 2.
6 S. N. Ezeanya, "Women in African Traditional Religion," *Orita: Ibadan Journal of Religious Studies* 10, no. 2 (1976): 105–21; Udobata Onunwa, "The

Paradox of Power and 'Submission' of Women in African Traditional Religion and Society," *Journal of Dharma* 13, no. 1 (1988): 31–8; Mary Nyangweso Wangila, "African Women in Traditional Religions: Illustrations from Kenya," in *Women and New and Africana Religions*, ed. Lillian Ashcraft-Eason, Darnise C. Martin, and Oyeronke Olademo (Santa Barbara: ABC-CLIO, 2010), 301–21.

7   Kyama M. Mugambi, *A Spirit of Revitalization: Urban Pentecostalism in Kenya* (Waco: Baylor University Press, 2020), 23–54.

8   See Chapter 3.

9   Nahashon W. Ndung'u, "The Akurinu Churches: With Special Reference to Their Theology" (PhD, Nairobi, University of Nairobi, 1994); Ndung'u.

10 For a book-length discussion on this, see Derek R. Peterson, *Ethnic Patriotism and the East African Revival: A History of Dissent, c.1935-1972* (New York: Cambridge University Press, 2014).

11 See also Nomatter Sande and Byron Maforo, "Pastoral Ministry from the Margins: Pastors' Wives in Apostolic Faith Mission in Zimbabwe," *Studia Historiae Ecclesiasticae* 47, no. 2 (2021): 1–14.

12 For a discussion on the Anglican church in Nairobi, see Lydia Mwaniki, *Gender and Imago Dei: Post Colonial African Reading of 1 Corinthians 11:1-16* (Borderless Press, 2018), 20–40.

13 Women in traditional society had a wider range of participation in societal affairs than what the colonial era offered. This posture continued in the decades immediately after independence. Pentecostal Christianity offered the most overt critique of this posture through the more equitable participation of women in leadership.

14 See, for example, Loreto Sisters work among European girls in Nairobi in 1926 "KNA/AV/12/321" (Kenya National Archives, 1926).

15 For example, sources from 1933 in Nairobi indicate a growing ministry to educate women for their role in Christian society. One women's day school averaged fifty to sixty daily attendees. See "Kenya Mission: CMS CRL Annual Report 1933-1934 01 63-84" (UK: Church Missionary Society, 1934), 56.

16 See "KNA/MSS/61/2/113."

17 Mwaniki, *Gender and Imago Dei: Post Colonial African Reading of 1 Corinthians 11:1-16*, 24.

18 Mwaniki, *Gender and Imago Dei: Post Colonial African Reading of 1 Corinthians 11:1-16*, 24.

19 For more on this, see Chapter 1.

20 See Pithon Kamau, "Woman's Guild," PCEA Gateway Church, https://www.pceagateway.org/woman-s-guild (accessed November 4, 2023); "Woman's Guild- Become a Member in PCEA Evergreen," http://www.pceaevergreen.org/guild.php (accessed November 4, 2023); "Mothers' Union- ACK," Https://Www.Ackenya.Org/ (blog), https://www.ackenya.org/blog-grid/board-of-mission/mothers-union/ (accessed November 4, 2023); "Mothers' Union– All Saints Cathedral Diocese," https://allsaintscathedraldiocese.org/mothers-union/ (accessed November 4, 2023).

21 Beecher held this position from 1960 to 1970 when Kenya became a separate province from East Africa and received its first archbishop, Festo Olang'.

22 "Mothers' Union - ACK."

23 Examples of this engagement are many. We name a few here: Musimbi Kanyoro, "Feminist Theology and African Culture," 1996, https://africabib.org/rec.php?RID=W00079934&DB=w; Esther Mombo, "Doing Theology from the Perspective of the Circle of Concerned African Women Theologians," *Journal of Anglican Studies* 1, no. 1 (2003): 91–103; Nyambura J. Njoroge, "A New Way of Facilitating Leadership: Lessons from African Women Theologians," *Missiology: An International Review* 33, no. 1 (2005): 29–46; Anne Nasimiyu-Wasike, "Christology and an African Woman's Experience," in *Jesus in African Christianity: Experimentation and Diversity in African Christology*, ed. J. N. K Mugambi and Laurenti Magesa (Nairobi: Acton Publishers, 1998), 123–35; Philomena Njeri Mwaura, "The Circle of Concerned African Women Theologians and Their Engagement in Public Theology: A Pathway to Development," *Pathways to African Feminism and Development, Journal of African Women's Studies Centre* 1, no. 1 (2015): 90–104; Damaris Parsitau, "Agents of Gendered Change: Empowerment, Salvation and Gendered Transformation in Urban Kenya," in *Pentecostalism and Development: Churches, NGOs and Social Change in Africa*, ed. Dena Freeman (London: Palgrave Macmillan, 2012), 203–21, https://doi.org/10.1057/9781137017253_9.

24 Rachel Angogo Kanyoro, *Groaning in Faith: African Women in the Household of God* (Nairobi: Acton Publisher, 1996), https://ixtheo.de/Record/1631939564; Rachel Nyagondwe Fiedler, *A History of the Circle of Concerned African Women Theologians 1989-2007*, 30 (Malawi: Mzuni Press, 2017); Hazel O. Ayanga, "Voice of the Voiceless: The Legacy of the Circle of Concerned African Women Theologians," *Verbum et Ecclesia* 37, no. 2 (July 8, 2016): p. 6, https://doi.org/10.4102/ve.v37i2.1580.

25 Ayanga, "Voice of the Voiceless"; Fiedler, *A History of the Circle of Concerned African Women Theologians 1989-2007*; Musimbi R. A. Kanyoro, "Threading More Beads in the Story of the Circle," in *African Women, Religion, and Health: Essays in Honor of Mercy Amba Ewudziwa Oduyoye*, ed. Isabel Apawo Phiri and Sarojini Nadar, (Eugene OR: Wipf &Stock, 2012), 19–42.

26 Wanjiru M. Gitau, *Megachurch Christianity Reconsidered: Millennials and Social Change in African Perspective* (Downers Grove: IVP Academic, 2018); Telesia Kathini Musili, "Being Grounded: Epistemological Concerns and Ethical Foundations of Feminism in Africa," in *Women Empowerment and the Feminist Agenda in Africa* (IGI Global, 2023), 76–95; Telesia Kathini Musili and Fancy Cheronoh, "Ethical Considerations for Community Based Psychosocial Accompaniment: Towards a Strengthened Mental Health Response amidst Covid-19 Pandemic," *East African Journal of Arts and Social Sciences* 4, no. 1 (2021): 1–10; Ishmael Opiyo Otieno, Stephen Akaranga Ifedha, and Edith Chamwama Kayeli, "Reflections on Divorce and Remarriage in Contemporary African Christianity," *East Africa Journal of Contemporary Research* 3, no. 1 (2023): 58–71.

27 For a fuller discussion on this, see Jason Bruner, *Living Salvation in the East African Revival in Uganda* (Rochester: University of Rochester Press, 2017); Peterson, *Ethnic Patriotism and the East African Revival*; Kevin Ward and Emma Wild-Wood, eds., *The East African Revival: History and Legacies* (Kampala, Uganda: Fountain Publishers, 2010).

28 See her autobiography Anne Jackson and Teresia Wairimu Kinyanjui, *A Cactus in the Desert: An Autobiography of Reverend Teresa Wairimu Kinyanjui*, 1st edition (Nairobi: Revival Springs Media, 2011).

29 *Word of the Year Service - January 2022* (Nairobi: FEM Family Church, 2022), https://www.youtube.com/watch?v=kJxg8Tn5n2M; *Word of the Year Service - January 2023* (Nairobi: FEM Family Church, 2023), https://www.youtube.com/watch?v=FkeSMuvTdW4.

30 Jackson and Kinyanjui, *A Cactus in the Desert: An Autobiography of Reverend Teresa Wairimu Kinyanjui*.

31 Kathy Kiuna, *Transformed Woman* (Nairobi: Jubilee Publishers, 2016).

32 See Kiuna, *Transformed Woman*; Prince Obasi-Ike and Esther Obasi-Ike, *Purpose and Promise-Driven Life* (Nairobi: Mustard Seed Publications, 2012).

33 See Travis R. Kavulla, "'Our Enemies Are God's Enemies': The Religion and Politics of Bishop Margaret Wanjiru, MP," *Journal of Eastern African Studies* 2, no. 2 (2008): 254–63; Loreen Maseno, "'The Glory Is Here!' Faith Brands and Rituals of Self-Affirmation for Social Responsibility in Kenya," *Alternation Journal*, no. 19 (2017): 252–67.

34 See JIAM, "Bishop Margaret Wanjiru," https://jiam.org/bishops-profile/ (accessed May 28, 2020).

35 Judy Wanjiru Mbugua, *See What God Has Done: Celebrating God's Faithfulness in Homecare Spiritual Fellowship* (Nairobi: Virtue Plus, 2021), 27–8.

36 Mbugua, *See What God Has Done*, 114.

37 "Pan African Christian Women Alliance Leadership Conference | Lausanne World Pulse Archives," https://lausanneworldpulse.com/lausannereports/1000/09-2008 (accessed December 29, 2023).

38 Linda Ochola-Adolwa, *Hatua* (Nairobi: Fearless Publications, 2009); "Who We Are," *Hatua Trust* (blog), https://hatuatrust.org/who-we-are/ (accessed December 26, 2023).

39 "Who We Are."

40 "Daughters of Zion," https://www.facebook.com/DozKenya/ (accessed October 15, 2015); "Queen Esthers Generation," n.d., http://queenesthersgeneration.com/qeg-mandate/.

41 It is worth noting here that Nigerian influence has found its way into churches in mass media, through the music and sermons. It is commonplace for Kenyan preachers to imitate the Nigerian accent to emphasize Christian messages, either seriously or in jest. See, for example, popular Nairobi comedian who imitates Nigerian preachers Sande Bush, whose stage name is Dr. Ofweneke. Grace Waruguru, "Dr. Ofweneke Biography and Everything about the Talented Comedian," Tuko.co.ke- *Kenya News*, July 8, 2020, https://www.tuko.co.ke/365635-dr-ofweneke-biography-real-nationality-tribe-education-life-story.html.

42 *Day 5: Occupy Conference 2023: Revival- Rev. Dr. Esther Obasike* (Nairobi: Deliverance Church Donholm, 2023), https://www.youtube.com/watch?v=Uj2WMD3kUiw; *The Birthing Position- Esther Obasike: DOZ September Edition* (Nairobi: Jubilee Christian Church, 2023), https://www.youtube.com/watch?v=HDucU1OogFw.

43 *Pastor Victoria Orenze: Ministration at DOZ Convention 2023* (Nairobi: Jubilee Christian Church, 2023), https://www.youtube.com/watch?v=n7ogxsO-SDU; *Sinach & JCC Worship Team- The Name of Jesus* (Nairobi: Jubilee Christian Church, 2020), https://www.youtube.com/watch?v=o2m8JvcErbo.

44 *Lesley Osei: DOZ Convention 2022: The Prophesied Lifting* (Nairobi: Jubilee Christian Church, 2022), https://www.youtube.com/watch?v=wpm8ys7AE2Q.

45 Kenya National Bureau of Statistics, *2019 Kenya Population and Housing Census: Volume I*, 7.

Chapter 8

1 "Sun, Light, Air," https://www.docomomo.pt/wp-content/uploads/2021/04/DocomomoJournal64_2021_YShariff.pdf (accessed November 2023).

2 https://nation.africa/kenya/life-and-style/lifestyle/where-the-devil-lives-and-rules-in-kenya-by-maverick-clergyman-531718 (accessed November 2023).

3 B. Knighton, *Religion and Politics in Kenya*. [edition unavailable] (Palgrave Macmillan US, 2009). https://www.perlego.com/book/3479376/religion-and-politics-in-kenya-essays-in-honor-of-a-meddlesome-priest-pdf (accessed 6 November 2023).

4 Paul Gifford, *Christianity, Politics and Public Life in Kenya* (London: Hurst, 2009), 241.

5 Galia Sabar, *Church, State and Society in Kenya* (London: Taylor and Francis, 2012), ch 3, section 1, para 6.

6 Sabar, *Church, State and Society*, ch 3, section 1, para 15.

7 Sabar, *Church, State and Society*, ch 3, section 1, para 13.

8 Sabar, *Church, State and Society*, ch 3, section 1, para 17.

9 Sabar, *Church, State and Society*, ch 3, section 2 para 9.

10 John Gatu, *Fan into Flame* (Nairobi: Moran, 2016), 189.

11 Gatu, *Flame*, 192.

12 Gatu, *Flame*, 200.

13 Gatu, *Flame*, 200.

14 Wanjiru Gitau, "The Transformation of a Young Continent: Dimensions of Africa Rising," *Contemporania* 9, no. 2 (May–August 2019): 406.

15 John Lonsdale, "Compromised Critics," in *Religion and Politics in Kenya*, ed. Ben Knighton (New York: Palgrave Macmillan, 2009), 74.

16 Lonsdale, "Compromised Critics," 107.

17. John Karanja, "Evangelical Attitudes towards Democracy in Kenya," in *Evangelical Christianity and Democracy in Africa,* ed. T. O. Ranger (Oxford: Oxford University Press, 2008), ch 2, section 11, paragraphs 3–4.
18. Oliver Kisaka, https://www.cnn.com/2010/WORLD/africa/08/04/kenya.constitution.churches/index.html (accessed November 14, 2023).
19. Oliver Kisaka, https://www.cnn.com/2010/WORLD/africa/08/04/kenya.constitution.churches/index.html (accessed November 14 2023).
20. Oliver Kisaka, https://www.cnn.com/2010/WORLD/africa/08/04/kenya.constitution.churches/index.html (accessed November 14, 2023).
21. "Cooperation and Confrontation," https://www.csis.org/analysis/kenya-cooperation-co-optation-and-confrontation (accessed November 15, 2023).
22. Kenya Gazette Supplement, Acts 2013, Act No. 42, Election Campaign Financing Act, 2013, December 27, 2013.
23. Doreen Ajiambo, "Kenyan Archbishop Denies Catholic Church Accepts Funds from Corrupt Politicians," *National Catholic Reporter,* March 11, 2019, https://www.ncronline.org/news/kenyan-Archbishop-denies-catholic-church-accepts-funds-corrupt-politicians (accessed November 16, 2023).
24. Sakaja Arthur Johnson provides a welcome relief to the story of political exploitation of the churches. Elected in 2022, Sakaja is open and sincere about his Christian faith, and his alignment with the AIC, in contrast with previous mayors and governors of the city. His campaign trail often included visits to churches, and his rhetoric reflected sensitivity to Christian themes. He also identified with the youth in a way that acknowledged this previously marginalized yet significant group.
25. Allan Muchiri, "Political Theology in the Making: The Responses of Kenyan Churches to Large Cash Donations by Politicians (2018-2022)" (unpublished PhD seminar paper, Africa International University, 2023), 5.
26. "Chinese Christians Find God and Religious Refuge in Kenya," CNN, https://www.cnn.com/2019/04/28/asia/china-christians-africa-kenya-intl/index.html (accessed November 17, 2023).
27. Joanne M. Moyer, A. John Sinclair, and Harry Spaling, "Working for God and Sustainability: The Activities of Faith-based Organizations in Kenya," *Voluntas, Internal Society for Third-Sector Research,* December 6, 2011, https://link.springer.com/article/10.1007/s11266-011-9245-x (accessed November 17, 2023).
28. "Climate Summit," https://laudatosimovement.org/news/african-climate-week-and-africa-climate-summits-statement-of-faith/ (accessed November 17, 2023).
29. "Kenyan Cult," https://www.cnn.com/2023/06/19/africa/kenya-starvation-cult-explained-intl-cmd/index.html (accessed November 17, 2023).
30. "Kenyans in Shock," https://religionunplugged.com/news/2023/5/1/kenyans-in-shock-demand-regulation-of-churches-as-83-dead-in-cult-inspired-fasting (accessed November 17, 2023).
31. "The Church in Politics," Church and Politics Summit, 2021, 9.
32. "Boniface Mwangi," https://risenetworks.org/yotw/youth-of-the-month-boniface-mwangi/ (accessed November 16, 2023).

33. "Truth will never die," https://thegroundtruthproject.org/truth-will-never-die-death-threats-for-kenyan-activist/ (accessed November 16, 2023).
34. "Boniface Mwangi," https://twitter.com/bonifacemwangi/status/1380041842318839809 (accessed November 17, 2023).
35. Anders Ese and Kristen Ese, *The City Makers of Nairobi* (London: Taylor and Francis, 2020), Epilogue, 23.

Chapter 9

1. "Yellow is the Color of Love for Kenyan Congregations," *Christian Century*, September 28, 2016.
2. https://kenya.un.org/en/sdgs (accessed April 29, 2024).
3. Kevin Dunn and Pierre Englebert, *Inside African Politics*, 2nd ed. (London: Lynne Rienner Publishers, 2019), 107.
4. Kenya National Bureau of Statistics, *2019 Kenya Population and Housing Census: Volume IV* (Nairobi: Government Printer, 2019), 422.
5. Kenya National Bureau of Statistics, *2019 Kenya Population and Housing Census: Volume IV*, 422.
6. Anne Cussac And Nathalie Goms, "Muslims in Nairobi: From a Feeling of Marginalization to a Desire for Political Recognition," in *Nairobi Today: The Paradox of a Fragmented City*, ed. Helene Charton-Bigot and Deyssi Rodriguez-Torres (Dar es Salaam: Mkuki na Nyota Publishers, 2006), 254.
7. Cussac and Goms, "Muslims in Nairobi," 254–5.
8. Dunn and Englebert, *Inside African Politics*, 107.
9. Cussac and Goms, "Muslims in Nairobi," 226, 256–7, 258.
10. Cussac and Goms, "Muslims in Nairobi," 226, 263.
11. Cussac and Goms, "Muslims in Nairobi," 259.
12. Cussac and Goms, "Muslims in Nairobi," 260.
13. Lawrence Oseje, "Muslim Perception of Christians in History and Its Effects on Current Christian-Muslim Relations in Kenya," *Impact: Journal of Transformation* 4, no. 2 (2021): 57. ISSN 2617-5576.
14. Cussac and Goms, "Muslims in Nairobi," 253.
15. William Patterson, "Islamic Radicalization in Kenya," *JFQ* 78 (3rd Quarter 2015): 18.
16. Hassan Ndzovu, *Muslims in Kenyan Politics: Political Involvement, Marginalization, and Minority Status* (Evanston: Northwestern University Press, 2014), 69.
17. Patterson, "Islamic Radicalization in Kenya," 18.
18. Cussac and Goms, "Muslims in Nairobi," 261–2.
19. Ndzovu, *Muslims in Kenyan Politics*, 97.
20. Dunn and Englebert, *Inside African Politics*, 109.

NOTES

21 Patterson, "Islamic Radicalization in Kenya," 21.
22 Ndzovu, *Muslims in Kenyan Politics*, 103.
23 Hassan Ndzovu, "Muslims and Party Politics and Electoral Campaigns in Kenya" (Institute for the Study of Islamic Thought on Africa (ISITA), Working paper No 09-001 March 2009), 2.
24 Dunn and Englebert, *Inside African Politics*, 114.
25 Cussac and Goms, "Muslims in Nairobi," 264.
26 In B. Knighton, *Religion and Politics in Kenya* (Palgrave Macmillan, 2009), 172.
27 Cussac and Goms, "Muslims in Nairobi," 266–7.
28 Patterson, "Islamic Radicalization in Kenya," 20.
29 Patterson, "Islamic Radicalization in Kenya," 19.
30 Ngala Chome, "From Islamic Reform to Muslim Activism: The Evolution of an Islamist Ideology in Kenya," *African Affairs* 118, no. 472: 536.
31 Patterson, "Islamic Radicalization in Kenya," 20. Patterson further noted that "In 2012, Kenya passed a tough antiterrorism bill called the Prevention of Terrorism Act 2012. Though the passage of this bill was not as controversial as some earlier iterations, it still elicited criticism from Kenyan human rights and Muslim groups." Patterson, "Islamic Radicalization in Kenya," 17.
32 Patterson, "Islamic Radicalization in Kenya," 16.
33 Oseje, "Muslim Perception of Christians in History and its Effects on Current Christian-Muslim Relations in Kenya," 58–9.
34 David Barrett et al., ed., *Kenya Churches Handbook* (Nairobi: Evangel Press, 1973).
35 See Michael Brislen, "Christian Perceptions of Islam in Kenya–As Expressed in Written Sources from 1998 to 2010" (Unpublished diss., University of Birmingham, 2013), 148.
36 Brislen, "Christian Perceptions of Islam in Kenya," 149.
37 Brislen, "Christian Perceptions of Islam in Kenya," 150.
38 Brislen, "Christian Perceptions of Islam in Kenya," 169.
39 Brislen, "Christian Perceptions of Islam in Kenya," 193.
40 Brislen, "Christian Perceptions of Islam in Kenya," 232.
41 Brislen, "Christian Perceptions of Islam in Kenya," 241.
42 Brislen, "Christian Perceptions of Islam in Kenya," 251.
43 [IRCK-2020-2024-STRATEGIC-PLAN https://interreligiouscouncil.or.ke/ova_doc/irck-strategic-plan-2020-2024/].
44 https://interfaithreflectionshome.blog/2022/03/24/faith-leaders-sign-a-declaration-to-fight-modern-slavery/ (accessed April 25, 2024).
45 https://interfaithreflectionshome.blog/2022/03/24/faith-leaders-sign-a-declaration-to-fight-modern-slavery/ (accessed April 25, 2024).
46 A Discussion with Francis Kuria, "Executive Director of Inter-Religious Council of Kenya," https://berkleycenter.georgetown.edu/interviews/a

-discussion-with-francis-kuria-executive-director-of-inter-religious-council-of-kenya (accessed April 25, 2024).
47 Jeremiah 29:7.
48 Robert Dowd, "Christianity, Islam, and Political Culture: Lessons from Sub-Saharan Africa in Comparative Perspective," (unpublished paper presented to American Political Science Association, August 2003), 14.
49 Robert Dowd, *Christianity, Islam and Liberal Democracy: Lessons from sub-Saharan Africa* (Oxford: Oxford University Press, 2015).

Conclusion

1 Aga Khan is the title of the supreme leader of the Ismailia sect of Islam that has important investments in the city of Nairobi. Ismailia's own several buildings in Nairobi. They also have a mosque and community center on the northern end of Moi Avenue, one of the main streets in the CBD. They also own and run schools in the Parklands area. The Aga Khan University Hospital is one of very few private institutions that offer courses in the medical sciences.
2 Nairobi's motto was changed at independence from Latin to Kiswahili, and it now reads *Ushauri Kwa Uaminifu* (Honest counsel).
3 The central shield had quartered green and gold colors. The green represented the agricultural wealth of the colony. The gold represented the mineral wealth of the nation. The central motif commemorated a stylized image of water, "representing the swamp that once inundated the Nairobi area and from which it received its Masai name, 'the place of cool waters.'" James Smart, *Nairobi: A Jubilee History 1900-1950* (Nairobi: The East African Standard, 1950), 104.
4 Smart, *Nairobi*, 104.
5 Smart, *Nairobi*, 104.
6 Smart, *Nairobi*, 104.
7 See Adriaan Van Klinken, *Kenyan, Christian, Queer* (Park, PA: Penn State University Press, 2021).
8 This area of ministry has attracted several academic studies in Kenyan universities Nancy Wagi Maina Nyambura, "Perceptions of Deaf Children and Their Parents on Spiritual Nurture Experiences at Church: A Case of Lugha Ishara Centre, Nairobi County" (PhD Thesis, Nairobi, Kenya, Daystar University School of Applied Human Sciences, 2022); Rachel CW Koigi, "Challenges in Translating and Transcribing Kenyan Sign Language The Case of Immanuel Christian School for the Deaf" (PhD Thesis, Nairobi, Kenya, Africa International University, 2014); Trajan Besigye, "Caring for People with Disabilities: The Christian Community in Nairobi" (PhD Thesis, Nairobi, Kenya, University of Nairobi, 2002).

Bibliography

Books

Anderson, Allan H. *Spirit-Filled World: Religious Dis/Continuity in African Pentecostalism*. Switzerland: Springer, 2018.
Barrett, David. *Schism and Renewal in Africa: An Analysis of Six Thousand Contemporary Religious Movements*. Nairobi: Oxford, 1968.
Barrett, David, George Mambo, Janice McLaughlin, and Malcolm McVeigh, eds. *Kenya Churches Handbook*. Nairobi: Evangel, 1974.
Berger, Peter. *De-secularization of the World*. Grand Rapids: Eerdmans, 1999.
Berger, Peter. *The Many Altars of Modernity: Toward a Paradigm for Religion in a Pluralist Age*. Boston: De Gruyter, 2014.
Bruner, Jason. *Living Salvation in the East African Revival in Uganda*. Rochester: University of Rochester Press, 2017.
Cox, Harvey. *The Secular City: Secularization and Urbanization in Theological Perspective*. Revised edition. Princeton: Princeton University Press, 2013.
Cussac, Anne and Nathalie Goms. "Muslims in Nairobi: From a Feeling of Marginalization to a Desire for Political Recognition." In *Nairobi Today: The Paradox of a Fragmented City*, edited by Helene Charton-Bigot and Deyssi Rodriguez-Torres, 269–304. Dar es Salaam: Mkuki na Nyota Publishers, 2006.
Dowd, Robert. *Christianity, Islam and Liberal Democracy: Lessons from Sub-Saharan Africa*. Oxford: Oxford University press, 2015.
Dunn, Kevin and Pierre Englebert. *Inside African Politics*. 2nd edition. London: Lynne Rienner Publishers, 2019.
Ese, Anders and Kristin Ese. *The City Makers of Nairobi: An African Urban History*. London: Routledge, 2020.
Fackler, P. Mark, Levi Obonyo, Mitchell Terpstra, and Emmanuel Okaalet. "Media and Post-Election Violence in Kenya." In *The Handbook of Global Communication and Media Ethics*, edited by Robert S. Fortner and P. Mark Fackler, 626–54. Malden: Wiley-Blackwell, 2011.
Fiedler, Rachel Nyagondwe. *A History of the Circle of Concerned African Women Theologians 1989–2007*, 30. Mzuzu, Malawi: Mzuni Press, 2017.
Gatu, John G. *Fan into Flame: An Autobiography*. Nairobi: Moran, 2017.
Gifford, Paul. *Christianity, Development and Modernity in Africa*. London: C Hurst & Co Publishers Ltd., 2015.
Gifford, Paul. *Christianity, Politics and Public Life in Kenya*. London: Hurst, 2009.
Gitari, David. *Troubled but Not Destroyed: Autobiography of Dr. David M. Gitari*. Pennsauken: BookBaby, 2014.
Gitau, Wanjiru M. *Megachurch Christianity Reconsidered: Millennials and Social Change in African Perspective*. Downers Grove: IVP Academic, 2018.
Githieya, Francis. *The Freedom of the Spirit, African Indigenous Churches in Kenya*. New York: Oxford University Press, 1997.

Gogan, Cothrai. *H.G.M., Holy Ghost Mission: The Spiritans in Nairobi, 1899–1999*. Limuru: Kolbe Press, 1998. http://archive.org/details/hgmholyghostmiss00goga.

Gray, Richard. *Black Christians, White Missionaries*. New Haven: Yale, 1990.

Hall, Samuel. *Youth Employment in Kenya*. Nairobi: British Council, 2017.

Jackson, Anne and Teresia Wairimu Kinyanjui. *A Cactus in the Desert: An Autobiography of Reverend Teresa Wairimu Kinyanjui*. 1st edition. Nairobi: Revival Springs Media, 2011.

Jenkins, Philip. *The Next Christendom: The Coming of Global Christianity*. Oxford and New York: Oxford University Press, 2011.

Johnson, Todd M. and Gina A. Zurlo, eds. *World Christian Encyclopedia*. 3rd edition. Edinburgh: Edinburgh University Press, 2020.

Kalu, Ogbu. *African Pentecostalism: An Introduction*. Oxford: Oxford University Press, 2008.

Kanyoro, Musimbi. "Feminist Theology and African Culture." In *Violence Against Women: Reflections by Kenyan Women Theologians*, edited by Grace Wamue and Mary N. Getui, 4–12. Nairobi: Acton Publishers, 1996.

Kanyoro, Musimbi. "Threading More Beads in the Story of the Circle." In *African Women, Religion, and Health: Essays in Honor of Mercy Amba Ewudziwa Oduyoye*, edited by Isabel Apawo Phiri and Sarojini Nadar, 19. Wipf & Stock Publishers, 2012.

Kanyoro, Rachel Angogo. *Groaning in Faith: African Women in the Household of God*. Nairobi: Acton Publishers, 1996.

Karanja, John. "Evangelical Attitudes towards Democracy in Kenya." In *Evangelical Christianity and Democracy in Africa*, edited by T. O. Ranger, 1220–617. Oxford: Oxford University Press, 2008.

Kiuna, Allan. *Anointed for the Marketplace*. Nairobi: Aura Publishers, 2012.

Kiuna, Kathy. *Transformed Woman*. Nairobi: Jubilee Publishers, 2016.

Kiuna, Kathy and Allan Kiuna. *Appointment with Destiny: A Moving Testimony of God's Love and Faithfulness*. Nairobi: Jubilee Publishers, 2006.

Knighton, Ben, ed. *Religion and Politics in Kenya*. New York: Palgrave Macmillan, 2009.

Kollman, Paul and Cynthia Toms Smedley. *Understanding World Christianity: Eastern Africa*. Minneapolis: Fortress, 2018.

Koonammakkal, Thomas. *Elements of Syro-Malabar History*. Kuravilangad: Beth Aprem Nazrani Dayra, 2012.

Lindenfeld, David. *World Christianity, and Indigenous Experience*. New York: Cambridge University Press, 2021.

Lonsdale, John. "Compromised Critics." In *Religion and Politics in Kenya*, edited by Ben Knighton, 57–94. New York: Palgrave Macmillan, 2009.

Magesa, Laurenti. *African Religion in the Dialogue Debate: From Intolerance to Coexistence*. Vol. 3. Munster: LIT Verlag Münster, 2010.

Magesa, Laurenti. *What Is Not Sacred? African Spirituality*. Nairobi: Acton Publishers, 2014.

Mbugua, Judy Wanjiru. *See What God Has Done: Celebrating God's Faithfulness in Homecare Spiritual Fellowship*. Nairobi: Virtue Plus, 2021.

McLeod, Hugh and Werner Ustorf. *The Decline of Christendom in Western Europe, 1750–2000*. Cambridge: Cambridge University Press, 2003.

Mejia, Rodrigo. *The Conscience of Society: The Social Teaching of the Catholic Bishops of Kenya: 1960–1995*. Nairobi: Paulines Publications Africa, 1995.

Miller, Donald E. and Tetsunao Yamamori. *Global Pentecostalism: The New Face of Christian Social Engagement*. First Edition, Includes DVD edition. Berkeley: University of California Press, 2007.

Morakinyo, Niyi. *The Seven Professional Nations (Full Version): Reconciling Them Back To God.* Nairobi: The Joshua Generation Trust, 2013.

Mugambi, J. N. Kanyua and Laurenti Magesa, eds. *Jesus in African Christianity: Experimentation and Diversity in African Christology.* Nairobi: Acton Publishers, 1998.

Mugambi, J. N. Kanyua and Laurenti Magesa, eds. *The Church in African Christianity: Innovative Essays in Ecclesiology.* African Challenge Series, no. 1. Nairobi: Initiatives, 1990.

Mugambi, Justus. *Five Decades of God's Faithfulness: The Amazing Story of Christ Is the Answer Ministries.* Nairobi: Evangel Publishing House, 2009.

Mugambi, Kyama M. *A Spirit of Revitalization: Urban Pentecostalism in Kenya.* Waco: Baylor University Press, 2020.

Mugambi, Kyama M. "Student Movements and Spiritual Identity in the Growth of Pentecostalism in Kenya." In *The Pentecostal World*, edited by Michael Wilkinson and Jörg Haustein, 82–93. London: Routledge, 2023.

Musili, Telesia Kathini. "Being Grounded: Epistemological Concerns and Ethical Foundations of Feminism in Africa." In *Women Empowerment and the Feminist Agenda in Africa*, edited by Maxwell Constantine Chando Musingafi, and Chipo Hungwe, 76–95. Hershey, PA: IGI Global, 2023.

Musya, Justus. *Inculturating the Eucharist in Africa.* Mauritius: Lambert Academic Publishing, 2011.

Mwaniki, Lydia. *Gender and Imago Dei: Post Colonial African Reading of 1 Corinthians 11:1-16.* Alameda: Borderless Press, 2018.

Nasimiyu-Wasike, Anne. "Christology and an African Woman's Experience." In *Jesus in African Christianity: Experimentation and Diversity in African Christology*, edited by J. N. Kanyua Mugambi and Laurenti Magesa, 123–35. Nairobi: Acton Publishers, 1998.

Ndung'u, Nahashon W. *Akurinu Churches in Kenya: Background, Development and Theology.* Nairobi: University of Nairobi Press, 2019.

Ndzovu, Hassan. *Muslims in Kenyan Politics: Political Involvement, Marginalization, and Minority Status.* Evanston: Northwestern University Press, 2014.

Ntarangwi, Mwenda. *East African Hip Hop: Youth Culture and Globalization.* Urbana: University of Illinois Press, 2009.

Ntarangwi, Mwenda. *The Street Is My Pulpit: Hip Hop and Christianity in Kenya.* Illustrated edition. Urbana: University of Illinois Press, 2016.

Nyamiti, Charles. "African Christologies Today." In *Jesus in African Christianity: Experimentation and Diversity in African Christology*, edited by J. N. K Mugambi and Laurenti Magesa, 17–40. Nairobi: Acton Publishers, 1998.

Nyamiti, Charles. *Christ as Our Ancestor: Christology from an African Perspective.* 11. Gweru: Mambo Press, 1984.Obasi-Ike, Prince and Esther Obasi-Ike. *Purpose and Promise-Driven Life.* Nairobi: Mustard Seed Publications, 2012.

Ochola-Adolwa, Linda. *Hatua.* Nairobi: Fearless Publications, 2009.

Omenyo, Cephas N. "Charismatization of the Mainline Churches in Ghana." In *Charismatic Renewal in Africa: A Challenge for African Christianity*, edited by Mika Vahakangas and Andrew Kyomo, 5–26. Nairobi: Acton Publishers, 2003.

Orobator, Agbonkhianmeghe E. "Small Christian Communities as a New Way of Becoming Church: Practice, Progress and Prospects." In *Small Christian Communities: Fresh Stimulus for a Forward-Looking Church*, edited by Klaus Krämer and Klaus Vellguth, 113–25. Phillipines: Claretian Communications Foundation, 2013.

Parsitau, Damaris. "Agents of Gendered Change: Empowerment, Salvation and Gendered Transformation in Urban Kenya." In *Pentecostalism and Development: Churches, NGOs and Social Change in Africa*, edited by Dena Freeman, 203–21. London: Palgrave Macmillan, 2012. https://doi.org/10.1057/9781137017253_9.
Peterson, Derek R. *Ethnic Patriotism and the East African Revival: A History of Dissent, c.1935–1972*. New York: Cambridge University Press, 2014.
Sabar, Galia. *Church, State and Society in Kenya*. London: Taylor and Francis, 2012.
Sivi, Katindi. *Youth Fact Book: Infinite Possibility or Definite Disaster?* Nairobi: Institute of Economic Affairs (IEA) and Friedrich-Ebert-Stiftung (FES), 2010.
Smart, James. *Nairobi: A Jubilee History 1900–1950*. Nairobi: The East African Standard, 1950.
Strachan, H. *The First World War in Africa*. Oxford: Oxford University Press, 2004.
Van Klinken, Adriaan. *Kenyan, Christian, Queer*. Pennsylvania: Penn State University Press, 2021.
Wangila, Mary Nyangweso. "African Women in Traditional Religions: Illustrations from Kenya." In *Women and New and Africana Religions*, edited by Lillian Ashcraft-Eason, Darnise C. Martin, and Oyeronke Olademo, 301–21. Santa Barbara: ABC-CLIO, 2010.
Ward, Kevin and Emma Wild-Wood, eds. *The East African Revival: History and Legacies*. Kampala, Uganda: Fountain Publishers, 2010.
Wariboko, N. *The Charismatic City and the Public Resurgence of Religion: A Pentecostal Social Ethics of Cosmopolitan Urban Life*. 2014 edition. New York: Palgrave Macmillan, 2014.
Zurlo, Gina A. *Women in World Christianity: Building and Sustaining a Global Movement*. 1st edition. Hoboken: Wiley-Blackwell, 2023.

Journals and Journal Articles

Ayanga, Hazel O. "Voice of the Voiceless: The Legacy of the Circle of Concerned African Women Theologians." *Verbum et Ecclesia* 37, no. 2 (July 8, 2016): 6. https://doi.org/10.4102/ve.v37i2.1580.
Barron, Joshua Robert. "Is the Prosperity Gospel, Gospel? An Examination of the Prosperity and Productivity Gospels in African Christianity." *Conspectus: The Journal of the South African Theological Seminary* 33, no. 1 (2022): 88–103.
Berger, Peter. "Secularism in Retreat." *The National Interest*, no. 46 (Winter 1996/97): 3–12.
Berman, Eli, Laurence R. Iannaccone, and Giuseppe Ragusa. "From Empty Pews to Empty Cradles: Fertility Decline among European Catholics." *Journal of Demographic Economics* 84, no. 2 (2018): 149–87.
Black, William. "Offended Christians, Anti-Mission Churches and Colonial Politics: One Man's Story of the Messy Birth of the African Orthodox Church in Kenya." *Journal of Religion in Africa* 43 (2013): 261–96.
Bosire, Mokaya. "Hybrid Languages: The Case of Sheng." In *36th Annual Conference on African Linguistics*, 185–93. Somerville: Cascadilla Proceedings Project, 2006.
Ezeanya, S. N. "Women in African Traditional Religion." *Orita: Ibadan Journal of Religious Studies* 10, no. 2 (1976): 105–21.

Gitau, Wanjiru M. "The Transformation of a Young Continent: Dimensions of Africa Rising." *Contemporania* 9, no. 2 (May–August 2019): 401–429.

Griffin, Beth. "Kenyan Bishops Keep up Campaign against Vaccine." *National Catholic Reporter* 51, no. 12 (2015): 6–7.

Healey, Joseph. "Small Christian Communities (SCCs) Promote Family Ministry in Eastern Africa." *Hekima Review*, 2013.

Hearn, Julie. "The 'Invisible' NGO: US Evangelical Missions in Kenya." *Journal of Religion in Africa* 32, no. 1 (2002): 32–60. http://www.jstor.org/stable/1581671 (accessed July 1, 2022).

Irvin, Dale T. "The Church, the Urban, and the Global: Mission in an Age of Global Cities." *International Bulletin of Missionary Research* 33, no. 4 (October 2009): 177–82.

Kavulla, Travis R. "'Our Enemies Are God's Enemies': The Religion and Politics of Bishop Margaret Wanjiru, MP." *Journal of Eastern African Studies* 2, no. 2 (2008): 254–63.

Maseno, Loreen. "The Glory Is Here! Faith Brands and Rituals of Self-Affirmation for Social Responsibility in Kenya." *Alternation Journal* 19 (2017): 252–67.

Miyokawa, Hiroko. "The Coptic Orthodox Mission in Kenya: An African Search for Identity and the Coptic Encounter with Africa." *Sophia Journal of Asian, African and Middle Eastern Studies* 39 (2021): 69–86.

Mombo, Esther. "Doing Theology from the Perspective of the Circle of Concerned African Women Theologians." *Journal of Anglican Studies* 1, no. 1 (2003): 91–103.

Moyer, Joanne M., A. John Sinclair, and Harry Spaling. "Working for God and Sustainability: The Activities of Faith-based Organizations in Kenya." *Voluntas: International Journal of Voluntary and Nonprofit Organizations* 23, no. 4 (2012), 959–99.

Musili, Telesia Kathini and Fancy Cheronoh. "Ethical Considerations for Community Based Psychosocial Accompaniment: Towards a Strengthened Mental Health Response amidst Covid-19 Pandemic." *East African Journal of Arts and Social Sciences* 4, no. 1 (2021): 1–10.

Mwaura, Philomena Njeri. "The Circle of Concerned African Women Theologians and Their Engagement in Public Theology: A Pathway to Development." *Pathways to African Feminism and Development, Journal of African Women's Studies Centre* 1, no. 1 (2015): 90–104.

Mwaura, Philomena Njeri. "Paul David Zakayo Kivuli and the Founding of the Africa Israel Church Nineveh." *Journal of African Christian Biography* 3, no. 4 (October 2018): 6–12.

Ndingi Mwana'a Nzeki, R. S. "People for Peace in Africa." *Wajibu* 5, no. 1 (1990): 2–3.

Nichols, Bruce. "Nairobi 1975: A Crisis of Faith for the WCC." *Themelios* 1, no. 3. https://www.thegospelcoalition.org/themelios/article/nairobi-1975-a-crisis-of-faith-for-the-wcc/.

Njeru, Ian, Yusuf Ajack, Charles Muitherero, Dickens Onyango, Johnny Musyoka, Iheoma Onuekusi, Jackson Kioko, Nicholas Muraguri, and Robert Davis. "Did the Call for Boycott by the Catholic Bishops Affect the Polio Vaccination Coverage in Kenya in 2015? A Cross-Sectional Study." *Pan African Medical Journal* 24, no. 1 (2016): 120. https://doi.org/10.11604/pamj.2016.24.120.8986.

Njoroge, John. "Missiological Context of the Eastern Churches." *International Review of Mission* 106, no. 2 (December 2017): 356–68.

Njoroge, Nyambura J. "A New Way of Facilitating Leadership: Lessons from African Women Theologians." *Missiology: An International Review* 33, no. 1 (2005): 29–46.

Odira, Teddy. "The Caged Bird Sings: The Impediments Faced by the Kenyan Music Industry." *Social Science Research Network*, 2022. Available online: https://papers.ssrn.com/sol3/papers.cfm?abstract_id=4424233.

Odundo, Akello A., Joyce A. Akach and Collins S. Makunda. "The Impact of Sauti Sol in The Globalization of Contemporary East African Culture." *Africa Design Review Journal* 1, no. 2 (2022).

Okoth, Grace Brenda W. "How Kenyans on Twitter Use Visuals as a Form of Political Protest." *Journal Kommunikation. Medien*, no. 12 (2020): 1–27.

Onunwa, Udobata. "The Paradox of Power and 'Submission' of Women in African Traditional Religion and Society." *Journal of Dharma* 13, no. 1 (1988): 31–8.

Otieno, Ishmael Opiyo, Stephen Akaranga Ifedha, and Edith Chamwama Kayeli. "Reflections on Divorce and Remarriage in Contemporary African Christianity." *East Africa Journal of Contemporary Research* 3, no. 1 (2023): 58–71.

Ouma, Marisella. "Copyright and the Music Industry in Africa." *Journal of World Intellectual Property* 7 (2004): 919.

Patterson, William. "Islamic Radicalization in Kenya." *JFQ* 78 (3rd Quarter 2015): 16–23.

Sande, Nomatter and Byron Maforo. "Pastoral Ministry from the Margins: Pastors' Wives in Apostolic Faith Mission in Zimbabwe." *Studia Historiae Ecclesiasticae* 47, no. 2 (2021): 1–14.

Shariff, Yasmin. "Modern Movement Houses in the Colonial Capital City of Nairobi." *Docomomo Journal* no. 62 (2021): 80–3. Available online: https://www.docomomo.pt/wp-content/uploads/2021/04/DocomomoJournal64_2021_YShariff.pdf (accessed November 2023).Shaw, Ian. "What Has Glasgow to Do with Nairobi? The Churches and Rapid Urban Growth in Twentieth-Century Nairobi: A Comparison with Nineteenth-Century Glasgow." *Studies in World Christianity* 20, no. 2 (2014): 166–86.

Waihenya, Waithaka and Ndikaru wa Teresia. "A Voice Unstilled: Archbishop Ndingi Mwana A Nzeki." *Journal of Hekima College*, no. 41 (2009): 172–3.

Online Articles

Ajiambo, Doreen. "Kenyan Archbishop Denies Catholic Church Accepts Funds from Corrupt Politicians," *National Catholic Reporter*, March 11, 2019. https://www.ncronline.org/news/kenyan-Archbishop-denies-catholic-church-accepts-funds-corrupt-politicians (accessed November 16, 2023).

Berkley Center. "A Discussion with Francis Kuria, Executive Director of Inter-Religious Council of Kenya." https://berkleycenter.georgetown.edu/interviews/a-discussion-with-francis-kuria-executive-director-of-inter-religious-council-of-kenya (accessed April 25, 2024).

CNN. "Muslim and Christian Youths Clash in Kenyan Capital." December 1, 2000. https://www.cnn.com/2000/WORLD/africa/12/01/kenya.riot.reut/index.html (accessed December 8, 2023).

Douglas Grant, Kevin. "'Truth Will Never Die' – More Death Threats for a Kenyan Activist." https://thegroundtruthproject.org/truth-will-never-die-death-threats-for-kenyan-activist/ (accessed November 16, 2023).

Feleke, Bethlehem and McKenzie, David. "How Faith Turned Deadly for Kenyan Cult Followers Who Chose Starvation as Path to Salvation." https://www.cnn.com/2023/06/19/africa/kenya-starvation-cult-explained-intl-cmd/index.html (accessed November 17, 2023).

Graves, Dan. "To Better Meet African Needs, Ajuoga Created a Home-grown Church." https://christianhistoryinstitute.org/it-happened-today/1/8 (accessed August 28, 2023).

Jenkins, Philip. "Christianity's Explosive Growth in Kenya." *Christian Century*. https://www.christiancentury.org/article/notes-global-church/christianity-s-explosive-growth-kenya (accessed July 1, 2022).

Kamau, Pithon. "Woman's Guild." *PCEA Gateway Church*. https://www.pceagateway.org/woman-s-guild (accessed November 4, 2023).

Marsh, Jenni. "Chinese Christians Find God and Religious Refuge in Kenya." *CNN*. https://www.cnn.com/2019/04/28/asia/china-christians-africa-kenya-intl/index.html (accessed November 17, 2023).

Muriuki, Muriithi. "Kenya: Torched Catholic Church Reopened." *The Nation*, March 31, 2003, sec. News. https://allafrica.com/stories/200303310163.html.

Laudato Si' Movement. "African Climate Week and Africa Climate Summit's Statement of Faith." https://laudatosimovement.org/news/african-climate-week-and-africa-climate-summits-statement-of-faith/ (accessed November 17, 2023).

Nagel Institute. "Engaging African Realities." https://nagelinstitute.org/project/engaging-african-realities/ (accessed February 25, 2023).

Nairobi Chapel. "Our Financials." *Nairobi Chapel Ngong Road*. https://nairobichapelngongroad.org/our-financials/ (accessed December 22, 2023).

Nation. "Where the Devil Lives and Rules in Kenya, by Maverick Clergyman." https://nation.africa/kenya/life-and-style/lifestyle/where-the-devil-lives-and-rules-in-kenya-by-maverick-clergyman-531718 (accessed November 2023).

Nzwili, Fredrick. "Some Kenyan Catholic Bishops Urge Caution on COVID-19 Clinical Trials." *Crux* (blog), May 7, 2020. https://cruxnow.com/church-in-africa/2020/05/some-kenyan-catholic-bishops-urge-caution-on-covid-19-clinical-trials/.

Nzwili, Fredrick. "Yellow is the Color of Love for Kenyan Congregations." *Christian Century*, September 28, 2016. https://www.christiancentury.org/article/2016-08/yellow-color-love-kenyan-congregations.

Osanjo, Tom. "Kenyans in Shock, Demand Regulation of Churches as 98 Dead in Cult Inspired Fasting." https://religionunplugged.com/news/2023/5/1/kenyans-in-shock-demand-regulation-of-churches-as-83-dead-in-cult-inspired-fasting (accessed November 17, 2023).

Osen, Gordon. "Russia-Ukraine Conflict Splits Kenyan Orthodox Church." https://www.the-star.co.ke/news/2022-02-18-russia-ukraine-conflict-splits-kenyan-orthodox-church/ (accessed August 18, 2023).

Samson, Grace. "Pan African Christian Women Alliance Leadership Conference." *Lausanne World Pulse Archives*. https://lausanneworldpulse.com/lausannereports/1000/09-2008 (accessed December 29, 2023).

Standard Entertainment and Lifestyle. "Ati Mum? Kathy Kiuna's Birthday Celebrations Spark Debate." https://www.standardmedia.co.ke/entertainment/local-news/2001335854/ati-mum-kathy-kiunas-birthday-celebrations-spark-debate (Accessed August 8, 2020).

TV47. "Kathy Kiuna Followers Trolled for Wishing Their 'Mum' a Happy Birthday." July 29, 2019. https://tv47.co.ke/2019/07/29/kathy-kiuna-followers-trolled-for-wishing-their-mum-a-happy-birthday/.
Waruguru, Grace. "Dr. Ofweneke Biography and Everything about the Talented Comedian." *Tuko.co.ke – Kenya News*, July 8, 2020. https://www.tuko.co.ke/365635-dr-ofweneke-biography-real-nationality-tribe-education-life-story.html.

Reports and Documents

African Union. *African Youth Charter*. Addis Ababa, Ethiopia: African Union, 2006. https://au.int/sites/default/files/treaties/7789-treaty-0033_-_african_youth_charter_e.pdf.
CITAM. "The Church and Politics Archives." *CITAM Valley Road*. https://valleyroad.citam.org/?wpv_sermons_category=the-church-and-politics (accessed December 22, 2023).
CITAM. "CITAM Business Forum (CBF) Conference 2022." *CITAM Valley Road*, November 13, 2021. https://valleyroad.citam.org/event/citam-business-forum-cbf-conference-2022/.
CITAM. "Financial Reports—CITAM::Christ Is the Answer Ministries." https://citam.org/financial-reports/ (accessed December 22, 2023).
The Constitution of Kenya. Nairobi: Government of Kenya, 2010.
Downie, Richard. "Kenya: Cooperation, Co-optation, and Confrontation." https://www.csis.org/analysis/kenya-cooperation-co-optation-and-confrontation (accessed November 15, 2023).
IRCK-2020-2024-STRATEGIC-PLAN. https://interreligiouscouncil.or.ke/ova_doc/irck-strategic-plan-2020-2024.
Kenya Gazette Supplement, Acts 2013, Act No. 42, Election Campaign Financing Act, 2013, December 27, 2013.
"Kenya Mission: CMS CRL Annual Report 1923-1924 01 42-61." UK: Church Missionary Society, 1924.
"Kenya Mission: CMS CRL Annual Report 1933-1934 01 63-84." UK: Church Missionary Society, 1934.
Kenya National Bureau of Statistics. *2019 Kenya Population and Housing Census: Volume I*. Nairobi: Government Printer, 2019.
Kenya National Bureau of Statistics. *2019 Kenya Population and Housing Census: Volume II*. Nairobi: Government Printer, 2019.
Kenya National Bureau of Statistics. *2019 Kenya Population and Housing Census: Volume III*. Nairobi: Government Printer, 2019.
Kenya National Bureau of Statistics. *2019 Kenya Population and Housing Census: Volume IV*. Nairobi: Government Printer, 2019.
"KNA/AV/12/321." Kenya National Archives, 1926.
"KNA/AV/12/329." Kenya National Archives, 1928.
"KNA/MSS/61/2/113." Kenya National Archives, 1943.
"KNA/NAT/ADM/3A/111." Kenya National Archives, 1950.
"KNA/PC /RVP/6A/15/10." Kenya National Archives, 1942.
"KNA/RN/6/5." Kenya National Archives, 1971.
"KNA/RN/6/6." Kenya National Archives, 1973.
"KNA/RN/6/7." Kenya National Archives, 1977.
"KNA/Secretariat/2/1." Kenya National Archives, 1940.
"KNA/TR/8/1733." Kenya National Archives, 1966.

Websites

All Saints Cathedral Diocese. "Mothers' Union." https://allsaintscathedraldiocese.org/mothers-union/ (accessed November 4, 2023).
All Saints' Nairobi. "All Saints' Cathedral." https://www.allsaintsnairobi.org/ministries/youth-and-young-adults-department/ (accessed November 2, 2023).
The Anglican Church of Kenya. "Mothers' Union." https://www.ackenya.org/ (accessed November 4, 2023).
Catholic University of East Africa. "Brief History," September 14, 2020. https://www.cuea.edu/?page_id=6827.
CNN. https://www.cnn.com/2010/WORLD/africa/08/04/kenya.constitution.churches/index.html (accessed November 14, 2023).
"Daughters of Zion." https://www.facebook.com/DozKenya/ (accessed October 15, 2015).
Dictionary of African Christian Biography. "Ajuoga, Abednego Matthew (B)." https://dacb.org/stories/kenya/ajuoga-abednego1/ (accessed August 28, 2023).
Dictionary of African Christian Biography. "Wellington Mulwa." https://dacb.org/stories/kenya/mulwa-wellington/ (accessed November 2023).
Hatua Trust. "Who We Are." https://hatuatrust.org/who-we-are/ (accessed December 26, 2023).
Interfaith Reflections. "Faith Leaders Sign a Declaration to Fight Modern Slavery," March 24, 2022. https://interfaithreflectionshome.blog/2022/03/24/faith-leaders-sign-a-declaration-to-fight-modern-slavery/ (accessed April 25, 2024).
Kenya Assemblies of God. "Home." https://kag.ke/ (accessed December 22, 2023).
Mater Misericordiae Hospital. "Mater Heart Run." https://www.materkenya.com/heart-run (accessed December 8, 2023).
Mavuno Church. "About Fearless Summit – Fearless Summit." https://fearlesssummit.org/about-fearless-summit/.
OLQP South B. "About." http://www.olqpsouthb.org/index.php/about/ (accessed July 29, 2019).
Orthodox Church of Kenya. "Holy Archdiocese of Nairobi – HOME." https://orthodox-church-kenya.org/ (accessed August 19, 2023).
Pacis Insurance, "Who We Are," May 13, 2023. https://www.pacisinsurance.com/about-us/who-we-are/.
PCEA Evergreen. "Woman's Guild – Become a Member in PCEA Evergreen." http://www.pceaevergreen.org/guild.php (accessed November 4, 2023).
"Pawa254." https://pawa254.org/ (accessed December 23, 2023).
"Queen Esther's Generation." n.d. http://queenesthersgeneration.com/qeg-mandate/.
Rise Networks. https://risenetworks.org/yotw/youth-of-the-month-boniface-mwangi/ (accessed November 16, 2023).
Strathmore University. "History," April 5, 2023. https://strathmore.edu/history/.
Strathmore University. "Opus Dei," April 5, 2023. https://strathmore.edu/opus-dei/.
Twitter. https://twitter.com/bonifacemwangi/status/1380041842318839809 (accessed November 17, 2023).
Vincentian Prayer House, Lavington, Nairobi. "Vincentian Congregation." https://www.vphnairobi.org/about-us/vincentian-congregation/ (accessed December 8, 2023).
United Nations. "Median Age in Africa 2000–2030." https://www.statista.com/statistics/1226158/median-age-of-the-population-of-africa/ (accessed November 2, 2023).
United Nations "Our Work on the Sustainable Development Goals in Kenya." https://kenya.un.org/en/sdgs (accessed April 29, 2024).

World Bank Data. "Kenya Data." http://data.worldbank.org/country/kenya (accessed March 27, 2017).

Videos

114. *The Early Days – Tedd Josiah (The Play House)*. The Play House. Nairobi: CTA – Cleaning The Airwaves, 2021. https://www.youtube.com/watch?v=6eYVNjBdG58.

344. *Kenya's First Gospel DJ & Getting On Family Radio – DJ Moz (The Play House)*. The Play House. Nairobi: CTA – Cleaning The Airwaves, 2021. https://www.youtube.com/watch?v=fleh9tY0j2o.

345. *Kubamba On Family FM, Ollovar Dance Crew, Missions & Much More! – DJ Moz (The Play House)*. The Play House. Nairobi: CTA – Cleaning The Airwaves, 2021. https://www.youtube.com/watch?v=wtGWDwjaJrA.

348. *The First Ever TSO (Totally Sold Out) Kubamba Event – DJ Moz (The Play House)*. The Play House. Nairobi: CTA – Cleaning The Airwaves, 2021. https://www.youtube.com/watch?v=ADD13EIMcug.

584. *Starting Hart With Tedd Josiah – Pete Odera (The Play House)*. The Play House. Nairobi, 2021. https://www.youtube.com/watch?v=zjnPnUB4Kew.

586. *How the Church Lost 5 Alive and Shut Out Hart – Pete Odera (The Play House)*. The Play House, 2021. https://www.youtube.com/watch?v=5qaEa7OIwHc.

721. *The Evolution of the Kenyan Music Industry – Rufftone (The Play House)*. The Play House. Nairobi: CTA – Cleaning The Airwaves, 2021. https://www.youtube.com/watch?v=fREmEuLwyvw.

The Birthing Position – Esther Obasike: DOZ September Edition. Nairobi: Jubilee Christian Church, 2023. https://www.youtube.com/watch?v=HDucU1OogFw.

CTA Cleaning the Airwaves: How It Started; Richard Astar Njau. Part 5. Nairobi: The Kenyan Entrepreneur, 2020. https://www.youtube.com/watch?v=ISGi3VLxu2Q.

Day 5: Occupy Conference 2023: Revival—Rev. Dr. Esther Obasike. Nairobi: Deliverance Church Donholm, 2023. https://www.youtube.com/watch?v=Uj2WMD3kUiw.

Lesley Osei: DOZ Convention 2022: The Prophesied Lifting. Nairobi: Jubilee Christian Church, 2022. https://www.youtube.com/watch?v=wpm8ys7AE2Q.

Pastor Victoria Orenze: Ministration at DOZ Convention 2023. Nairobi: Jubilee Christian Church, 2023. https://www.youtube.com/watch?v=n7ogxsO-SDU.

Sinach & JCC Worship Team – The Name of Jesus. Nairobi: Jubilee Christian Church, 2020. https://www.youtube.com/watch?v=o2m8JvcErbo.

Word of the Year Service – January 2022. Nairobi: FEM Family Church, 2022. https://www.youtube.com/watch?v=kJxg8Tn5n2M.

Word of the Year Service – January 2023. Nairobi: FEM Family Church, 2023. https://www.youtube.com/watch?v=FkeSMuvTdW4.

Interviews

Gichinga, John. Interview by Kyama Mugambi, August 18, 2018.
Nyabera, Rev Fred. Interview by Mark Shaw, August 2023. Nairobi, Kenya.

Odera, Gowi. Interview by Kyama Mugambi, December 21, 2023.
Okeno, Bishop Rose. Interview by Mark Shaw, August 2023. Nairobi, Kenya.
Wathang'a, Joshua. Interview by Kyama Mugambi, December 16, 2022.
Mathenge, Moses. Interview by Kyama Mugambi, December 28, 2023.

Other sources

Besigye, Trajan. "Caring for People with Disabilities: The Christian Community in Nairobi." PhD Thesis, University of Nairobi, 2002.

Brislen, Michael. "Christian Perceptions of Islam in Kenya–As Expressed in Written Sources from 1998 to 2010." Unpublished Dissertation, University of Birmingham, 2013.

Dowd, Robert. "Christianity, Islam, and Political Culture: Lessons from Sub-Saharan Africa in Comparative Perspective." unpublished paper presented to American Political Science Association, August 2003.

Koigi, Rachel C. W. "Challenges in Translating and Transcribing Kenyan Sign Language the Case of Immanuel Christian School for the Deaf." PhD Thesis, Africa International University, 2014.

Muchiri, Allan. "Political Theology in the Making: The Responses of Kenyan Churches to Large Cash Donations by Politicians (2018–2022)." Unpublished PhD seminar paper, Africa International University, 2023.

Munuku, Anne Wangari. "Influence of Twitter Hashtags on the Formation of Public Opinion on Socio-Political Issues in Kenya." PhD Thesis, JKUAT-COHRED, 2019. http://ir.jkuat.ac.ke/handle/123456789/4899.

Ndung'u, Nahashon W. "The Akurinu Churches: With Special Reference to Their Theology." PhD, University of Nairobi, 1994.

Ndzovu, Hassan. "Muslims and Party Politics and Electoral Campaigns in Kenya." Institute for the Study of Islamic Thought on Africa (ISITA), Working paper No 09-001, March 2009.

Nedumparambil, George Joseph. "A Search of the Roots of Syro-Malabar Church in Kerala." PhD Thesis, Würzburg, Universität Würzburg, Dissertation, 2013, 2015.

Nyambura, Nancy Wagi Maina. "Perceptions of Deaf Children and Their Parents on Spiritual Nurture Experiences at Church: A Case of Lugha Ishara Centre, Nairobi County." PhD Thesis, Daystar University School of Applied Human Sciences, 2022.

Omangi, Sherlyne. "An Assessment of Residential Neighborhood Satisfaction: A Case of Bahati Estate, Eastlands, Nairobi, Kenya." Unpublished PhD dissertation, University of Nairobi, 2016.

Roberts, Mara J. *Conflict Analysis of the 2007 Post-Election Violence in Kenya*. September, 2009.

Samper, David Arthur. "Talking Sheng: The Role of a Hybrid Language in the Construction of Identity and Youth Culture in Nairobi, Kenya." PhD, University of Pennsylvania, 2002.

United Nations, "Definition of Youth: United Nations Youth," United Nations Department of Economic and Social Affairs (UNDESA), 2013.

Index

Accra 103
Addis Ababa 78
Africa Inland Church (AIC) 3, 12, 14–15, 39–40, 49–52, 71, 77, 100, 116, 119, 121, 144
Africa Inland Mission (AIM) 9, 42
Africa International University 16, 134
African Israel Church Nineveh (AICN) 12, 44, 59
Agikuyu 41
AICPA 39
Ajuoga, Abednego Matthew 40, 44–6, 49, 51
Akurinu 40, 42, 44, 51, 59
Alexandria 12, 73–4
All Saints' Cathedral 7–8, 95
Anglican Church of Kenya (ACK) 20, 45, 102
Arabic 129
Arathi 40–2
artivism 123
Association of Member Episcopal Conferences of Eastern Africa (AMECEA) 31
Australia 73

Bahati 37–9, 52
Balokole 45, 48, 52
Batiya 49
Beecher, Leonard 102
benga 85
Berger, Peter 2, 20–1, 83, 138
Bohra 127
Buruburu 60, 88

Cairo 50, 73, 75
Canada 12, 19, 43, 60
capitalism 1, 135
Catholic University of East Africa 30–1

Chai 114
chapati 7
charism 32
charisma 58, 68, 93, 103–5
charismatic 2–3, 18, 32–4, 44, 54, 56, 58, 60, 65, 67–8, 70, 83, 88, 90–1, 94, 99–101, 104–5, 122, 144
Chrisco (Christ Coworkers Fellowship) 135
Christian Council of Kenya (CCK) 12
Christian Union (CU) 89–91
Christ is the Answer Ministries (CITAM) 65–6, 93, 106, 119, 122
Christological 81
Churches of Christ in Africa (CCA) 40, 45–6, 51
Church of Scotland Mission (CSM) 9–11, 71
Church of the Province of Kenya (CPK) 79
circumcision 71–2
Clean the Airwaves (CTA) 94
clergywoman 107
coalition 113, 116–17, 121–2
colonial 7, 10, 12, 23–5, 27–8, 32, 35, 41, 47–8, 71, 73, 88, 99, 101, 110, 117, 123, 128, 133, 143
Constantinople 69
Constitution of the Kenya Review Commission (CKRC) 131
contraception 29
Coptic 2–3, 50, 70–1, 75–7, 81
Coptic Orthodox Church (COC) 70, 75, 77, 79
Creed 81, 83
Cyprus 73–4

Daddy 92
Daystar University 16

INDEX

Deliverance church (DC) 18, 41, 57, 61, 87, 95, 119, 122
Democracy 111, 115, 117, 121, 131, 139
Derg 78–9
Dini 42–3, 47
DJ 85, 92–3
DNA 21
Don Bosco 95. *See also* Salesians

Eastlands 2, 37, 59–61, 88, 95
Eastleigh 17, 127, 131, 135
Egypt 50, 70, 75, 77
Eldoret 46
Elim 60
Embakasi 2
Empire 9–10
England 13, 72
Escrivá, Josemaria 30
Ethiopia 46–7, 75, 78–80
Ethiopian 3, 40, 70–1, 77–82
Ethiopian Orthodox Tewahedo Church (EOTC) 70, 77–82
Eucharist 38–9, 80–2
Evangelical Alliance of Kenya (EAK) 15, 20, 136
Evangelistic ministry churches (EMCs) 62–3

Fadhili 107
Faith Evangelistic Ministries (FEM) 62, 104
fascists 78
Finland 73
Francis, Pope 25
Full Gospel Churches of Kenya (FGCK) 57

Garissa 118, 125, 132, 137, 139
Gathinji 114
Gatu, John 15, 40, 46–9, 52, 113–14, 123
Gatundu 28, 113
GEMA (Gikuyu, Embu, and Meru peoples) 113
German East Africa (GEA) 10
Ghana 103
Gikomba 60
Gitari, David 14, 115–16

Glasgow 17
Global Anglicans Future Conference (GAFCON) 17
Gospel Missionary Society (GMS) 47
Gothic 7

Haile Mariam, Mengistu 78–9
Hekima University College 31
Hindu 2, 116, 136, 144
Hindu Council of Kenya (HCK) 136
Historic mission churches (HMCs) 16, 18, 33, 56, 58, 67, 70, 86, 90, 94–5, 99–103, 143, 145
HIV 50, 107, 119
Holy Family Minor Basilica 23
Holy Ghost Mission (HGM) 9
homosexuality 110
Hurlingham 80

International Christian Center (ICC) 60, 65
International Fellowship of Evangelical Students (IFES) 89
Inter-Religious Council of Kenya (IRCK) 136–7
Islamic Party of Kenya (IPK) 130
Islamize 135
Islamophobia 133
Ismael 137
Israel 12, 40, 42–3, 59
Italian 27, 30, 47, 78

Jamia 127, 141, 144
Jerusalem 88
Jesuit 31–2
Johera 45–6
John Paul II, Pope 25
Jubilee Christian Center 63–4, 107
Jumuia 34, 67

Kabaka 45
Kabete 12, 28, 45, 47
Kadhi 117, 127, 130–1
Kahdi 135
Kahuhia 12
Kamba 12, 14
Kambii 47
Kambui 71
Kangemi 32

INDEX

Kanjii, Mbugua 92
Karen 16–17, 21–2, 31–2, 56, 96, 104
Karing'a 72
Kasarani 2, 32, 89
Kawangware 32–3
kayamba 26
Kayo, Joe 57, 61
Kayole 97
Kencom 141
Kenya African Democratic Union (KADU) 113
Kenya African National Union (KANU) 14, 111, 116, 129
Kenya Assemblies of God (KAG) 60, 95
Kenya Commercial Bank (KCB) 141
Kenya Conference of Catholic Bishops (KCCB) 28–9, 136
Kenya Missionary Council (KMC) 12
Kenyans on Twitter (KOT) 94
Kenya Students Christian Fellowship (KSCF) 91
Kenyatta, Jomo 2, 13, 28, 72, 111–12, 129
Kenyatta, Uhuru 39, 118
Kenyatta International Conference Center (KICC) 120
Kenyatta University (KU) 90, 103, 133
Kerala 33
keshas 91
Khariji 126
Kiambu 40–2, 46–7, 71
Kibaki, Mwai 28, 116–17
Kibanda 7
Kibera (Kibra) 16–17, 32, 59, 125, 127, 139
Kigara 71
Kikuyu 11–13, 27–8, 37–42, 46–7, 59–60, 71–3, 77, 113–14
Kikuyu Central Association (KCA) 72
Kikuyu Independent School Association (KISA) 72–3
Kikuyu Karing'a Education Association (KKEA) 72
Kilimani 17, 70, 80
Kinship 34, 64, 91, 101, 105
Kirore 71–2
Kisumu 9, 70

Kitonga, Arthur 61
Kiuna, Allan 63–4, 105–6
Kiuna, Kathy 63–4, 105–6
Kivuli, Zakayo 40, 42–4, 49, 52
K-Krew 85, 92–3. *See also* Kubamba
Koran 127, 132
Koranic 127
Korogocho 32
Koventha 33
Kubamba 85, 93. *See also* K-Krew
Kuna Nuru Gizani 62
Kuyper, Abraham 19–20

Lambeth 17
Langata 17, 32
laymen 122
laywomen 100
LGBTIQ 144
liberalization 57, 62, 111
Liberalized 63, 87, 92–3
Lisbon 84
Lodwar 16
Lonsdale, John 115
Loreto 30
Lunatic Express 9
Luo 42–3, 45, 59, 77, 114, 127
Lutheran 49, 102

Maasai 143
Maathai, Wangari 120
madondo 7
madrasas 129
Magesa 31
Magina 60
Makarios 73–5
Makumira 49
Malaria 119
Malawi 86, 122
Malindi 121, 128
Mandarin 120
Mandera 137
Mang'u 28
MAP 4–6
Maringo 88
Marxist 78
Mater Misericordiae 31
Mathare 32
Media and entrepreneurial churches (MECs) 63

INDEX

Methodist 9, 11, 16, 45, 102, 119, 121
Moi, Daniel Arap 13–15, 28–9, 115–16, 118, 121, 129–30
Mombasa 9, 12, 15, 24, 72, 128, 137
Mothers' Union 102
Muge, Alexander 14, 115
Muntu 13
Musyimi, Mutava 14, 115

Nairobi Baptist Church 14, 16
Nairobi Chapel 85, 93
Nairobi Youth Network (NAYNET) 95
Nandi 43
National Cohesion and Integration Commission (NCIC) 138
National Council of Churches of Kenya (NCCK) 12, 14–15, 20, 44, 113, 115–17, 119, 122, 132, 136
nationalism 13, 46–7, 77, 82
nationalist 40, 51
National Muslim Leaders Forum (NAMLEF) 136
National Rainbow Coalition (NARC) 116
Nazi 11
Nazirite 41
ndengu 7
Newer Pentecostal Charismatic churches (NPCCs) 60–1, 64–5
New Zealand 109
Ng'ang'a, Joseph 40
NGO 16, 120, 122
Nigeria 139
Nigerian 107
Nilotic 59
Njiri, Peter 60
Njoya, Timothy 115, 123
Nomiya 43, 59
nongovernmental 35
nonviolence 15
Nunciature 28–9
Nyanza 43, 45
Nyeri 28
Nzeki, Ndingi Mwana a' 29

Odinga, Raila 117
Olang, Festo 12–13
Opus Dei 30

Organization of African Instituted Churches (OAIC) 44, 49–51, 77, 136
Oriental 81
Orthodox 2, 12, 40, 58, 69–83, 91, 144
Orthodoxy 3, 19, 58, 68–71, 73–84

Pacis Insurance 26–7
Padwick, John 44
Pakistani 127
Pan African Christian Women Alliance (PACWA) 107
Parklands 65, 127
Parliament 23, 109–10, 114–16, 118, 123, 130, 134
pathology 58, 68
patriarchal 69, 99, 101
Patriarchate 12
Pentecostal Assemblies of Canada (PAOC) 43–4, 60
Pentecostal Assemblies of God (PAG) 12, 60
Pentecostal Evangelistic Fellowship of Africa (PEFA) 57, 60
Persia 128
pluralism 2–3, 14, 21–2, 52, 82–3, 87, 89–90, 96, 101, 108, 134, 138–9, 144
pneumatology 105
postcolonial 130, 143
postindependence 3
Presbyterian Church of East Africa (PCEA) 12, 15, 48, 51, 109–10, 113–15, 119, 121, 133
Progressive Pentecostal Churches 64, 66
Prophet 40–2, 49, 59, 100, 137
Prophetic 14, 51, 104, 115, 122–3, 143
Pumwani 127

Quaker 43

Ramadan 132
Rebmann, Johann 9
Redeemed 61, 107, 119
Redeemed Christian Church of God (RCCG) 107
Redeemed Gospel churches (RGC) 61

reformist   127
revival   7–8, 12–13, 40, 44–9, 51–2, 55, 89, 100, 104, 114, 141
Rironi   24
Riruta   127
Roho   3, 40, 42–4, 51
Rufftone   92

Safari   9
Sahara   86, 126
Saharan   115, 126, 139
Salafism   129
Salesians   95. *See also* Don Bosco
Satan   110, 135
Savannah   24
Scottish   27
secessionist   40, 45, 126
sectarian   21, 82
secular   1–3, 21, 23, 25–6, 29, 54–5, 57–9, 64–5, 83, 86, 88–9, 94, 99, 129, 134, 138
secularization   20–1, 89, 91
segregated   12, 30
seminary   70, 74–5
Seventh Day Adventist (SDA)   42, 136
sexuality   17
Shakahola   121
Sharia   135
Sheikh   53
Sheng   85, 87–8, 93, 95
Shia   126–8, 136
slavery   137
Somali   127–9, 131–2
Soviet   79
St. Paul's University (formerly St. Paul's United Theological College)   16, 44, 46, 48
Strathmore University   30
Sufism   127
sukuma   7
Sunnah   127
Sunni   126–8
Supreme Council of Kenyan Muslims (SUPKEM)   127, 129–31, 136
Swahili   7, 9, 21, 25–6, 32, 34, 37–8, 40, 43, 48, 53, 55, 57, 63, 69, 79, 85, 87, 97, 114–15, 128

synod   102
Syro-Malabar   33

Tanzania   49, 86, 130
televangelist   57, 104
television   38, 54, 62–3, 85, 88, 93–5
terrorism   15, 118, 130, 133
terrorist   15, 118, 132, 138
Tewahedo   70, 77
Theological Education by Extension (TEE)   49–50
Theophilos, Abuna   78–9
Thogoto   10, 71
Tigoni   77, 79
totalitarian   78
traditionalists   2, 47
Tukutendereza Yesu   45
Turkana   70

Ufungamano House   116–17
Uganda   2, 12, 44–5, 47, 72–3, 86, 139
Uhuru Park   23, 25, 56–7
UK's Department for International Aid (DFID)   86
Ukambani   9
Ukraine   75
Ukrainian   75
ummah   131
Umoja   61, 88
United Kingdom (UK)   86
United Nations (UN)   2, 86, 119, 125
University of Nairobi (UoN)   91, 98, 103
utopia   54

Vincentian   32–4, 67

Wahhabi   129
Wanjiru, Margaret   62–3, 106, 134
Westgate   15, 118, 131
Westlands   56, 127
Woman's Guild   102

Zambia   86
Zanzibar   11
Zion   107